THE GOSPELS

AS

HISTORICAL DOCUMENTS

THE GOSPELS
AS
HISTORICAL DOCUMENTS

PART III

THE FOURTH GOSPEL

BY

VINCENT HENRY STANTON, D.D.

FELLOW OF TRINITY COLLEGE
REGIUS PROFESSOR OF DIVINITY IN THE UNIVERSITY OF CAMBRIDGE

WIPF & STOCK · Eugene, Oregon

Wipf and Stock Publishers
199 W 8th Ave, Suite 3
Eugene, OR 97401

The Gospels as Historical Documents, Part III
The Fourth Gospel
By Stanton, Vincent Henry
ISBN 13: 978-1-60608-277-5
Publication date 02/04/2009
Previously published by Cambridge UP, 1920

PREFACE

IN this volume, for reasons which I have given in the Epilogue, I bring this work to a close, in spite of a different plan which I sketched in the preface to my first volume. The present volume is occupied with the Fourth Gospel, as the last was with the Synoptic Gospels. Questions, however, relating to the authorship of the Fourth Gospel came before us to a considerable extent in the first volume owing to their connexion with the history of the reception of the four Canonical Gospels in the Church, which was the special subject of that volume. In the present volume I am principally concerned with the form and character of the Fourth Gospel itself, though I have had occasion to add a little to what I before wrote on its use in the Church, and the tradition about John son of Zebedee.

Possibly an explanation may be due from me to any readers of the two former volumes who have felt some interest in my work, with regard to the long delay—no less than eleven years—since the publication of my last volume. This has to a considerable extent been caused by the intricate nature of the problems which the subject presents, and the amount of controversial literature dealing with them, requiring to be mastered. But in addition to this I have often found it impossible even for some months together to work at them at all owing to official duties. The recovery of threads which have been dropped has often been a difficult and laborious task ; but I hope that there has been some gain in one's having been compelled to come back even to the same parts of the subject repeatedly, and to weigh more than once conclusions already before arrived at.

My aim in this volume has not been, except incidentally, to throw light upon the subject-matter of the Fourth Gospel, but to ascertain—so far as can by way of a preliminary study be done, and needs to be in order to determine our attitude towards it from the outset in using it—whether it has a right to be treated as an independent historical witness alongside of the Synoptic Gospels, having drawbacks indeed in this character as they have, though largely different ones, but whose testimony cannot any more than theirs be disregarded. I am convinced that this right belongs to it, which in recent times has been and still is denied by many.

As a far fuller study than any attempted here of the actual contributions made to our knowledge of the Life and Work of Jesus Christ by each of the four Gospels I may mention *The Fourfold Gospel* by Dr E. A. Abbott.

V. H. STANTON.

CAMBRIDGE,
August 18, 1920.

TABLE OF CONTENTS

CHAPTER I

THE PRESENT POSITION OF THE QUESTION OF THE ORIGIN OF THE FOURTH GOSPEL

	PAGES
Small progress towards agreement as compared with that made in respect to the Synoptic Gospels	1–3
Theory of F. C. Baur	3–5
The position of C. Weizsäcker	5–7
E. Schürer's review of the results of criticism	7–8
B. F. Westcott on the Fourth Gospel	8
Criticism during the past thirty years	9–13
The significance of the Partition-theories	13, 14
Mysticism and History	14, 15
The wide differences of view on the date and authenticity of this Gospel which still exist	15, 16

CHAPTER II

THE STRUCTURE OF THE GOSPEL AND THE QUESTION OF ITS INTEGRITY

The authorship of chapter XXI	17–27
Notes on chapter XXI	28–32
Question of the integrity of chapters I–XX:	
Alleged accidental displacements and textual corruption	32, 33
Theories as to the growth of the Gospel through the work of different hands	33–44
Some general remarks on these theories	44–50
Probable influence of preceding oral teaching upon the form of the Gospel	50–2
Some crucial passages discussed	52–7
Instances of parenthetic comments	57–62
Reflections added to reported discourses	62–4
Conglomerates	64–6
Question of interpolations and dislocations	66–73
ADDITIONAL NOTES:	
Theories as to accidental transpositions of certain passages in the Fourth Gospel	73–5
Comparison of order of narratives in Tatian's *Diatessaron*	75–6

CHAPTER III

THE PLACE OF THE FOURTH GOSPEL IN THE JOHANNINE LITERATURE

PAGES

The Apocalypse of John:
    Structure of the Apocalypse 77–80
    Date and authorship of the Apocalypse 80–3
The First Epistle of John:
    Relation of the First Epistle to the Gospel of John in point of date and authorship 83–103
The Second and Third Epistles of John:
    The writer's description of himself 103–4
    The Second Epistle is addressed to a particular Church . 104–5
    Question whether the writer of these two Epistles was the same as of the Apocalypse, First Epistle, or Fourth Gospel 105–8
    John the Elder 108–9

ADDITIONAL NOTE:
    John the Presbyter and the Fourth Gospel, by Dom J. Chapman, O.S.B. 110–1

CHAPTER IV

THE ATTRIBUTION OF THE AUTHORSHIP OF THE GOSPEL TO JOHN THE SON OF ZEBEDEE

The evidence alleged against residence in old age of John son of Zebedee in Ephesus examined, and compared with that for it . 112–22
The significance to be attached to the fact that Irenæus, the Muratorian Fragment and Eusebius do not offer evidence to demonstrate the authenticity of the Fourth Gospel . . 123–32
The indications of authorship, actual or supposed, in the Fourth Gospel itself:
    The notice at end of chapter XXI 132–4
    The allusions before chapter XXI to the disciple whom Jesus loved 134–9
    "He that saw bare record" 139–40
    "We beheld his glory" 140–3
    The disciple known to the high priest 143–4
    The beloved disciple's home 144
    The anonymity of the beloved disciple 144–5
    Apostleship and discipleship 145–6
Conclusion 146

Table of Contents

CHAPTER V

THE ENVIRONMENT IN WHICH THE FOURTH GOSPEL WAS PRODUCED AND THE AUTHOR'S OWN ANTECEDENTS

	PAGES
The writer's relation to Paulinism cannot here be discussed	147–8

§ 1. Acquaintance with things Jewish in general and with localities in Palestine:

The Judaism of the Dispersion	149–50
The evangelist's attitude to the Jews	150–1
His silence as to the scribes does not shew ignorance	151–2
The Hebraic style of the Gospel	152
The knowledge of the Old Testament shewn	152–3
Acquaintance with the ideas of later Judaism and with Jewish customs	154–5
Acquaintance with localities in Palestine	155–60

§ 2. Alexandrian Judaism:

Divers views as to the extent to which the evangelist had been affected thereby	161
The Logos-doctrine in the Prologue compared with that of Philo	162–6
The doctrine of the Prologue compared with that of the remainder of the Gospel	166–79
The use of allegory in the Fourth Gospel	179–82

ADDITIONAL NOTE:

Bp Westcott and Prof. Rendel Harris on the derivation of the Logos-idea in the Prologue	182–6

§ 3. Gentile religious thought and feeling:

The Mystery-religions	187–92
Tendencies in the philosophy of the age	192–4
Pre-Christian Gnosticism	194–6
The Mysteries and Christianity	197–200

ADDITIONAL NOTE:

The question of the influence of the Mystery-religions on Christian rites, ideas and worship	200–1

§ 4. Gnosticism commonly so called:

The type of Gnosticism referred to in the Gospel and First Epistle of John	201–7
This type a very early one	208

CHAPTER VI

THE FOURTH GOSPEL AND THE SYNOPTICS

	PAGES
The fourth evangelist should not be held to be put out of court as a historical witness by the Synoptics	209–14
The question of the fourth evangelist's acquaintance with the Synoptic Gospels	214–9
The fourth evangelist knew only St Mark	219–20
The object of the comparison now to be undertaken	220–1
The work of John the Baptist	221–3
The formation of a band of disciples	223–5
Early belief that Jesus is the Christ	226–7
Visits of Jesus to Jerusalem	228–33
First visit to Jerusalem	233–5
Journey through Samaria	235–6
The Galilean Ministry	236–42
The final departure from Galilee and the last months of Christ's Ministry	242–5
The supper at Bethany	245–7
The Last Supper	247–57
The Garden	257–8
The Arrest	258–9
Jesus brought before Annas and Caiaphas	259–60
The trial by Pilate	260–2
The Condemnation and Crucifixion	262–3
The Utterances of Jesus in the Synoptics and Fourth Gospel on His Person and Mission	263–76
EPILOGUE	277–88
INDEX	289–93

CHAPTER I

THE PRESENT POSITION OF THE QUESTION OF THE ORIGIN OF THE FOURTH GOSPEL

WHEN I entered upon the treatment of the subject of the origin and composition of the Synoptic Gospels, it was possible for me to begin by stating, and briefly giving reasons for, several conclusions which, after long controversy, had won a very large amount of assent. Nothing of the kind can be attempted in the case of the Fourth Gospel. Some of the chief arguments that have been employed again and again for and against its genuineness and historical trustworthiness for a hundred years[1] are employed still, and yet often without producing conviction. Theories to account for its special phenomena, propounded seventy, sixty, or fifty years ago, are held still with greater or less modifications, and among the representatives of these different opinions there are men of undoubted ability, knowledge of the subject, and honesty of purpose.

It is easy to see why investigation and discussion should thus far have been so much more fruitful in obtaining results in the case of the Synoptic Gospels than in that of the Fourth. The problem in regard to the former which presented itself most conspicuously, and in the solution of which there has been the greatest amount of success, was the comparatively limited one of accounting for the combination of differences with abundant and striking resemblances; and any theories on the subject had to be tested by these differences and resemblances themselves, largely of a merely verbal kind, which did not allow of a great diversity of impressions and interpretations on the part of the investigators. The Fourth Gospel, on the other hand, holds an isolated position. The contrast between it and the other three is one of the strange phenomena to be

---

[1] For the date marking the beginning of the controversy I refer of course to Bretschneider's *Probabilia de Evangelii et Epistolarum Joannis Apostoli indole et origine*, A.D. 1820.

explained. The problem of its origin is also a complex one. The evidence in respect to it is of different kinds, and yet a final judgment cannot be passed on the weight to be attributed to the different portions of that evidence apart from a consideration of the other portions. For instance, trustworthy as the tradition in favour of Apostolic authorship may be held to be, this authorship could not be thereby proved if the character of the Gospel should appear to be incompatible with it. Hence after a balancing of different parts of the evidence, and different probabilities, against one another, the judgment as to one or another may need to be revised—a difficult process even if bias can be avoided. But more serious still, the conclusions reached will on more than one important point be affected by the views that are held as to the development of Christian belief, and the true scope and significance of such development, in a very obscure period of its history; and without reference to these questions there can be no final decision.

But inquiry and controversy could not well be, and have not been, altogether fruitless; and it is necessary that we should ascertain the position to which the Johannine problem has been brought through them, if we would know how most usefully to direct our own efforts.

E. Schürer, in a survey which he made some thirty years ago of the position reached at that time in the criticism of the Fourth Gospel[1], maintained that the progress towards agreement which had taken place was matter for satisfaction and promising for the future. I fear that he exaggerated the extent and significance of the measure of agreement attained even then; and the "mutual approach" from different sides which he hoped would continue has not done so in any decided manner.

The experience of the past may, therefore, well seem discouraging to those who would labour in this field. But on close consideration, there will, I think, appear to be ground

---

[1] See *Vorträge der theologischen Konferenz zu Giessen*, 1889, that by Schürer being *Ueber den gegenwärtigen Stand der johanneischen Frage*. This lecture was reproduced in a slightly altered form in the *Contemporary Review* for September, 1891. This article was also reprinted a few years later, with a brief postscript, as no. 18 in the series of *Essays for the Times*, published by F. Griffiths. In the sequel all references will be to this last edition.

for hoping that its further investigation may not be profitless or unattractive. No one, indeed, who would endeavour to form the best judgment of which he is capable on this subject, the importance of which is at least equal to its difficulty, can avoid going over ground that has already been often trodden. But in spite of all the sameness that there has been, and must to a considerable extent continue to be, in the points that are discussed in this controversy, and the manner in which they are discussed, it appears to me that attention has been directed in recent years to features in the Gospel which need to be more fully considered than as yet by most critics they have been; and that partly in consequence of this, partly also of a certain change of attitude among those who look at the subject from the side of orthodox belief, a point of view is suggested from which the study of the Fourth Gospel acquires fresh interest and the combination of elements of truth contained in different theories becomes more easy.

We will presently turn to the summary of results given by Schürer[1], and then from the time of his survey pass to the period succeeding. But it will be desirable first to dwell for a little while on a couple of outstanding personalities in the time preceding.

In order to make clear the points at issue even in present-day controversy, it will, I believe, be advisable to give here a fairly full statement—a somewhat fuller one than that supplied in Schürer's essay—of Baur's view of the origin of the Fourth Gospel[1]. The influence of the ideas of Baur, which lasted long in its full original strength, and still in a measure continues on this particular subject, although it came to be curtailed far earlier in regard to the New Testament and Early Church History in general, needs to be recognised more clearly than it often seems now to be.

---

[1] The following account is based on the section of his *Die kanonischen Evangelien* (published 1847), which deals with the Gospel of John. To it all the references given are made. Baur had treated the subject of the composition and authorship of this Gospel before, but less completely, in the *Theologische Jahrbücher* for 1844. Baur's views were also, as Schürer observes, put forward to some extent about the same time, and in some instances a little before himself, by pupils of his own. See Schürer's essay above referred to, p. 13.

The theory of F. C. Baur

Baur[1] maintained that this Gospel is to be interpreted and judged in every part with reference to its master-thought. That thought is the manifestation of the Divine Logos in the Person of Jesus, through which a separation is effected among men according as by their belief in Him or their unbelief they shew themselves to be children of light or of darkness, while the faith even of those who believed, containing as it did an element akin to unbelief in so far as it needed the support of external signs, had to undergo a process of purification. The whole significance of the narrative lies for him in its being the form in which this thought is set forth[2]. The Gospel is not in the proper sense history. Wherever the Fourth Gospel conflicts with the Synoptic Gospels the preference is to be given to the latter. Whatever the defects of these Gospels as historical records may be, their authors at least intended to write a history and the author of the Fourth Gospel did not. In spite of the fact that the greater part of the contents of the Fourth Gospel differs from that of the Synoptic Gospels, there is no good reason for thinking that the evangelist either relates what he knew as an eye-witness, or had an independent source of information, written or oral. On the contrary, there are many indications that he has found his historical material, so far as it is to be accounted historical, solely in the Synoptic Gospels, though he has altered both the course of events and particular features in the narratives in the freest possible manner. And the preference is to be given to their accounts where they conflict with his, even where his are in themselves equally probable, or more probable, because of the far clearer marks of "tendency" which characterise his whole work, and which render all his statements of fact suspicious[3]. But there is frequently, also, apart from the more startling character of some of the miracles that he relates, a lack of verisimilitude in his representations of the actions both of Jesus and of the parties and individuals among the Jews with whom He is brought into contact. The discourses more particularly, which constitute such an important part of this Gospel, cannot have been spoken in the form in which, or on the occasions on which, they are

---

[1] Baur, *ib.* pp. 80, 238.   [2] *Ib.* pp. 176 f., 180, 183 f., 243.
[3] P. 132; pp. 239–280.

here given. In them the purpose of the evangelist, not to be a mere chronicler of actual history but to work out the Logos-idea, appears with special clearness[1].

That an apostle should have written a work of this character, in which the interests of history are completely subordinated to those of doctrinal teaching, is, Baur holds, not absolutely inconceivable but in the highest degree improbable. It would have been almost impossible for one who was an eyewitness to suppress to such an extent his personal reminiscences for the sake of his idea[2]. But account has also to be taken of the fact that the stage of doctrinal development that has been reached in this Gospel, both in regard to Christology and as regards the Universalism of the Gospel and the attitude adopted to Judaism and the Law, presupposes the stage illustrated by the Pauline writings. Now all that we know from the New Testament about John the son of Zebedee (apart from the character of the writings attributed to him) seems to shew that he was not likely to have attained to this point of view[3]. Lastly there are signs in the Gospel that it stands in a relation not only to fully developed Gnosticism, but to the Paschal controversy and to Montanism, which must point to A.D. 160–170 as the time of its composition[4].

Let me next speak of C. Weizsäcker, not that his influence has been comparable to that of Baur, or (it may be) that he was of equal originality of mind, or that there were not other men of great ability among the writers of the middle part of the nineteenth century on New Testament subjects; but because he is the chief representative of a distinct view, that of *mediate* Johannine authorship—that is to say, that the author was a disciple of the Apostle, not the Apostle himself, and not a mere reporter.

Schürer does not seem to me to do full justice to what this view implies. After mentioning various writers who were defenders of the authenticity of the Fourth Gospel as the work of the Apostle John, but who "did not all, by any means, vouch for the full and unconditional historicity of the contents," he proceeds:

[1] Pp. 280–310. [2] Pp. 328 f.
[3] Pp. 311–327, 329 ff. [4] P. 373.

"Weizsäcker went furthest in the acknowledgment of the subjective character of the Gospel account in his valuable *Investigations respecting the Gospel History*, 1864. He sought to show that the portrait of Christ, as here drawn, bears a double character throughout. True, it was based on historical reminiscences. But these were treated everywhere with great freedom. The historical and the ideal, tradition and theological reflection, were here blended into an indissoluble unity, so that every link of the account allowed of a double interpretation. The historicity of the narrative was to all intent, however, abandoned, and Weizsäcker concluded his investigations with the admission that the Apostle himself was not the author, but that a disciple had composed the Gospel from the traditions of his Master[1]."

But to hold that "a disciple had composed the Gospel from the traditions of his Master," or even that "the historical and the ideal, tradition and theological reflection, were here blended into an indissoluble unity," is not the same thing as "to abandon to all intent the historicity of the narrative." "Historicity" may be of different degrees. A writing affected by the subjectivity of the writer, even to the full extent here supposed in the case of the Fourth Gospel, may yet be a most valuable document in the hands of an interpreter with a true instinct for history, such as Weizsäcker was, for the purpose of obtaining light upon the history recorded in it. It is so as regards particular points or features in that history; it is so even more when we are seeking to form a true general conception of what Jesus was from the broad impression which He made upon His followers. More cannot be claimed for the Synoptic Gospels, and never has been for the second and third, than that they convey to us the testimony of immediate disciples of Jesus, as reported by those who heard them. In maintaining that the Fourth Gospel was not composed by the Apostle John, but by a disciple of his, Weizsäcker only reduces it to the same level as those others. It is true that the views of the author of the Fourth Gospel, and other circumstances, have left a mark upon its form and contents far exceeding the effect of any such influences in the case of the other Gospels. The

[1] *Ib.* p. 15.

character and degree thereof are matters to be decided by investigation of the Gospel. The theory of "mediate" Johannine authorship of the Apostle John leaves open the possibility of estimates of its historical character and value which vary considerably. The difference between Weizsäcker's early work, his *Investigation respecting the Gospel History* (1864), and what he writes on the subject of the Fourth Gospel in his *Apostolic Age of the Christian Church*[1], which has often been commented on, may illustrate this, though I think it may be due in part to the difference of aim in the two books[2]. The present writer at least, in reading the former work, has often felt that he was being brought directly into contact with historical fact by Weizsäcker's expositions of passages of the Fourth Gospel. In the later work Weizsäcker is simply concerned with setting forth the genesis of this Gospel, and he dwells upon the relation to Judaism, and the influence of the Logos-doctrine, which are to be observed in it, both of which he considers to he incompatible with authorship by the Apostle John himself. But he insists at the same time no less strongly that the phenomena of the Gospel are inexplicable unless we assume that it is " based upon the outlook of an original apostolic faith and rests upon its authority[3]." Moreover, he considers it probable that the developments seen both in the Fourth Gospel on the one hand and the Apocalypse on the other had begun under the eye of the Apostle John[4].

We may now notice that "mutual approach" of which Schürer speaks. He points out that the theory of the origin of the Fourth Gospel propounded by F. C. Baur and the early members of his school had been modified in certain respects at the hands preeminently of Keim, as seen in vol. I of his great work, *The history of Jesus of Nazara*, published in 1867. It had come to be "recognised that the Gospel is at least some 30 to 40 years older than Baur admitted; that it arose not 160–170 A.D., but at latest about 130 A.D.; that it was not simply a

[1] First edition 1886, 2nd edition 1892; Eng. trans. 1894.
[2] Schürer, *ib.* p. 19, asserts that Weizsäcker has "so changed his earlier position, that he is now distinctly to be reckoned among the opponents of the genuineness of the Gospel." He is adverse to "the genuineness" only in the same sense as before.
[3] See 2nd edition, pp. 537 f.   [4] *Ib.* pp. 518 and 538.

poetical product, but that to a greater or less extent it used other traditions which were existing parallel to the Synoptics; and, finally, that even the difference between the Johannine and Synoptic picture of Christ, whilst great, is not so marked as Baur had drawn it[1]." And he observes that in this revised form the theory had "more and more won acceptance[2]." There had also, he remarks, been concessions on the conservative side, to the effect that in the Fourth Gospel "the historical material had undergone some remodelling through the subjectivity of the evangelist." After mentioning Luthardt and Grau as early examples of this tendency, he adds that "the two most respected defenders of the genuineness in recent decades, Beyschlag and Weiss, go still further in the same direction[3]."

In our own great commentator, also, on the Gospel and Epistles of St John, Brooke Foss Westcott, the influence of Baur was apparent, though in a different way. He made no formal concessions on the question of historicity; he was not manifestly free in his treatment of the text on particular points. But he sought to meet Baur's theory by absorbing what seemed to him to be true in it, without departing from his own standpoint as to Apostolic authorship and the essential historical truth of the record. He did not shrink from recognising any of the traits of a more developed Christology than that of the Synoptics which could be pointed out in the Fourth Gospel, because this more developed form was in his view the right unfolding of simpler statements elsewhere, and therefore such an unfolding as even an original disciple of unusual discernment would have been capable of giving. But I must add that I do not think he ever closely grappled with the question whether it was *probable* that one of the Galilean twelve would, even in later years, so have presented his testimony.

We have now to consider what has been added to our knowledge of the subject and how the orientation of students of it has been, or should be, affected, through the work and the controversy of the last thirty years[3].

[1] *Ib.* pp. 17 ff.   [2] *Ib.* p. 20.
[3] Even in Schürer's latest republication of the substance of this lecture he takes account of no work later than 1889 except on one point of external evidence. Many writers, however, on the Johannine question since his time, have

The work of the last thirty years 9

It will be convenient to allude first to certain views on particular points which were put forward in the decade following the time of Schürer's review. In 1892[1] Harnack published an important article on the relation of the Prologue in the Fourth Gospel to the Gospel as a whole, in which he contended that after the Prologue the author no longer concerns himself with the idea of the Logos any more than he uses the name. This view has not so far met with much favour. But his arguments have not, it seems to me, received the attention they deserve[2], or been satisfactorily answered. And if his contention is true, or even largely true, its significance is great both for the history of the development of Christian doctrine and for our estimate of the historical character of the Gospel.

Next, in 1896, we have the theory as to the authorship of the Fourth Gospel, which had been advocated not many years before by Delff, and made by him the starting-point of his whole view of the Gospel[3], adopted, though not pressed to all the same consequences, by Bousset in his work on the Apocalypse: namely, that the evangelist was not John, the son of Zebedee, but the other disciple of the Lord of the name of John whom Papias mentions. Bousset has treated the same subject again more fully in two articles in the *Theol. Rundschau* for 1905. On this later occasion he again maintained that there had been an eminent John in the Province of Asia, in order to explain the belief (due, he holds, to a confusion) which is found there in the second half of the second century as to an Ephesine residence of the Apostle John. But he made the

reviewed the course of the controversy, down to the times when they severally wrote. To mention three: M. Loisy gave a sketch of it in his own graceful and effective manner, in the Introduction to his *Commentary* on the Fourth Gospel, published in 1903; *The Criticism of the Fourth Gospel*, dealing largely with the history of that criticism, was the subject of eight lectures by Prof. Sanday, published in 1905; A. Meyer in three articles in the second volume of the *Theologische Rundschau* (that for A.D. 1900) reviewed the literature on the Johannine problem that had appeared in the ten years (1889–99) following the date of Schürer's review, and has continued to review "Johannine literature" from time to time since in articles in the same journal.

[1] See *Zeitschrift f. Theologie u. Kirche* for that year; also see his *Dogmengeschichte*, I, p. 109, n. 1, in the 4th edition.

[2] There has been one careful examination of the theory, that by J. Grill in *Untersuchungen über die Entstehung d. vierten Evangeliums*, 1902.

[3] See my vol. I, p. 163 n.

personal connexion of this John, who had actually been a prominent figure there, with Jesus and with Palestine a slenderer one than he did before, and his part in the production of the Gospel also slighter[1].

Questions relating to external evidence, including that now referred to, have already been the subject of discussion in my first volume. But I must return to this one in a chapter of the present volume.

The remaining theory, to be noticed here, which was proposed in the last decade of the last century, will bring us back to the subject of the evangelist's purpose. According to Baldensperger[2], to whom I here allude, the confutation of a sect of disciples of John the Baptist, who exalted him as a rival to Jesus, claiming that he was the promised prophet that should come into the world, and even the Messiah, was the one great object of the composition of the Fourth Gospel whereby its whole contents are affected. Jesus is asserted to be, not merely the Christ, but the Logos in the Prologue, and implicitly again and again in the Gospel, with the express intention of exalting him immeasurably above the Baptist[3]. Again, John's baptism is allusively depreciated in various ways, as in the story of the feet-washing on the eve of the Passion, and in the stress the evangelist lays upon the death and the blood of Jesus which alone, he would say, have atoning power, in contrast with the ceremonial washings of which his opponents made so much[4]. The evangelist is engaged in defending the faith of a community

---

[1] In *Die Offenbarung Johannis*, pp. 45, 46, Bousset writes: "Only a one-sided criticism which overshoots its mark can ignore the fact that the Gospel of John supplies, as compared with the Synoptics, an independent and in many respects superior account so soon as Jerusalem becomes the stage of the Gospel drama," and goes on to say that he considers this phenomenon to be accounted for by the connexion of the Gospel with the Jerusalemite disciple. He also declares (p. 45, n. 3), that "here once for all I turn away from the criticism which treats the historical matter in John's Gospel as fiction. This criticism must first solve the riddle how generally such a confident, independent, different tradition as compared with the Synoptics could arise, had not the authority of an eye-witness stood behind it." He does not in the later articles referred to explain the reasons for the change of view there apparent.

[2] *Der Prolog d. vierten Evangeliums, sein polemisch-apologetischer Zweck*, 1894.

[3] E.g. see pp. 57, 58, 89 (end of § 7), 90 ff., 93 ff.

[4] Pp. 59–74.

The work of the last thirty years

to which he belongs and which is being attacked by the members of another community. It is quite a mistake to look in this work for a carefully thought out system of doctrine, such as critics have supposed it to contain. In a controversial work, such as this is, that must not be expected. In controversy one seizes upon and uses any weapons that come to hand and seem likely to be serviceable. All the Christological ideas in the book do not harmonise with one another. There is a unity in the book, but it is not of a theoretic kind; it is simply that which comes from its practical aim[1]. As to another point, namely that it is not to be regarded as a work of history, criticism has been substantially right. At the same time, Baldensperger adds, the writer of a controversial work, if he hoped to convince, would be constrained to appeal only to what was in the main held among his fellow-believers. He could not rely on stories that he had himself invented. Hence Baldensperger is prepared to allow of the presence in the Fourth Gospel of traditions that are historically sound[2]. Nor does he doubt that the evangelist himself believed earnestly in the Logos-doctrine. How he had arrived at this belief Baldensperger does not consider.

Though this theory has not won a large measure of assent as a comprehensive explanation of the phenomena of the Gospel, such as its author claimed that it was, yet it derives importance from a certain typical character which it has, owing to the endeavour of a more or less novel kind which is made in it to connect the Gospel with the time when it was produced.

Schürer, as we have seen, noted a certain change that had taken place in the Tübingen position; but it consisted simply in some concessions, in consequence of which, he adds, that theory had in the main won acceptance more and more. Those concessions may have been to some extent the result of a change of method in the investigation of the problem, though Schürer does not indicate this. But at any rate from the closing years of the last century onwards such a change has been noticeable among many of those who might be regarded as the natural heirs of the Tübingen tradition, and who are at all events in nowise concerned for the defence of conservative views of the

[1] Pp. 157–159.   [2] Pp. 160–162.

Gospel. Thus we find Jülicher in the 3rd and 4th editions of his "Introduction" to the New Testament, published in 1901[1], repudiating as "a one-sided opinion which is now out of date" the one which he had himself espoused in the 1st and 2nd editions published in 1894, that the Fourth Gospel is "a philosophical fiction by a theologian of Asia." It is still in his view devoid of independent worth as a record of the life and teaching of Christ, but he insists now that it is to be regarded as "a work born out of the needs of its time." What he means by this statement is in his 5th and 6th editions, published in 1906, rendered still clearer through its being immediately followed by a reference to Baldensperger, with whom thus far he is in agreement. But he does not consider that a controversy with a sect of disciples of John the Baptist can by itself account for all the peculiar features of the Fourth Gospel. He finds an explanation rather in the acute opposition and controversy existing at the time and place where the Gospel was written between the Christian Church and the unbelieving Jews, who among other modes of attack magnified the Baptist to the disadvantage of Jesus.

The view expounded by Wrede in his *Charakter und Tendenz des Johannes-Evangeliums*, 1903, is very similar, and it is there argued at greater length. A. Meyer[2], also again in close connexion with a notice of Baldensperger, in concluding the last of his three articles for the decade 1889–99, observes that "In point of fact the determination of the historical relationships of the Fourth Gospel is the way on which a serviceable result in this whole complicated question may be expected." And he declares that "to have pressed into the foreground and energetically grappled with" the task of understanding what the writer desired to be and was to his time "is the merit of the more recent research[3]." It may well seem that these attempts which have now been mentioned at connecting the Fourth Gospel with controversies of the time in reality fail far more than Baur's treatment does in bringing out what are obviously its chief thoughts. It must, also, be observed that Baur, too,

[1] § 31. 4 (same section in all the editions).
[2] *Theologische Rundschau*, II, pp. 340 f.
[3] Cp. also J. Grill's remarks in his preface on the work still required for a truer understanding of the Gospel and its genesis.

The significance of the Partition-theories 13

did not overlook the question of the time and circumstances which fitted his view of the Fourth Gospel. Nevertheless, those other attempts to explain the purpose with which it was written arose in consequence of a defect in Baur's reasoning. Baur and his school were far too much disposed to imagine the evangelist as a philosophic theologian whose object, to which he closely adhered, was the exposition of a great theme. Only after forming their notion of the work under the influence of this conception of the author's purpose did they consider its relation to its time. The perception that it might be desirable to postpone the construction of a theory about the Gospel as a whole and its genesis, till there had been a fuller consideration in detail of the contents, and of the relation which different parts might have to particular circumstances and readers, has had effects both upon conceptions of the purpose of the Gospel and on the setting deemed appropriate for it, some of which have been happier than those earlier instances. This change in the attitude and method of criticism has naturally been more marked and has shewn itself earlier in some writers than in others. And it still remains to be seen whether it will have any influence, as it seems to me it should, in leading those who deny that the Fourth Gospel has value as a historical record of the Character, Life and Teaching of Jesus, to retreat from that opinion. Yet the change is even in itself and so far as it has gone a significant one, and would be so if only because a different view of the relation of the Fourth Gospel to Gnosticism may fairly be placed to its account. "The principal error" (in Baur's theory), says Loisy, "consisted in seeing in the Fourth Gospel a kind of compromise between fully developed Gnosticism and the primitive Christian tradition, whereas it takes its place quite certainly, and in the most natural manner, where Gnosis is entering upon its career[1]." The truth of this observation will be widely admitted[2].

The Tübingen view and reasoning have been challenged in a still more radical fashion by the Partition-theories which were put forward in the last decade of the nineteenth and in the first of the present century, and have been much discussed.

[1] "Au début de la Gnose." See Loisy, *Le Quatrième Évangile*, p. 40.
[2] I do not say universally, see below, p. 15.

Necessarily they profoundly affect also the traditional view of the authorship of the Gospel as a complete work by the Apostle John. Judgment has, I think, on the whole gone against them. We must, however, examine them with some care in the next chapter. It is a troublesome subject of inquiry, owing to the multitude of particulars on the investigation of which a decision must depend, and as being concerned to a large extent, though not exclusively, with form rather than with the writer's thoughts. Yet a better knowledge of the mode in which the Gospel was composed can hardly fail to throw light on the process of preparation for writing, and to shew us the author more clearly in his relation both to his materials and to those whom he desired to instruct, and so also to his age, and thus far at least to increase the historical value of the work for us, namely as a document illustrative of the age in which it appeared. The analysis of its structure may even turn out to have some bearing upon its historical value in a more important sense, namely as a source of evidence in regard to its professed subject, the Self-revelation and the Ministry of Jesus.

The principal object of the present work is to be a contribution towards the ascertainment of the value of the Fourth Gospel in that latter sense. It must be regretfully allowed that those who believe themselves entitled to speak in the name of Criticism for the most part deny that the Fourth Gospel has any independent value in this sense, i.e. that it adds anything trustworthy to the statements of the Synoptic Gospels[1]. And there are writers who are plainly concerned for the edification of the Christian people who have so fully convinced themselves of the rightness of this conclusion of Criticism that they evidently hold that they can best render service to the faithful by insisting upon the value which the Fourth Gospel has simply as a record of spiritual experience. That is to say, they would have the author regarded as a great Christian mystic, and not along with this as a historian; so that, it would seem, his meditations are valuable in the same way as those of other great Christian mystics which have been preserved to us, and not in any essentially different way. Yet plainly the hope thus held

---

[1] E.g. see A. Meyer in *Theol. Rundsch.* VII (1904), p. 526.

Wide differences of view continue

out to us that the Fourth Gospel in losing its value as a historical record may not lose that which it has as a spiritual instructor and companion may too probably prove fallacious. The spiritual experience of the writer of the Fourth Gospel himself, and that of Christian mystics in all generations, has been intimately bound up with belief in the historic truth of the appearing of Jesus Christ in the world, according to the main lines of the representation given of it in the Fourth Gospel. It may well be doubted whether the two are, for clear thinkers, separable; and the fact of this connexion supplies an exceedingly strong reason for striving with scrupulous care to obtain a right decision as regards the soundness of the belief in the historical record.

To return to the position of Criticism. If the date to be assigned for the composition of the Gospel, though earlier by some decades than that proposed by Baur, is still to be as late as that for which Schmiedel[1] argues, namely between A.D. 132 and 140, it would no doubt not only be impossible that the author should be one of the first generation of Christians, but highly improbable that in years gone by he could to any considerable extent have had personal contact with any such. But the case is altered if with Jülicher[2] and many others who speak scarcely more favourably than Schmiedel does of the historicity of the Gospel, the date assigned is early in the second century[3]. It must not, however, be supposed that all competent judges of historical evidence agree with them. Let me name Prof. Loofs in Germany as a writer whose position as a historian of Christian doctrine is high. He without hesitation treats the Fourth Gospel as giving the testimony of the Apostle John[4]. Among English writers I will mention the late Prof. James Drummond[5], and Prof. Sanday, who, in *the Criticism of the Fourth Gospel*[6], even decided for actual authorship by the Apostle.

[1] *Das vierte Evangelium*, p. 26.   [2] *Einleit.* pp. 385 f.
[3] Cp. statement by H. J. Holtzmann, *Hand-Com.*, 3rd edition, p. 13, "Eine Reihe von Gelehrten stimmt in der Angabe 100-125."
[4] See the few but valuable pages by him on the Fourth Gospel in his little treatise *Die Auferstehungsberichte und ihr Wert*, 3rd edition, 1908, pp. 36-9; and his volume of lectures entitled, *What is the truth about Jesus Christ?* 1913, pp. 97-111.
[5] *An Inquiry into the Authorship and Character of the Fourth Gospel*, 1903.
[6] Published 1905.

16 *Origin of the Gospel still "sub judice"*

I have given in this chapter only a sketch of the history of controversy on the problem of the Fourth Gospel and reviewed broadly its present position. It is best that fuller notices of the history and present state of opinion on individual points should be reserved till we come to their actual discussion.

From the names on each side among recent, and in most instances still living, writers whom I have mentioned, it will be evident that the relation of the Apostle John to the Gospel, and its historical character, are still subjects for earnest inquiry.

CHAPTER II

THE STRUCTURE OF THE GOSPEL AND THE QUESTION OF ITS INTEGRITY

THE great majority of critics of all schools, no less than the adherents of tradition, have regarded the Fourth Gospel (with the exception at most of its last chapter) as the work of a single author. The partition-theories which have now and again in the past been put forward have made comparatively little impression. Recently, however, the attempts made to distinguish in the Fourth Gospel between a fundamental document, or Grundschrift, have been carried out so systematically and have been urged with so much vigour, that they have compelled attention, and it has become almost a necessity that anyone should reckon with them, who endeavours to discuss in a thorough manner the problems connected with the Fourth Gospel.

But before we examine the question of compositeness as regards the Gospel generally it will be well to discuss the provenance of the last chapter. The consideration of this matter will prepare us in some respects for that more general one. It has also an importance of its own, because the value of the statements contained in that chapter respecting the authorship of the Gospel depends upon the answer to it.

THE AUTHORSHIP OF CHAPTER XXI

Long before the Johannine authorship of the Gospel generally was disputed, Hugo Grotius in 1641 propounded the view that after the Apostle's death this chapter was added by the Ephesine Church. And among critical students of the New Testament in the same and the next century he found some to follow him, though the majority still maintained that it was an addition by the Apostle himself[1]. So also since the beginning of active controversy on the authorship of the Fourth

---

[1] See Eberhardt (*Ev. Joh. ch. xxi*, pp. 8 ff.), who gives a good account of the history of opinion on the subject.

Gospel, there have been among those who have maintained the Johannine authorship of the remainder of the Gospel some who have not claimed it for this chapter. Lücke[1] may be mentioned as an early and notable instance. And coming down to our own time, it is significant that Zahn, while holding that the contents of ch. xxi was derived from the Apostle John, is of opinion that it did not proceed directly from his pen like the rest[2]. On the other hand writers so competent as Lightfoot[3] and Westcott[4] have contended for the authenticity of ch. xxi, with the exception of the last two verses.

Some of the strongest reasons for thinking that ch. xxi is not by the same author as the remainder of the Gospel hold only if the remainder is by the Apostle John; that is to say, they are primarily objections to the Johannine authorship of ch. xxi. It is, therefore, to be noted that some who reject the Johannine authorship of any part of the Gospel hold that the last chapter is by the same author as the rest. Among older critics who are of this opinion I may mention Hilgenfeld[5], and among recent ones Jülicher[6] and Eberhardt[7]. The last named attributes the authorship of the whole Gospel to a personal disciple of the Apostle. Nevertheless the majority of those who reject the Johannine authorship of any part of the Gospel hold also that the last chapter is by a different author from the preceding part[8].

On the supposition that the author of this Appendix was a different man the further question arises whether anything can be said as to the time when and the place where it was added. Was it, for instance, composed soon after the main

---

[1] See his *Commentary*, 1843, II, pp. 805 ff.
[2] *Einleitung*, II, p. 487.　　[3] *Biblical Essays*, pp. 194 ff.
[4] *Com. on St John, in loco.*　　[5] *Einleit.* p. 717.
[6] *Einleit.* pp. 387 ff. It would be more correct to say that he holds the arguments for and against identity of authorship to be very evenly balanced.
[7] *Ev. Joh. ch. xxi*, 1897.
[8] See Scholten, *Kom.* (German trans.), 1869; Schmiedel, *Encycl. Bibl.* II, p. 2543; Loisy, *Le Quatrième Évangile*, 1903, pp. 925-952; A. Klöpper, *Zeitschrift f. Wiss. Theol.* 1899, pp. 337 ff.; H. J. Holtzmann, *Hand-Commentar*, 1908, pp. 308 ff.; B. W. Bacon, *The Fourth Gospel in Research and Debate*, 1910, chs. vii and viii; Tiele, *Annotatio in Locos Nonnullos Evangelii Joannei*, 1853, pp. 115-154, who argues for the Johannine authorship of chs. i-xx, makes it his aim simply to state the arguments *pro* and *con* as regards the Johannine authorship of ch. xxi.

The authorship of Chapter XXI

part of the Gospel in the Church to which this had been first given, or considerably later in other surroundings? Several of those who have decided against identity of authorship have refrained from speaking definitely on these other points. The view has, however, been advocated by H. J. Holtzmann, and more recently by Prof. Bacon, that it was added in Rome near the middle of the second century for the purpose of commending the Gospel to the Church there[1].

These various views must now be considered. That there are many links connecting ch. xxi both in its style and thought and subject-matter with chs. i–xx is undeniable. It appears to me, also, that of the differences alleged to prove that the writer is not the same several are without force. Every writer uses fresh words when he has to say things such as he had not had occasion to say before, and sometimes varies his modes of expression even when he has the same or very similar things to say. Nevertheless, I believe that there are sufficient grounds for rejecting not only the Johannine authorship of the last chapter, but also the identity of its authorship with that of the rest of the Gospel even on the assumption that the rest too is not by the Apostle.

It is, in the first place, more natural that the contents of ch. xxi should have been added by a different hand than that the addition should be an after-thought by the writer who had brought his work to such an impressive and (it would seem) carefully planned termination at xx. 30 and 31. The need for correcting a mistake as to the death of the beloved disciple might indeed have been felt later, but this is only one point in the appended chapter. There is much else in it which might suitably have been included in the body of the work. It is not easy to assign a reason why it should not have occurred to the author of the Gospel to relate it till after he had completed his Gospel in the way that he originally intended. As an objection to the Johannine authorship of the chapter I would observe that it is more natural to suppose the explanation of the saying in regard to the future of "the disciple whom Jesus loved" (*vv.* 22, 23) to have been given after his death, than

---

[1] See Holtzmann, *ib.* p. 314, and Bacon, *ib.* Loisy also is inclined to adopt this theory. *Ib.* pp. 934, 940, 943; but he does not write confidently.

that it should have been given by that disciple himself before his death in anticipation of the possibility that he might not live till the Parousia. So long as life lasted the old man himself, and others, would be likely to cherish the hope that the Lord would return before he died. Further, *v.* 24, as is generally admitted, must be from another hand than his, and yet it seems to be very closely connected in thought with what precedes; and moreover it supplies, together with the verse following, a suitable ending to the Gospel. It is improbable that the writer who had first concluded his work so effectively with *vv.* 30, 31 of ch. xx should have left his work with such an abrupt termination as he would have done if it ended with xxi. 23, which those are compelled to suppose who assume Johannine authorship down to this point. It is certainly best to regard these verses as an integral part of the Appendix, and there is no reason for separating them from it if the writer of xxi. 1–23 was not the Apostle. But if so any indication of authorship in these verses will serve for the Appendix as a whole. Now I do not think we have here quite the same accent of conviction founded on immediate personal knowledge of the facts as in i. 14. At least a slightly greater distance from the facts is implied in the case of those who bear testimony to the witness and declare that they know he speaks the truth, than of those who testify directly to the facts.

Next as to particular features in *vv.* 1–23: it has frequently been pointed out, and I think with truth, that there is a lack of self-consistency and life-likeness, and (to use a favourite modern term) "convincingness" in portions of the narrative, chiefly in the fishing scene, as to the parts played by Simon Peter and the other disciples in hauling in the nets and the purpose for which the fish were wanted, but also to some extent in the statement that Simon Peter saw the beloved disciple following Christ though there has been no indication of any movement on the part of Jesus (*v.* 20). This want of clearness and naturalness[1] tells of course especially against the writer having been an eye-witness. But if someone who was not himself an eye-witness composed the whole Gospel, as we have it,

---

[1] This defect was also noticed by de Wette, 1842 (quoted by Eberhardt, p. 13).

The authorship of Chapter XXI

and included therein what he had learned from different sources of information, the qualities referred to above might in different parts be present in greater or less degree according to the character of the source upon which he was depending.

Difference of authorship from the rest of the Gospel, alike if it was by the Apostle or by another, is however suggested by a certain difference of attitude to the expectation of the Parousia involved in the stress that is laid upon such a saying as that recorded in xxi. 22, as compared with the form in which Christ's teaching on the subject of His Coming is given in xiv. 2, 3, 18, 19 etc.

Other differences of point of view between ch. xxi and chs. i–xx are urged, the reality of which is to my own mind more doubtful. Of these I shall speak when considering the relation of the Appendix to the rest of the Gospel in regard to time and doctrinal associations. But it may now be observed, that even comparatively slight peculiarities of style and phraseology, such as there are in ch. xxi, though they would be of little weight by themselves, have force when taken in conjunction with the considerations which I have already mentioned. Together they seem to me to render it the most probable view that ch. xxi is by a different hand from chs. i–xx even on the assumption that these are not written by the Apostle John.

In comparing the characteristics of the Appendix with those of the Gospel it is necessary to bear in mind that the Gospel generally may have been revised and edited by the hand which added the Appendix, and this has been in point of fact maintained. No one, however, supposes that all the similarities and connecting links between the last chapter and the bulk of the work can thus be accounted for. And the obvious explanation of their presence seems to be that the addition was made not many years after the completion of the rest, by a writer belonging to the same region, more probably even the same circle[1], as that in which the preceding work was produced, that is to say in Ephesus or its neighbourhood. The

[1] Cp. Lücke, *ib.* p. 828, "Der Inhalt wie die Form mag dem Joh. Kreise angehören."

features in question, however, have been attributed to imitation[1]. Prof. Bacon even remarks of the writer, "Of course this editor adjusts his own style to that of the work he edits. Such was the literary method of his time[2]." One would be glad to know what instances of this "literary method of his time" Prof. Bacon has in mind, so that one might consider whether they seem to be really to the point. I have not been able to think of any that support his assumption. Indeed, I should have been more disposed to say that it was not thought necessary at that time, in making an addition to an older record, to attempt to secure such an agreement in style with the original work, for effecting which, at least as regards the subtler resemblances that may be observed in the present instance, close study would be required. Prof. Bacon would, I think, have made a better suggestion, and one equally good for his own purpose, if he had said that his editor had first, through lovingly meditating upon and copying the original work, acquired to a great extent its style. But the view which I have above put forward that he belonged to the same portion of the Church, and approximately to the same time, may claim to be in itself even more probable.

Further, from the nature of the references "to the beloved disciple" in the Appendix it seems clear, that here at least some actual person must be in view, whatever may be the case in the earlier references[3]. But if so, it is more natural that the need for an explanation of his having died before the coming of Christ should have been felt near the time of his death, and in the Church in which he had been revered, rather than a generation or two later in a different part of the world[4].

There is one other consideration to be mentioned in favour of the view that the addition of ch. xxi to the Gospel was not long delayed, which has rightly, as it seems to me, been held by many students to possess great weight, namely that no good evidence is forthcoming that the Gospel was ever known

---

[1] M. Loisy, on the other hand (*ib.* pp. 926 ff.), attempts to distinguish between a "source" used in this chapter, and the editor's alterations.

[2] *Ib.* p. 200.

[3] For discussion of the latter question see below, pp. 54 ff., 134 ff.

[4] Cp. Beyschlag, *Zur Johanneischen Frage*, p. 17, quoted by Eberhardt.

The authorship of Chapter XXI

without the Appendix[1]. Prof. Bacon indeed exclaims triumphantly:

"Those who make this plea shew slight appreciation of the power a canonized writing exerts, as shewn, e.g. in the history of the Massoretic text of the Old Testament, toward the suppression of earlier and uncanonical forms. How many examples are left to us of the 'many narratives' which Luke aimed to supersede, and has actually superseded? How many of the *Logia* of Matthew? How many of the Diary incorporated by 'Luke' in Acts? How many of Romans without the Epistle of commendation of Phœbe, and without the doxology so variously placed, but in the printed texts appearing as Rom. xvi. 25–27? How many examples have we of Mark unsupplemented? How many of Revelation without the framework provided by its Asian editor[2]?"

But—not to go back to the history of the Old Testament—those instances of earlier Christian documents being absorbed in later ones, were of a different character and moreover belong to a time before the close of the first century A.D. That no traces of the earlier forms should be left in such cases is a very different thing from what Prof. Bacon supposes, viz. that the main part of the Fourth Gospel was edited and had an Appendix added to it in the middle of the second century, some 20 to 40 years after it had originally been written, when the Christian Church had greatly grown and the copying of Christian writings must have begun to be more or less actively practised. The instances of the Doxology at end of Romans and the present ending of Mark do not strengthen his position, because in the former of these cases there is textual evidence

---

[1] So, for instance, Klöpper, *Zeitschr. f. Wiss. Theol.* 1899, p. 381, though he could have had no inducement for doing so in his view of the subject-matter of the Appendix, and of its purpose.

[2] *Ib.* pp. 211 f. Prof. Bacon says "that the earliest known reference to the Fourth Gospel seems to know it *not* as supplemented by the Appendix," p. 215. This "earliest known reference" is Mk xvi. 9. I do not myself think that this can with any confidence be taken as a reference to the Fourth Gospel. The same tradition might well be known both to the compiler of the Supplement to Mk, and to the fourth evangelist. Moreover, while it is true that the former does not shew any knowledge of the appearance in Jn xxi, he also shews none of xx. 19–end. Mk xvi. 12 ff. are based on Lk. xxiv. 13–end, or on a tradition common to both.

of the words being variously placed, and in the latter of a different ending. It is, therefore, an important fact that there is no similar evidence in the case of the Appendix of the Fourth Gospel.

But we have still to examine the positive reasons that are alleged for supposing that ch. xxi is from the hand of an editor who wished to commend the work to the Church of Rome. He felt, it is said, that an account of an appearance of the Risen Lord to His disciples in Galilee must be added in order to satisfy those who had been accustomed to the Markan narrative which was contained in the original sequel to Mk xvi. 8.

It must, however, be remarked that as the appearance of Jesus to his disciples in Galilee was there the first, since the disciples were directed to go thither to meet Him, whereas here it is expressly stated to have occurred subsequently to those in Jerusalem, no great amount of pains is shewn to adjust the accounts. Moreover, in view of the close correspondence between Matthew and Mark almost up to the point where the original Mark breaks off, it is most probable that we possess still the original ending of Mark embodied with other matter in the ending of Matthew[1]. And there are no signs of correspondence here with the Appendix in the Fourth Gospel.

In the argument to shew that Jn xxi is derived from Mk's original ending the mediating link is found in the concluding verses of the fragment of the *Gospel of Peter* which was recovered not many years ago. There, although we are not told that the women remained silent as to an appearance to them, the disciples are described as leaving Jerusalem without apparently having heard that the Lord had risen, while the fragment breaks off with the beginning of a fishing scene. From this ignorance of the disciples, together with the fact that Peter is specially mentioned in the message through the women as given in Mk v. 8, it is inferred that the fishing scene in Jn xxi, and that of which we have the beginning in the *Gospel of Peter*, were derived from the lost ending of Mark. Against this view it may, I think, well be urged, *first*, that we must suppose Christ's promise to have been fulfilled, even though the women did not report it, and that the sequel in Mt. was more truly a fulfilment

[1] See vol. II of the present work, p. 202.

The authorship of Chapter XXI

of this promise than that in John xxi, where only seven disciples were present. To this the fact that Peter is the object of special notice hardly supplies a sufficient make-weight. *Secondly*, little stress ought to be laid on the agreement of the *Gospel of Peter* because the writer may well have taken his fishing scene from Jn xxi. That he should have done so would accord with the use that has been made of all four Canonical Gospels in other parts of that fragment. The assumption, therefore, that the appearance on the shore of the Lake of Galilee in Jn xxi was derived from Mark's lost ending appears to be a very precarious one.

This is not the place to discuss the relation to one another and the respective values of the different narratives of Appearances of the Risen Christ. But it may be observed that there do not exist any indications that the traditions of Appearances in Jerusalem and Galilee respectively were ever dominant in particular places or districts outside of Palestine. When men heard in early days a fresh narrative, which seemed to come to them on good authority, they would not be slow to receive it, and would not feel any strong critical solicitude for adjusting it precisely with what they had received before. Even supposing that a member of the Ephesine Church had as such been bred in the knowledge only of the Appearances related in Jn xx, he need not have felt any repugnance to accepting and recording the narrative given in ch. xxi, if he came across it. In other words, there is nothing improbable in the idea that the latter should have been added to the rest by one living amid the surroundings where the preceding account had been committed to writing. As for Rome, the great centre to which traditions and systems of teaching were brought from all parts of the world, Christians there must have become accustomed to combining as best they might the "Jerusalemite" and "Galilean" accounts of Appearances long before the middle of the second century.

We are supposed to have another, and even perhaps more direct, concession to feeling in Rome in the commission given to Simon Peter in xxi. 15–17. The singling out of Peter to receive this commission while nothing is said to the other disciples, several of whom were present, is a point which should be dispassionately considered. It has generally been regarded by conservative non-Roman commentators as designed by Christ, alike to deepen his penitence and to reassure him, after his peculiarly conspicuous fall. And the correspondence between the threefold inquiry as to his devotion to his Master and the threefold denial, and the allusion that there appears to be in the question "lovest thou Me *more than these*" to the protestation recorded at Mk xiv. 29, Mt. xxvi. 33, "Though all shall be offended yet will not I," justify this explanation. But it may not, and probably does not, exhaust the significance of the incident, in view of the position among the Twelve and in relation to the Church which Peter held in his own life-time, and the words addressed to him at Mt. xvi. 18, 19. On the other hand Roman Catholic interpreters and certain modern critics are not warranted in reading into the commission given to Peter in Jn xxi. 15–17 a conception of Simon Peter's "primacy" resembling, if not indeed virtually identical with, the present Roman notion of it. Roman Catholic commentators have often taken "the sheep" whom Peter was to feed as "other pastors," and "the lambs" as the faithful generally. M. Loisy admits that this is unsound exegesis. Yet he clings to the view that rule over and the guidance and instruction of the other Apostles are implied in the charge here given to Peter[1]. But neither he nor anyone else, so far as I am aware, has given any good reason for thinking so. In the New Testament, and in all early Christian literature up to the latter part of the second century, Peter appears only as *primus inter pares*, not as *Episcopus episcoporum*. If he is singled out here to receive the charge from Christ to feed His flock it is as the representative of the whole body, privileged to hold this position because he would be preeminent in a work in which all had a share. Further, there is not the slightest indication that he was to have a special successor in his position, which is a necessary point in the Roman theory. Thus even if it could be shewn that the narrative of the charge to Peter was derived from the lost ending of Mark, there would be little ground for supposing that its introduction was designed to favour claims made in Rome.

But further the suggestion that this account of a charge given specially to Simon Peter to feed Christ's flock was framed with the intention of humouring the Church of Rome in its

[1] Pp. 942 f.

The authorship of Chapter XXI

claims on behalf of its bishop, and so to win acceptance for the Gospel to which it was appended, appears to involve a flagrant anachronism. There is positive evidence that such claims were not then made in the letter of Irenæus to Victor near the close of the century, in which he contrasts the pretensions of the latter with the attitude of Anicetus to Polycarp some 40 years before[1].

Finally, it is scarcely conceivable that one who (according to the theory of those who suppose the Appendix to have been added about A.D. 150) desired to get the Fourth Gospel recognised as the work of the Apostle John and as part of his scheme for securing this sought to commend it to Roman Christians, whose views as to the Gospel narrative and as to a Petrine supremacy had been moulded by Mark[2], should have proceeded so tentatively both as to the points he conceded and as to those which he wished to see accepted. He had, it is true, a very delicate task to perform. He had to correct an impression which might be gathered from the main body of the Gospel that Peter was inferior to the beloved disciple. And yet while he exalted Simon Peter, all the more must he lay stress on the preeminence of that other disciple in his own sphere[3]. But he was anxious to succeed, and according to the theory in question he did succeed. Yet how could he have done so by such means? How could such extremely slight adjustments to the Synoptic story have satisfied those who were wedded to it? How could such obscure indications of the personality of the evangelist have served to establish the Johannine authorship? As Jülicher truly observes, "in conflicts of this kind one needs weapons sharpened to a finer edge[4]."

Although, therefore, ch. xxi was by a different hand from chs. i–xx, there appears to be no good ground for interposing a long interval between the composition of the one and the other.

---

[1] Cp. Eus. v. 24.

[2] Bacon, p. 221: "We can scarcely see how it were possible otherwise for the transition to be made from a mystical Ephesian Gospel, accompanied by no higher claims than those embodied in Jn i–xx and the inclosing Epistles, to a catholic Gospel of general acceptation and admitted apostolic authority."

[3] Bacon, p. 200, refers to Jn xxi, as "a new and special account of the Apostolic Commission based upon the ancient Roman form, distributing its responsibilities between Peter and John."

[4] See Jülicher, *Einleit.* p. 389.

NOTES ON CHAPTER XXI

These notes are based mainly, though not exclusively, on an examination of the works referred to in the notes on p. 18 above of Scholten, Tiele, Eberhardt, Klöpper, Schmiedel, Loisy, and also Wellhausen, *Das Evang. Joh.* 1908, pp. 96 ff. They do not pretend to exhaust the evidence. Naturally, however, I have noticed especially those features which seem to me most significant. But in some instances I have also criticised the critics, because it seems to me that one of our greatest needs in the field of the study of Historical Criticism is a clearer understanding—at least as applied to the New Testament and Christian origins, whatever students in other fields have to say about theirs—as to what is, and what is not, sound critical method.

v. 1. μετὰ ταῦτα. Some features of the account in *vv.* 1-14 of an appearance of the Risen Christ, placed here after the Appearances in ch. xx, would better suit a first Appearance. In *vv.* 1-3 there is no sign that the disciples realise that they have received a great commission. We get rather an impression of listlessness. Their surprise also at seeing Jesus, the slowness of Peter to recognise Him, and the attitude of all at *v.* 12, are strange after the events already narrated.

Linguistically, however, μετὰ ταῦτα, in introducing a fresh narrative, is Johannine, though it occurs also several times in Luke. ἐφανέρωσεν ἑαυτόν: φανεροῦν reflexively is not elsewhere used of an Appearance of the Risen Lord, but we have ἐφανερώθη at *v.* 14 and at Mk xvi. 12 and 14. The word is a favourite one in Jn and is used reflexively at vii. 4; cp. also ii. 11 for the idea. It is not used in the other Gospels except in the Appendix to Mk. A point of contact with Mk xvi is the use of φανεροῦν of the Resurrection, Mk xvi. 12, 14, Jn xxi. 14, and reflexively at Jn xxi. 1 (bis). The use of ἐπὶ with gen. τῆς θαλάσσης is different from that at vi. 19. τῆς Τιβεριάδος : at vi. 1 we have the phrase τῆς θαλάσσης τῆς Γαλιλαίας τῆς Τιβεριάδος. It would not be unnatural that a writer, who had once given both the older name and that by which the lake was best known at a later time to strangers, should on a subsequent occasion be satisfied to give the latter only. But it would also be quite possible that the author of the Appendix should have introduced τῆς Τιβεριάδος in the earlier passage as an explanatory note.

v. 2. Σίμων Πέτρος, used five times in this chapter and twelve in

Notes on Chapter XXI

remainder of Gospel is used only besides at Mt. xvi. 16, Lk. v. 8, and 2 Pet. i. 1, though ὁ λέγομ. or ὁ ἐπικαλ. Πέτρος occurs a few times. ὁ λεγόμενος Δίδυμος occurs also at Jn xi. 16 and xx. 24, not elsewhere; Ναθαναήλ, in Jn i. *vv.* 45 ff., not elsewhere; ὁ ἀπὸ Κανὰ τ. Γαλ., Cana, Jn ii. 1, 11, iv. 46, not elsewhere. It is not, however, indicated in Jn i that Nathanael was of Cana. Schmiedel observes: "that Nathanael belonged to Cana is certainly the result of a false combination of i. 46 and ii. 1." But there might perfectly well be a tradition (true or false) of this kind in a particular part of the Church. On the other hand, the "sons of Zebedee" are not mentioned in Jn i–xx ἐκ τῶν μαθητῶν αὐτοῦ δύο : "the use, which is Hebraic rather than Greek, of ἐκ instead of the partitive gen. is very common in John" (*Eberh.*); see i. 35, vi. 8, etc. and contrast Mk xiv. 13, Lk. vii. 19, xix. 29. There is no similar enumeration of disciples elsewhere in this Gospel, nor does the evangelist elsewhere usually mention those who are not going to speak or act.

v. 3. Wellhausen notes that πιάζειν is nowhere else used in the Gospel for the taking of fish. But the word itself is specially common in this Gospel, and as there is no other fishing scene there was no opportunity for using it of catching fish.

v. 4. πρωίας δὲ ἤδη γινομένης : at xviii. 28, and xx 1 πρωΐ is used (*Schmiedel*). But the meaning conveyed is not precisely the same ; moreover πρωΐ is used at Mt. xx. 1, and πρωΐας δὲ γενομένης at xxvii. 1, and yet this difference has not so far as I know been traced to a difference of source. ἔστη εἰς (τὸν αἰγιαλόν), cp. xx. 19.

v. 5. παιδία: the disciples are not elsewhere so addressed, but we have the very similar address τεκνία at xiii. 33. Both παιδία and τεκνία are used in 1 Jn in addressing believers. The address in the other Gospels which is most nearly analogous is τὸ μικρὸν ποίμνιον at Lk. xii. 32. προσφάγιον, ἅπ. λεγ.; we have ὀψάριον at vi. 9, 11, and at xxi. 9, 10, 13, and not elsewhere in N.T. ἀποκρίνεσθαι is most commonly joined with λέγειν, e.g. ἀποκριθεὶς εἶπεν, or (as frequently in Jn) ἀπεκρίθη καὶ εἶπεν. Its use by itself is more common in Jn than elsewhere. With the present verse cp. esp. i. 21.

v. 6. βάλετε…ἔβαλον οὖν : "constructio est prorsus Joannea" (*Tiele*). ἰσχύειν: not elsewhere in Jn. ἀπό : "the causal ἀπό is found only here, and in place of the partitive ἀπό (*v.* 10) ἐκ is elsewhere used" (*Wellhausen*).

v. 7. ὁ μαθ. ἐκεῖνος ὃν ἠγάπα ὁ Ἰησοῦς: also at *v.* 20 ; cp. xiii. 23, xix. 26. ἐπενδύτην, ἅπ. λεγ. διαζωννύναι : also at xiii. 4, 5, not elsewhere in N.T. ἦν γὰρ γυμνός: "the parenthetic form of the subordinate

Notes on Chapter XXI

proposition is thoroughly Johannine...especially with γάρ" (*Eberhardt*). To "the disciple whom Jesus loved" quickness of spiritual perception is attributed; to Simon Peter promptness of action. This corresponds exactly with the characteristics of the two at xx. 4–8, if (as is frequently assumed) it is implied there that on that occasion Peter was not convinced.

v. 8. τῷ πλοιαρίῳ ἦλθον (without prep.) and τὸ δίκτυον τῶν ἰχθύων are both strange expressions.

v. 9. ὡς οὖν: Johannine, see iv. 1, 40; xi. 6; xviii. 6; xx. 11; not in Synoptics.

vv. 9–13, with which comp. also *vv.* 4–6. The narrative lacks clearness and simplicity. The disciples are bidden to catch fish for their meal and, even after they have seen fish being cooked when they land, to bring it, and although it is with the former apparently that they are fed. The parts also of Simon Peter and the rest of the disciples in dragging the net (*vv.* 9–11) are not made clear. There is also "something apocryphal" in the large and precise number—153. The narrative at Lk. v. 4 ff. is more natural.

v. 12. τολμᾶν: not used elsewhere in Jn. In the other Gospels, however, it is only used in Mk xii. 34, and parallels, and Mk xv. 43. ἐξετάζειν: not elsewhere used in this Gospel, but the situation is quite peculiar; the disciples are smitten with awe in the presence of Him Who, hard as it is to understand, they are convinced is their Lord risen from the dead. The use of a stronger word than ἐρωτᾶν is natural in the circumstances.

οὐδείς...μαθητῶν: "Insolita mihi videtur constructio. A Joanne enim οὐδείς semper genitivo qui ab eo pendet arcte jungitur, et idem ille post οὐδείς non genitivo uti solet, verum præpositione ἐκ sequente genitivo. Cæterum in universo genitivus partitivus, qui dicitur, ab evangelista quarto potissimum in constructionem cum præpositione ἐκ sequente genitivo dissolvitur" (*Tiele*).

v. 14. τρίτον: this is supposed not to agree with ch. xx, where three Appearances have already been recorded; only two, however, of these were *to the disciples*. Also the note of the number of times resembles the note at the end of the account of the miracle at Cana (ii. 11), and of that of healing the child of the court-official (iv. 54). Nevertheless it is true that the narrative in this chapter is taken from the tradition of Appearances in Galilee, while those in ch. xx are taken from that of Appearances in Jerusalem. And further the difficulty which the disciples experience in believing that it is indeed their Risen Lord would suit a first Appearance better than the third.

Notes on Chapter XXI

It may be added that each of the accounts of Appearances in ch. xx concludes with some spiritual teaching important for believers generally; there is none such after *v.* 13. The conversation which follows at *vv.* 15 ff. is of a more individual character, and is separated from *vv.* 1–13 by *v.* 14.

ἐγερθείς: at xx. 9, ἀναστῆναι is used. This has been noted by more than one writer on differences between this chapter and the remainder of the Gospel. For reference to Scholten, who lays stress on the connexion with ἠγέρθη at ii. 22, see p. 488. Bacon (*ib.* p. 198, n. 2) remarks, "Among the more important (differences), because involving a difference of conception, is the return of the Appendix (and the interpolated section, ii. 13–22) to earlier usage in referring to Jesus' resurrection (xxi. 14, Jesus 'was raised,' ἠγέρθη; xx. 9, he 'rose,' ἀνέστη, in accordance with the idea of x. 18)." The verdict of the Concordance, however, seems to be that there was no distinction of this kind between the two words, at least as to the date of use. ἀναστῆναι and ἐγερθῆναι are both repeatedly used of the Resurrection of Christ in Mk; moreover at Mk xii. 25, ἀναστῆναι *is used of the resurrection of the dead generally.* In Lk. the two words are used of Christ about equally, and ἀναστῆναι more generally of rising from the dead at xvi. 31. In St Paul's Epp. ἐγείρεσθαι is the commoner word; but in 1 Thess. (probably his earliest Ep., or one of the earliest) ἀνέστη is used of Jesus at iv. 14; and ἀναστήσονται, *ib. v.* 16, of the dead in Christ.

vv. 15–17. Σίμων Ἰωάνου three times: we have Σίμων ὁ υἱὸς Ἰωάνου at i. 42; neither elsewhere. It has been held that this charge to Simon Peter is designed to give him a higher place relatively to "the beloved disciple" than that which Peter occupies in chs. i–xx. At the same time the expressions "*my* sheep," "*my* lambs," remind us of x. 1 ff., where Jesus is represented as the Good Shepherd. The dimins. are not, however, used elsewhere for the members of the flock. On the other hand, πλέον τούτων seems like an allusion to Mt. xxvi. 23, rather than to any incident in the Fourth Gospel. "Formulam non-Joanneam esse credo...Ni fallor, Joannes scripsisset πλεῖον ἢ οὗτοι, cf. iv. 1" (*Tiele*).

v. 16. πάλιν δεύτερον: same phrase occurs at iv. 54; at Mt. xxvi. 42 and Ac. x. 15 we have πάλιν ἐκ δευτέρου.

v. 19. Many such comments are introduced throughout the Gospel; this one is similar to xii. 33. On the other hand there is a shade of difference from it in the application of the phrase δοξάζειν τ. θεόν, which may perhaps justify Lücke's remark that the expression "appears Johannine, but belongs in fact to the later ecclesiastical Greek."

v. 20. The amplified designation of the beloved disciple is peculiar. ἀκολουθοῦντα: ἀκολουθεῖν is here used apparently without the special connotation of ἀκολουθεῖ in *vv.* 19 and 22. That injunction to Simon Peter reminds one, however, of xiii. 36–38. Wellhausen seems to forget that passage when he speaks of the idea of "following Jesus to death through martyrdom" as a peculiarity of ch. xxi.

The expectation of the Parousia seems to be of a more usual kind than that in Jn xiv.

v. 23. τοὺς ἀδελφούς: at xx. 17, "my brethren" are the disciples, here members of the Christian body of a later time. But the difference is a natural one in the different context.

v. 25. οἶμαι: this common Greek expression is not elsewhere used in the N.T.

THE ALLEGED SIGNS OF DIFFERENT HANDS IN CHS. I–XX

The difficulties of the inquiry in which we have just been engaged are slight in comparison with those of an examination of the imperfections of arrangement, repetitions, illogical connexions, contradictions between various statements, comments which shew a misconception of the sayings which they seek to interpret or apply, differences of doctrinal outlook, which with more or less apparent reason are pointed out in the body of the Gospel itself, and of the inferences which in recent times have been drawn from them as to the combination of different sources in the Gospel, and the attempts which have been made to distinguish between a fundamental document and extensive interpolations. Yet this task must be faced.

Before entering upon it two other lines of speculation may be mentioned which deal with *some* of the same phenomena, but which it will not, I think, be necessary to discuss at length.

1. It has been supposed by some that there have been *accidental displacements* of the original text, and ingenious suggestions have been put forward as to the manner in which these accidental displacements have occurred[1]. But the cases

---

[1] See Additional Note, pp. 73 ff.

of Chapters I-XX

in which such an explanation will serve are but few, out of many where alterations in the original form of the Gospel may on equally good grounds be suspected. If these phenomena generally are to be effectively dealt with it can only be on some hypothesis which gives opportunity for somewhat freer and more varied treatment of different passages. In some instances also, as we shall presently see, the restoration to its supposed original position of a passage held to have been displaced, if it would remove some difficulties, would create fresh ones, to meet which further omissions or other remedies would be required.

2. Similarly, we may decline to consider Blass's numerous conjectural emendations of the text. There does not appear to be any sound reason for assuming that the Fourth Gospel was peculiarly unfortunate in the circumstances of its transmission[1].

On the other hand in connexion with the hypothesis of different sources, and of editing, motives are at least alleged for changes which have led to the presence of incongruities, and their probability or their improbability can be discussed. And, further, on the most extensive view that anyone could venture to take of the corruption of the text in the course of its transmission, it would hardly be possible to explain thus all the phenomena that should be considered together.

In comparison, then, with the two hypotheses just mentioned, that of there being the signs of different hands in the Gospel may fairly be said to hold the field, and the discussion of the theories which involve this larger hypothesis will, at least, serve to bring before us the facts which the other two seek to account for, as well as other facts along with them.

It will be convenient, I think, for most of my readers, if I first give some account of the chief theories of recent times which assume the compositeness of the Gospel[2]. The first to be noticed is that of H. H. Wendt, originally set forth by him

[1] For Blass's view see his *Das Joh. Evang.* p. 179.
[2] For some account of the earlier theories of the same kind the reader may see Wendt's work, published 1900 (immediately mentioned in the sequel), pp. 45 ff.; also Bousset's art. in the *Theol. Rundschau* for 1909 (mentioned below, p. 44 n. 1), pp. 1-6.

in the first edition of *Die Lehre Jesu*, 1886, and again in a separate work, *Das Johannesevangelium, eine Untersuchung seiner Entstehung und seines geschichtlichen Wertes*, A.D. 1900; and urged once more in another work devoted to the subject, *Die Schichten im vierten Evangelium*, A.D. 1912. Wendt's position bears a good deal of resemblance to that of Weisse in an earlier generation, but he has worked out and defended his view more systematically.

In his latest exposition he starts from a group of instances in the Fourth Gospel in which sayings attributed to Jesus are followed by comments on the part of the evangelist, which are not made from the same point of view as the sayings, and could not have been "devised and drafted in their context" by the same person. The instances which he specially adduces are ii. 21 f.; vii. 37 ff.; xii. 32 f. (cp. xviii. 32), xviii. 9 (cp. xvii. 12). There is, he also urges, a family likeness in the misinterpretations[1].

From this contrast he passes to a still broader one between the narrative portions of the Gospel generally and the discourses of Jesus. He notes in particular a difference of terminology in regard to the miracles of Christ. The word $\sigma\eta\mu\epsilon\hat{\iota}\alpha$ used repeatedly both by the Jews and by the evangelist is used twice only by Jesus, namely at vi. 26, and in a more or less depreciatory manner in the saying at iv. 48. The word He commonly employs is $\ddot{\epsilon}\rho\gamma\alpha$, which is used besides with reference to them only in the remark of His brethren at vii. 3 and in the mere repetition by the Jews of a phrase used by Jesus Himself at x. 33. With this difference of language a different estimate of the importance of the miracles is associated. The general term "works," if it includes the miracles, embraces also much besides. In two of the passages where Jesus appeals to His "works," He dwells in close connexion therewith upon His "words." His "works" are in point of fact parts of that one "work" which the Father gave Him to accomplish and are—so Wendt contends—"to be understood in the same sense[2]."

Closely connected with this difference in the place assigned to the miracles is a different view of what is implied in

[1] See *Schichten*, pp. 23 f. and *Jo. Ev.* pp. 62 ff.
[2] See *Jo. Ev.* pp. 60 f. and *Schichten*, p. 40.

Soltau's theory

believing. In the discourses it is conceived as "the practical recognition of the Divine significance of Jesus for salvation, which is completed through the appropriation and following of His preaching." For the evangelist, on the other hand, it signifies "the theoretical conviction of the Divine nature and power of Jesus, as produced principally through the impression made by his wonderful works and the evidences of His supernatural knowledge[1]."

Further, Wendt finds that the discourses do not always arise naturally and suitably out of the circumstances described in the pieces of narrative that introduce them. It will readily be admitted that the words at Jn vi. 30, "what sign doest thou,... what dost thou work?" come strangely from those who had on the preceding day, according to the account in our Gospel, witnessed the feeding of five thousand. Among other examples insisted upon by Wendt, I may mention the discourse in v. 17 ff. which, as also vii. 19–24, is, according to him, founded upon a different view of the manner in which the Sabbath had been broken from that in v. 1–16[2].

The conclusion drawn by Wendt from his observations is that the fourth evangelist had before him a source composed of *logia* of Jesus. In order to make these more generally serviceable he provided a framework of narrative for the whole, and descriptions of the occasions on which different discourses were spoken, and introduced glosses upon some of the sayings. In the composition of his Gospel he also sought to take account of the interest which the Christian community to which he belonged felt in the Apostle John, and to compare him with Simon Peter, while he also kept before himself certain dogmatic aims[3].

Next in order of time among recent critics to propound a theory of the composite origin of the Fourth Gospel was W. Soltau[4], and there is an affinity in an important respect between his views and those of Wendt. Like the latter Soltau holds that the Discourses in the Fourth Gospel existed as a

[1] *Jo. Ev.* p. 138.   [2] *Jo. Ev.* pp. 68–70, and *Schichten*, pp. 43–9.
[3] *Jo. Ev.* pp. 223 ff., cp. *Schichten*, pp. 80 f.
[4] *Unsere Evangelien, ihre Quellen und ihr Quellenwert*, 1901. He set them forth again in an article in *Theol. Stud. und Kritik.* for 1908, pp. 177–202, without substantial change. The references in what follows are to this later exposition.

separate collection before the remainder of the Gospel was compiled[1]. But this remaining matter was not simply supplied in order to be a framework for the Discourses, as Wendt suggested, but was composed as an independent work. The compiler of this work, however, whom Soltau calls "the evangelist," knew the Discourses, as is shewn by his having introduced fragments from them into his narratives[2]. Later, either he himself, or an editor—which must be a matter for further inquiry—inserted the Discourses themselves into the Gospel[3]. But in the Gospel, apart from the Discourses, different elements are to be distinguished by the differences in their relations to the Synoptic Gospels. Certain narratives, to which Soltau gives the name of Johannine legends, shew no trace of dependence upon, or knowledge of, the Synoptics[4]. There are others, on the contrary, which agree closely with the latter[5]. Once more there is a group, called by Soltau "antisynoptic," in which knowledge of the Synoptics is revealed by one or more traits or phrases, while these have been placed in a widely different setting. Soltau attributes the composition of this last set of narratives to "the evangelist" himself, and considers that the writer who was substantially faithful to the Synoptic Gospels in one set of narratives could not have treated them so differently in another[6]. He holds, therefore, that "the evangelist" found the "Johannine legends" and the "Synoptic narratives" already combined in a document which he used in framing his Gospel[7]. He is confident that henceforth these conclusions can alone lay claim to scientific recognition[8].

The indications of compositeness on which Wellhausen[9], to whom we will next turn, relies, are for the most part different and of a different kind. He lays stress upon actual contradictions and repetitions, or (to use the technical term) "doublettes"—or what appear to him to be such—alike in the narrative portions and the discourses. These cannot, he contends, be

[1] Pp. 180–182.   [2] Pp. 183 f.   [3] Pp. 200 ff.
[4] Pp. 187 f.   [5] Pp. 184 f.   [6] P. 189.
[7] P. 195.   [8] P. 202.

[9] Wellhausen first called in question the unity of the Fourth Gospel in a *brochure* entitled *Erweiterungen und Änderungen im vierten Evangelium*, pub. 1907. His views on the subject, in a much more fully developed form, were set forth by him in *Das Evangelium Johannis*, in the following year.

Wellhausen's theory

explained as mere lapses on the part of one who was the author of the whole Gospel. "A writer may be negligent and maladroit, and once in a way even a little forgetful, but he must know what he means and cannot lose forthwith all idea of what he has himself said[1]."

Again, Wellhausen's conception of the primitive document embodied in the Gospel differs widely from Wendt's. The latter, as we have seen, held it to be a collection of discourses; the analogy of the Matthæan *Logia* may have been present to his mind. Wellhausen's "foundation-document," on the other hand, resembled more the Marcan outline, in that he supposed the work of Jesus in Galilee to have been first described in it, without being preceded or interrupted by the account of any visit to Jerusalem, and the time spent in Jerusalem and Judæa only after that spent in Galilee. He bases this view on vii. 3, 4, which passage, as he maintains, implies that up to this time Jesus had only laboured in Galilee, and is incompatible with the preceding journeys to feasts and the chronology resting thereupon[2]. Accordingly he holds that those passages relating to Jerusalem and Judæa in the first six chapters of the present Gospel, which for one reason or another he considers to have been taken from the basal document, have been wrongly transferred from the time after to that before the turning point in the ministry of Jesus indicated at the beginning of ch. vii. The cleansing of the temple in ch. ii is not only out of place but had no place in the basal document; it could not be fitted into the course of events leading to the Passion as they were there represented. The incidents and teaching in ii. 23–iv. 3 of which the scenes are laid in Jerusalem and Judæa were also wanting to it. The visit to Samaria, of which an account is given in ch. iv, was originally described, like that in Luke, as taking place when Jesus was journeying from Galilee to Jerusalem, instead of in the opposite direction[3]. v. 1 is an editorial statement; in the basal document the miracle described in v. 2–16 followed immediately upon the account of the journey through Samaria. The discourse in v. 17–end must belong to a different occasion, since it does not really deal with the offence then given. Portions of it come from a

---

[1] See *Ev. Jo.* p. 4.   [2] P. 5.   [3] P. 20.

discourse of which other portions are preserved in chs. vii and viii[1]. The statement at viii. 59 is from the basal document though probably the clauses in the latter half of the verse should be inverted, and so should read, " But Jesus went out of the temple and hid himself." This attempt on the part of the Jews to stone Jesus excludes the possibility of the continued public Appearances related in ix. 1–x. 39, none of which consequently formed part of the basal document[2]. On the other hand, "the Lazarus-story was the turning point in its narrative[3]," though it has been much elaborated. xi. 45–57 are not original. The many miracles do not belong to the basal document, nor does the High Priest Caiaphas. The idea of sacrifice is also foreign to it. And the flight to Ephraim (*vv.* 54–57) is but a variant of x. 40–42[4]. In ch. xii, also, "the basal document is nowhere to be found[5]." Something may however have fallen out, which came between the Raising of Lazarus and the Feet-washing. The substratum of the farewell discourse so far as it is contained in ch. xiv was supplied by the basal document. The words "Arise, let us go hence" at xiv. 31 conclude it. Chs. xv and xvi are a later paraphrase of xiv, and xvii is in many ways peculiar.

In the account of the arrest, the trial by Jewish authorities and Peter's denials there have been various interpolations from the Synoptic Gospels in the basal document, in such wise that the connexion has been disturbed and there is great want of lucidity. Through the story of the trial by Pilate, Wellhausen renounces the attempt to thread his way, though he criticises the scenes separately[6]? Finally, the basal document ended at the same point as, according to Wellhausen, the original Mark did, viz. at the finding of the empty grave by the women and the appearance of an angel to them[7].

So far as to the general outline of Wellhausen's basal document. But it will be well also to refer to *some* of the passages that he omits from it, which have not yet been mentioned or not expressly so. In ch. i, *vv.* 22–24 and 25–28 are variants, and so are 29–31, and 32–34[8]. In the former pair the first is the later, in the latter the second. The numbering of the two

---

[1] Pp. 24, 25.   [2] P. 45.   [3] P. 50.   [4] P. 54.   [5] P. 58.
[6] Pp. 80, 83.   [7] P. 93.   [8] Pp. 9 ff.

Wellhausen's theory

miracles in Galilee (ii. 11, iv. 54) is not original; that would have been unnecessary since the second miracle was related immediately after the first[1]. In ch. v, *vv.* 19–29 are an insertion, *vv.* 43–47 are amplifications, and there are secondary touches even in the parts of which the substratum is from the basal document[2]. In ch. vi the discourse 26 ff. is not of one casting and *vv.* 22–25 have been provided as an introduction to it in order to connect it with the preceding narrative[3]. In ch. vii *vv.* 33–44 are an insertion, for 45 ff. completes the account begun in 31, 32. In the interpolated pieces different persons are in question and 40–44 is plainly a variant of 25–30[4]. The substratum, taken from the basal document of the discourse in ch. viii, is to be found only in *vv.* 21, 25, 26, 38, 39, 40, 44, 59[5]. Lastly, in ch. xiv, Wellhausen distinguishes the sources of different passages, according to the manner in which the functions of the exalted Jesus and the Paraclete are represented in them. In the one set Jesus, after He has gone to heaven, will not Himself come to men on earth; but the Paraclete is promised in His stead who is to abide for ever with the Church (*vv.* 1–4, 16, 26 ff.). In the other "the exalted Jesus Himself is the principle of life in the Church; the Paraclete is superfluous and in fact disappears (*vv.* 5–15, 18–24). The latter preponderate, and consequently the attempt is made to bring the Paraclete where He appears into a subordinate position relatively to Jesus (*vv.* 16, 26)." This second representation in which the immanent Jesus is the principal figure is the later, and is that which we have in the paraphrase—"so for brevity to call it"—in chs. xv and xvi[6].

Finally, the work of recasting, amplification and revision was not carried out by one hand only or even by two. It was a process in which many took part. Within the passages marked as not belonging to the basal document there are incongruities to be observed and variants and developments. And one addition gave rise to another[7]. With regard, however, to the significance from a historical point of view of this whole process of revision the following remark of Wellhausen is very important:

[1] P. 24.   [2] Pp. 25 f.   [3] P. 30.   [4] P. 38 f.
[5] P. 45.   [6] P. 77.   [7] See p. 100.

"Literary criticism (*die Literarkritik*) is of far more limited significance for the historical relations of the Fourth Gospel than for Exegesis. In spite of its different strata it can be historically regarded as essentially a unity. It should be assumed that the amplifications for the most part originate from the same circle within which the basal document arose and found its first readers[1]."

E. Schwartz[2], to whom I now pass, has much in common with Wellhausen, so that it will not be necessary to dwell on his views at the same length. But I will notice a few points. In the first of his Articles on "*Aporien* in the Fourth Gospel" he investigates the passages in which the "beloved disciple" appears, and comes to the conclusion that none of these belonged to the original Gospel. Two of them—that in the account of the Last Supper, and the scene in which Jesus committed His Mother to him—were introduced by the first and chief "elaborator" (*der Bearbeiter*) of the Gospel, for whom nevertheless, this disciple was only a typical figure. A later interpolator, the author of ch. xxi, identified him with the Ephesine John. To this later hand also the definite article and the description, "whom Jesus loved," are due in the narrative of the race to the grave (ch. xx. 2), whereby it was suggested that "another disciple" who brought Peter into the high priest's house was the same person[3]. The "elaborator" was also, he holds, the author of the First Ep. of John and probably of the Second and Third; the later interpolator made some slight changes in these, and introduced the name of John into the Apocalypse, and succeeded in getting the view accepted that these four writings as well as the Gospel were the work of the Apostle John[4].

Schwartz draws the same inference from vii. 3 f. that Wellhausen does, as to the form of the original Gospel. But, further, he has a theory of his own as to the motive for the introduction by a later hand of repeated visits of Jesus to Jerusalem for Jewish feasts, and the implication at viii. 57, that He was nearer fifty than thirty years of age. These changes were, he

[1] P. 119.
[2] See four articles on *Aporien im vierten Evangelium* in *Nachrichten d. Gesellschaft d. Wissenschaften zu Göttingen, philolog. hist. Klasse*, for 1907, 1908.
[3] *Ib.* 1907, pp. 361 ff.   [4] *Ib.* p. 368.

E. Schwartz's theory

holds, aimed at Valentinus and the early members of his school, who (as may be gathered from Irenæus) put a mystical interpretation, in accordance with their doctrine of Æons, upon the duration of Christ's Ministry, when it was assumed that it lasted only one year, and upon His age as thirty years. The reviser in this case cannot in Schwartz's opinion have been the author of the First Epistle, in which (he thinks) there is no antignostic tendency, and must therefore have been the "interpolator," the author of Jn xxi.

It has been seen then that according to Schwartz two hands at least must have been engaged in bringing the basal document of the Fourth Gospel to the present form of that Gospel. It may be added that he regards it as highly probable that there were other re-touchings of smaller extent[1].

Drastic as Wellhausen is in what he does not allow to have formed part of the original Gospel, Schwartz is even more so. In the narrative of the Crucifixion, for instance, he considers that the view that Jesus was Himself the Paschal Lamb is the only trait that can with any degree of certainty be traced to it[2].

Schwartz's view of the significance of the revision of the Gospel relatively to the life and thought of the Church presents a contrast with that suggested by the words of Wellhausen quoted above at the end of the notice of his work on the Fourth Gospel. "We have not here," Schwartz writes, "a collection of the additions, which the Christian community half unconsciously and naively made to the recollection of the disciples on the subject of the Lord. There is no continued growth here of a tradition which, if it does not keep firm hold on past events, is yet itself a living event. A poet of strong powers of thought and marked individuality, who has undertaken to raise an altogether new song concerning the excellencies of his God, is present here[3]."

B. W. Bacon agrees with Wellhausen and Schwartz in holding that the Fourth Gospel reached its present form through a long redactional process. But he expresses himself doubtfully as to the prospect of obtaining wide assent for many of the results that can be gained by critical analysis[4]. In his recent treatment

---
[1] *Ib.* 1908, p. 559.   [2] *Ib.* 1907, pp. 357, 361.   [3] *Ib.* 1908, p. 557.
[4] *The Fourth Gospel in Research and Debate*, pp. 481, 495, 521.

of the subject he has laid great stress on the connexion between the Appendix and various passages in the preceding twenty chapters as a means of ascertaining the revision which an earlier form of the Gospel has undergone[1]. Previously he had directed attention to the seeming disarrangements in the Fourth Gospel, as he does again in his recent work; and he has maintained that they were the result not of accident, but of "deliberate editorial adaptation[2]." His special contribution to the discussion of the subject has been an investigation of the arrangement of passages from the Fourth Gospel in Tatian's *Harmony*. He finds that Tatian has in several respects remedied defects in the order of the Gospel as we have it; and he submits that this is far less likely to have been due to critical acumen on his part than to his having been acquainted through an extra-canonical source with the form in which the Johannine material existed before being brought into the shape in which we have it, and as he also in his day had it[3].

I will conclude this notice of Bacon's treatment of the subject now before us, as I did that of each of the last two writers mentioned, by quoting words of his own on the broad significance of the conclusions reached. "It (the Fourth Gospel) has," he writes, "a history of growth and development, of revision, recasting, cancellation and supplementation. Proofs of this process rightly viewed can make this Gospel of all the greater value to the true student of Christian origins, because, like the varied 'scriptures of the prophets' given 'by divers portions and in divers manners' it will be seen to epitomize, as no mere individual's work could do, the inner life of one of the greatest branches of the Church[4]."

The article by R. Schütz[5] on the first portion of the Gospel according to St John, though but a slight investigation of its subject, deserves to be named, as he appears to have been the

---

[1] He speaks of the "redactional" process supposed by the "Revisionists" as "*centering* in the Appendix." This is far from representing the method pursued by Wellhausen or even by Schwartz, even though the latter begins with a discussion of the passages in the Gospel in which the beloved disciple is mentioned.

[2] See *Journ. of Bibl. Lit.* 1894, pp. 64–76.

[3] See Additional Note below, pp. 75 f.   [4] *Fourth Gospel*, p. 527.

[5] *Zum ersten Teil d. Johann. Evang.*, and *Zeitschr. f. d. Neutest. Wissenschaft* for 1907, pp. 243 ff.

first to publish the view that in the earliest form of the Fourth
Gospel no visit of Jesus to Jerusalem was recorded before that
for the Feast of Tabernacles, which we now have in ch. vii.

For the latter part of the Gospel we have a careful study
by Prof. M. Goguel of the sources of the narrative of the Passion[1]. He seeks to distinguish later from earlier elements by
such marks as the following:—signs of the tendencies as time
went on to harmonise different accounts, and again to relieve
the Romans of responsibility for the death of Jesus in order
that it might weigh more heavily upon the Jews; or again to
exalt the Twelve and efface anything unfavourable to them; or
again to extend the sphere of the marvellous; lastly signs of
doctrinal development[2]. Having applied these criteria, he
gathers together his observations and infers from them what
he can as to the process of revision that has taken place. But
he does not put forward a theory so definite as that of either
Wellhausen or Schwartz.

F. Spitta's work, *Das Johannes-Evangelium als Quelle der
Geschichte Jesu*, which appeared in 1910, certainly does not
lack in painstaking thoroughness. He is more conservative
than any of the other writers whom I have noticed, with the
exception possibly of Wendt. He holds that the basal document
in the Gospel was by John the son of Zebedee, and that the
general outline (in regard, for instance, to the earlier visits to
Jerusalem) as well as much of the contents of our present
Gospel, were derived from it. He is satisfied also to assume
that the Gospel was brought to its present form by a single
"elaborator" (*Bearbeiter*), viz. the man who added ch. xxi[3]. This
man supplemented it from other sources as well as with his
own remarks and amplifications, and he changed the order,
especially in various parts of the discourses[4].

Before closing this account of the "analytical" criticism of the
Fourth Gospel, it will be proper to mention two New Testament
scholars of high position who regard it favourably, though they
have not put forth any specific theories on the subject.
D. W. Bousset, in two articles, to the first of which I have already

[1] *Les Sources du Récit Johannique de la Passion*, par Maurice Goguel, 1910.
[2] See pp. 6 ff.   [3] See pp. 16 ff.
[4] Some of these alleged changes will presently come before us.

had occasion to refer, on the question of the unity of the Fourth Gospel[1], without accepting by any means all the views of Wellhausen and Schwartz, expresses his opinion that they "have rendered it probable that both the narratives and the discourses have undergone revision to a far greater extent than has been hitherto supposed[2]." And that "perhaps we must accustom ourselves to regard the Fourth Gospel as the work of a school, not of an individual man[3]." Again, E. von Dobschütz has made an interesting application of the principle of "strata" in the Gospel according to St John in the fourth of his lectures on *The Eschatology of the Gospels*[4].

It would not be possible in a work like the present, which aims at dealing comprehensively with the Johannine problem, to examine minutely and separately all these theories, of which I have given some account, and the arguments alleged in support of them[5], but we must endeavour to come to some conclusions in regard to them.

In attempting to judge of the question now before us it is important that we should not apply tests of unity of authorship which are inappropriate. It ought not to be imagined that unity of authorship would imply that we should find the succinctness of statement, and the logical arrangement designed to avoid tautology, which would satisfy the mind of an educated Westerner[6]. There would be no good reason to expect these qualities in the work of a Jew, whose Hellenic training (so far as he had received any) had not been of a thorough kind, whose temper was specifically that of a mystic, and whose

---

[1] *Ist das vierte Evangelium eine literarische Einheit? Theol. Rundsch.* for 1909, pp. 1 f. and 39 f.
[2] *Ib.* p. 59.   [3] *Ib.* p. 64.   [4] Pp. 195 ff.
[5] They are very fully and carefully examined by B. Weiss, *Das Johannes-Evangelium als einheitliches Werk*, and by C. Clemen, *Die Entstehung des Johannes-Evangeliums*, both pub. in 1912. A. Meyer's arts. in *Theol. Rundschau* for 1910, pp. 15 ff. and pp. 63 ff. are a briefer but to my mind very effective criticism. I would appeal especially to the first of Meyer's articles and to Clemen for support in what I urge in the present chapter.
[6] The remark by H. J. Holtzmann in an Art. entitled, *Unordnungen und Umordnungen im vierten Evangelium* (in *Ztsch. f. d. Neutest. Wiss.* 1902, p. 55), is important. "The critics too frequently take as their standard of measurement their own logic, their own attention to detail, their own exactness in regard to sequence, in a word a gospel such as they themselves would have written." Cp. also his *Einleit. in d. Neutest.* p. 313.

mind was absorbed by two or three great subjects of thought. Such a writer would not seek to produce conviction by dialectical reasoning, but by presenting again and again, under slightly varying aspects, the few great truths which he felt to be vital, for contemplation by the minds and spirits of men, just as he was wont to contemplate them himself in order to realise their power. The art itself of such a man, so far as he could be said to have any art, would consist in keeping his two or three great themes as long as possible before the eyes of his hearers or readers, by combining repetitions with partial changes of language. It is possible, therefore, to be far too ready to imagine that, where a subject in the Fourth Gospel after being dropped is again dwelt upon, there must have been dislocation, either accidental or intentional, and that, to get the original order we must bring the passages into close proximity.

Thus far as to arrangement in the Gospel generally and as to order in the narratives. Next let me say a few words as to a complaint that in the narrative portions links are not supplied which are necessary for a complete and clear account of what happened; as, for instance, Wellhausen objects that at ii. 1 we find ourselves in Galilee, though only an intention of Jesus to go there has been recorded (i. 43) and not His actual departure for His journey thither and arrival there[1]; and again, that Martha goes to her house to tell Mary that Jesus is calling for her (xi. 28), and that she is next heard of at the grave of Lazarus, without our having been told that she returned with Mary to Jesus or went direct to the grave[2]; again, that at xviii. 29 Pilate is suddenly introduced without it being explained who Pilate is[3]. Now even the most practised writers of history or fiction sometimes fail *per incuriam* to clear up every point in what they narrate; or they purposely leave something to the intelligence and imagination of their readers. In the instances just given and in others the explanations which, it is said, should have been given might only have served to make the style ponderous. But, further, there is no ground for assuming that a Christian of the end of the first or beginning of the second century, who undertook to write a gospel, would

[1] *Ev. Jo.* p. 12.   [2] *Ib.* pp. 5 and 51.   [3] *Ib.* p. 83.

be a practised writer. His writing would not improbably be marked to some extent by the defects common in oral accounts of occurrences, in which there are often gaps in the information supplied, and everything is not related in the right order. It should, further, be observed that in the Fourth Gospel incidents are related mainly for the spiritual instruction which they can be made to afford, or because they will serve as an introduction to teaching on some great truth. It is specially important to bear this in mind in connexion with that group of narratives of which Schwartz somewhere says that they "run into the sand"—the story of Nicodemus in ch. iii, which ends without a hint as to the effect the words of Jesus produced upon him, the incident of certain Greeks desiring to see Him, with regard to whom we are not told whether they were admitted to His presence or not, and other instances.

A sign of diversity of authorship has also been found in the mode of treating the Synoptics. Soltau, as we have seen, maintains that a writer who has given accounts in the Fourth Gospel of incidents, some of the features of which seem to be taken from the Synoptics while in material respects, such as those of time or place or both, the Synoptics are wholly disregarded, cannot be the same as the one who has included narratives in which in the main the Synoptics are closely followed. The idea that in the former class of cases the Johannine narrator has taken suggestions from the Synoptic Gospels, but has freely altered many of the circumstances to suit his own purpose is one which many critics have held and hold, who have not felt any difficulty in supposing that the same writer in certain other cases was faithful to the Synoptic accounts. For my own part, I believe that if a writer of what professed to be history could pay so little heed to the statements of those who, it is assumed, were his only authorities, there would be nothing strange in his treatment of those authorities being wholly arbitrary, so far as historical considerations were concerned, i.e. that he might follow them or not as suited his purpose in connexion with the instruction which he desired to give. But it seems to me far more natural to suppose that when the Johannine writer departs widely from the Synoptics in narratives which in certain points resemble what they relate, he is following an independent tradition, though the form of his account has been influenced through his recollection of the Synoptics, or through an affinity at some point between the partially divergent traditions which he and they represent. Thus, for instance, it would be no strange thing that the evangelist should have heard a story of the healing of a lame man in Jerusalem which shared with the Synoptic story of the healing of a paralytic the trait that the Saviour bade him "Take up his bed, arise and walk"; and if it did not, the evangelist in imagining the incident might well have supplied this trait from the similar incident in the Synoptics without fancying the whole incident to be the same, and to have been wrongly placed in Galilee. And a writer who so far used, or was influenced by, the Synoptics would not be inconsistent, if in other cases where he was uninfluenced by an independent tradition, he adopted their accounts more fully and strictly.

The contention that a description is inherently improbable is also at times urged by the "analytical" critics in order to prove that different hands have been at work upon it, or that the whole of it proceeds from an interpolator. But the lack of verisimilitude might equally be due to the evangelist not having formed for himself a true conception of all the circumstances and of the course of events. The signs of this may be hard to reconcile with his having been an eye-witness of the events, but this question should not be confused with that of unity of authorship. The older critics of the "analytical" school have been accused of being biassed in their criticism by the desire of finding a writing by the Apostle John embodied in the present Gospel, and their having determined what it contained according to their own predilections. There is ground for this charge, and Wendt and Spitta are also in a measure open to it. But it must be added that Wellhausen and Schwartz likewise have their own arbitrary notions about their *Grundschrift* and what it could contain[1].

So far I have insisted that the demand for freedom from inequalities and incongruities in the Fourth Gospel, in order that it may be regarded as the work of one author, shall not be an excessive one and of an unsuitable kind, and I believe

---

[1] E.g. see Schwartz, *ib.* pp. 516, 526.

that we shall also find an additional reason for this in a view of its composition presently to be put forward. But I now go on to observe that, as all must admit, the Fourth Gospel possesses very special characteristics of thought and point of view and spirit and style, to be found broadly speaking in every part of it. Those views as to the unity of authorship which have been so widely accepted could not have been so, and could not for so long have held their ground, if the common impression as to the appearance of unity had been a mere delusion; and no theory of the composition of the work which does not take account of the fact that the appearance in question does exist, and supply a reasonable explanation of it, can possibly be regarded as satisfactory. Presumably it was because of the characteristics which I have just mentioned that Wellhausen in a passage which I have quoted[1] declares that, "In spite of its different strata the Fourth Gospel can be historically regarded as a unity. It should be assumed that the amplifications for the most part originate from the same circle within which the basal document arose and found its first readers." But it is surely most unlikely, however special the conditions in some Christian community at the end of the first or the beginning of the second century were, that it should have contained several members with qualities of mind and spiritual temper which would have made them capable of writing pieces of the Fourth Gospel. It is not surprising that Schwartz[2], whose analysis of the Gospel into elements is not less elaborate, should hold that something more than the latter supposition offers is wanted in a theory of the Gospel that can stand, and that accordingly, as we have seen in the passage quoted from him above, he attributes much to a reviser who, he declares, was "a poet of strong powers of thought and marked individuality who has undertaken to raise an altogether new song." But it is certain that interpolations into a document from other documents, or even insertions from his own pen and the revision of forms of expression in other parts, is not the plan on which such a man is wont to work. Nor would a wholesale revision have produced the work which is in our hands. For the characteristics to which reference has been

[1] See p. 35 above.   [2] See p. 41 above.

made belong to the warp and woof of the work, and Schwartz[1] does not mend matters by his assumption that large portions of the basal document were actually omitted. For the general tendency of early editions and copyists was to make additions, not omissions, and in particular in the case of a document for which some reverence must have been felt, wholesale omission is very improbable, and it would have been difficult to secure consent for it.

The simpler analyses of Wendt and Soltau, according to which the narrative portions of the Gospel were devised by a writer (or according to Soltau more than one) into whose hands the discourses had come, in order to form a framework for the latter, stand condemned for a similar reason to that which is fatal to the more elaborate theories of Wellhausen and Schwartz. There is too much homogeneity in the whole work. The connexions between narratives and discourses are of too subtle a kind, the interlacing is too intricate, for the most skilful hand to have fitted the one into the other as a mere frame. In form even they often cannot be sharply distinguished. The narratives contain pieces of conversation, and the discourses are interrupted by questions and objections. More important by far, there are ideas which are common both to the narratives and the discourses, there are truths which the work as a whole is designed to illustrate and enforce. The subject of the whole is the manifestation of the Son of God among men together with the probation for men that this entailed, the grounds of faith, the nature of it, the causes of the lack of it. This great conception is reflected in the general arrangement of the matter as well as in the different parts. When the account of the rejection of Jesus by different classes in the Jewish people through giving way to false attractions of the world and unworthy fears has been concluded, Jesus is shewn at the last in the midst of the faithful little band, the call of several of whom had at the beginning been recorded, and who had been loyal throughout, and He gives them the promise of enduring spiritual support and of true bliss.

Spitta's view is less open to objection than the others which we have noticed just because he leaves more to the original

[1] *Ib.* 1907, p. 361; 1908, pp. 179 f., 183.

writer. But I believe that he assigns too large a part to the "reviser," and that he divides between different elements with a precision and confidence for which there is not sufficient justification.

We must, then, endeavour to form an idea of the history of the composition of the Fourth Gospel which shall give better promise than the theories of the analytical writers do of explaining the different kinds of phenomena in it, some strongly suggestive of unity of authorship, others which have been held, though too confidently, to conflict therewith.

In inquiries into the origin of the Synoptic Gospels, the question of the part played by oral tradition received in the past a large amount of attention. The verdict of the great majority of students of the Synoptic problem has come to be that oral tradition cannot account for the actual resemblances between the Synoptic Gospels. In that conclusion I fully concur. But I have contended that the period of oral teaching did much to prepare the way[1] for the composition of the first written narrative of Gospel facts, and to determine its shape, and also to establish it as a type for other writings which followed and made use of it, and that through oral teaching likewise the Sayings of Jesus were at first collected and transmitted[2]. It seems to me also that many of those who, like myself, rejected "oral theories" in their customary forms occupied themselves too much with hypotheses about documents in their endeavours to solve the Synoptic problem, and paid too little regard to the preparation made in the period of oral teaching for the subsequent writing of the Synoptic Gospels. I now submit that the effects of a period of oral teaching both on the teacher himself who became the author of the Fourth Gospel, and on the form and character of the material which stood ready for his use when he began to compose it, go far to account for those features in it with which we are now dealing.

The influences which operated must, however, be conceived differently from those at work in the case of the Synoptic Gospels; the time was later, the needs were not the same; the conditions were evidently peculiar; the evangelist was an altogether exceptional man. Let us suppose that in the Christian

---

[1] See vol. II, especially pp. 131-5.   [2] *Ib.* pp. 61 ff.

teaching on the form of the Gospel

community in which ultimately the Fourth Gospel saw the light it was customary not merely to repeat utterances of Christ, but to paraphrase them with a view to bringing out their meaning, and to combine fragments of His teaching which had been handed down separately, joining them together in such a way as to form longer and more continuous pieces. Let us, further, suppose that there was one preeminent teacher in this Church, subsequently the fourth evangelist, who made it his practice to give instruction in this way. He may also himself have been the disciple of a revered teacher[1], who had done likewise, and whose reports and paraphrases of Sayings of Jesus he repeated and expanded. Incidents in the work of Christ were also made themes for meditation and exposition by this teacher, who was to become the author of the Fourth Gospel, and it may be by the teacher who preceded him, and the favourite method of meditation or exposition on incidents consisted in recording along with them teaching of Christ to which, it was believed or suggested, they had given rise. All this would be in general accord with the idea of Hebrew Midrashim. Through repetition on different occasions these paraphrases and expositions would become more or less fixed in form, all the more because they were intended to represent teaching given by Christ. Similarity of ideas and of spirit had been imparted to the whole body of this material by the teacher through whose mind and lips it had passed and by whom it had been accumulated. But this would not be incompatible with the existence of shades of doctrinal difference here and there. Such would naturally appear owing to progress of reflection in the teacher's mind in instructions given during a course of years. But he himself might have been very little conscious of them and in many instances not have thought that pieces which differed in this way needed to be adjusted to one another. The appearance of a particular set of incidents in the collection would be largely due to their having been found specially suitable as texts. From the nature of the case when the collection both of discourses, and of incidents to which teaching was

---

[1] This has already been suggested in what has been said in ch. 1 on Weizsäcker's theory of "mediate" Johannine authorship, and the question of the reasons for it will come before us in subsequent chapters.

appended, was made into a book, some of those imperfect joinings and varying stages of doctrinal development which criticism has noticed in the Fourth Gospel would be found in it. The author himself would not have been particularly solicitous to avoid them. But also it would be marked by a real unity—not indeed such a unity as it would have had if it had proceeded as it were at one jet from the brain of a great thinker, not such a unity as Baur and his followers imagined they found in the Fourth Gospel, that of a work by a man who has been the first to grasp a new idea, which he has set himself to expound, moulding his whole composition to serve this purpose, subordinating to this end every other consideration—but such a measure of unity of thought and feeling as we actually find in it.

It is not, however, necessary to suppose that all the material of the kind that I have indicated, which was in existence at the time when the design of putting together such matter in a book was formed, was included in the first draft of it. Not only may some pieces resembling the rest have been known through oral communication, but they may have been already committed to writing, or they may have been so afterwards. It would have been natural enough that, in an age when the multiplying of books was a laborious and expensive matter, individuals should have written down pieces of limited extent which they had heard delivered, perhaps by the same teacher who was the author of the Gospel, or by someone in imitation of him, and that some such pieces should subsequently have been embodied in the Gospel itself. Owing to the conditions, also, under which books were then transmitted the addition of marginal glosses which afterwards found their way into the text would not be improbable. I contend only that such changes cannot, on account of that homogeneity with which the work impresses us, have been very considerable, or of a kind seriously disturbing to the general treatment of the theme.

But an examination of particular passages will be necessary in order that we may form some idea of the probable, or possible, extent of the alterations in the original draft. The first that I take shall be a statement which, according to Wellhausen and Schwartz, is of far-reaching significance for the whole present form of the Gospel.

Some crucial passages discussed 53

They argue that the counsel—if it is not a challenge—of the brethren of Jesus, in vii, *vv.* 3 and 4, that He should go to Judæa in order that His works might be seen, is a relic of an earlier form of the Gospel, according to which up to this point He had not during His Public Ministry gone up to Jerusalem. It must be added that this fragment itself has not, in their view, wholly escaped emendation; οἱ μαθηταί σου has been supplied as the subject for θεωρήσουσιν, with a view to harmonising the word a little better with the preceding part of the Gospel as it now stands. Originally the subject was not expressed, and the people of Judæa were intended.

As there is no textual evidence for the omission of οἱ μαθηταί σου, the reasonable thing to do first is to consider what sense can be made of the passage with this term included, after comparing other passages in our present Gospel. There can be no doubt that in two previous places (Jn iv. 1, and vi. 60ff.) the term (μαθηταί) is used in a general sense of those who had a certain measure of faith in Jesus, though they had not become like the twelve constant attendants upon His teaching. In the former of these places disciples that He made in Judæa are in question. Further we read a little before this of "many who believed on his name when he was in Jerusalem at the passover." Probably such believers should not be distinguished, or not sharply so, from those who were disciples in the general sense that I have indicated. Most likely, then, "the disciples" meant in vii. 3, 4 were at least partly persons resident in Judæa, who had been impressed by the works and teaching of Jesus on occasions when He had visited it. But disciples from other parts of the land, even from Galilee itself, may have been included. Jerusalem was a great *rendezvous* at the times of the feasts. Galileans themselves are said to have welcomed Him when He returned from Jerusalem after His first visit to it during His Ministry, because of what they had there witnessed. Similarly, those from various parts of the province, who could not constantly attend upon His teaching, as well as from more remote districts, would meet Him again there. For them too, the proclamation of His Mission, and miracles wrought in vindication of it, in the capital would have special significance. Does then the fact that Jesus is represented as having exercised His Ministry in Jerusalem and Judæa before make it unsuitable that He should be urged to do so again? Surely not. The "disciples" who resided there, or whom He would find gathered there, would need to have their faith confirmed. They would soon begin to regard Him as a "lost leader" if He lingered long in obscurity.

Wellhausen and Schwartz further insist that, according to vii. 3, 4, the brethren of Jesus advised a removal of His place of abode from Galilee to Judæa, whereas in the sequel there is question only of a visit for a feast. I am unable to see the importance of this observation. A removal that was to be permanent might well begin with a visit for a feast. And in point of fact, according to our present Fourth Gospel, Jesus, after going up to the feast that was then near, did not return to Galilee, but spent several months in Jerusalem and Judæa, or on its borders.

There are other difficulties which every reader must have felt in the context of the passage that we have been considering; but it is not necessary that we should discuss them in the present connexion. I may add that Bousset, who sees much more force than I do in the objections of Wellhausen and Schwartz to which I have referred, thinks they may be removed by supposing that an editor has introduced some glosses here and there, and that this is to be preferred to the theory that there has been a wholesale recasting of the Gospel[1].

I will take next the three passages[2] in which—in addition to the notices in ch. xxi—the "disciple whom Jesus loved" appears under this express designation. And I will ask the reader to bear in mind that the question here before us is simply whether these passages, or the mention of the beloved disciple in them, belong to the original Gospel, and not any of those questions relating to this figure which bear upon the authorship of the Gospel; these will be discussed later[3].

Schwartz maintains that the difficulties which have been felt in understanding the Johannine account of the Last Supper are due to the fusion in it of two stories, one of the Feet-washing, and another later one based upon the Synoptic

---

[1] *Theol. Rundschau*, 1909, pp. 49–52.
[2] xiii. 23, xix. 26, xx. 2.   [3] See below, pp. 134 ff.

Some crucial passages discussed

prediction of the betrayal at the Last Supper, but altered from it. The accounts of the Feet-washing and the Supper appear to him to be incompatible, as also the answer of the Lord to the beloved disciple, followed by the giving of the sop to Judas, with the absence of suspicion on the part of the disciples at *vv.* 27 ff.

It is no doubt strange that the Feet-washing did not precede supper, instead of coming after Jesus and His disciples had taken their places at the table. But its introduction where it occurs may have been intended to draw all the more attention to it. Besides we do not know whether the washing of the feet before such a meal would be regarded as indispensable in the class to which the disciples and Jesus Himself belonged. Be this, however, as it may, this point does not, surely, help to shew that the combination of the Feet-washing with supper is unoriginal. On the contrary it tells against that supposition. If it was contrary to custom that the feet should not have been washed before the meal began, it would have seemed even stranger to a reviser in 100–130 A.D. than to us, and it would have been perfectly easy for him in joining the story of the Supper to an earlier one of the Feet-washing to have indicated that the Supper followed.

Further, it has been urged, not only by Schwartz but by others, that the statement regarding Judas at *v.* 2, at least if understood in the sense ordinarily given to it, is inconsistent with that at *v.* 27. This is not clear to me. There is a difference between the phrases used which may imply that an evil suggestion at first instilled had in the interval taken complete possession of the traitor's mind. But even if a contradiction is admitted, it remains to be asked which statement is the earlier. That in *v.* 2 could be removed from its context without any difficulty. Moreover, there seems to be a connexion between the reference to Judas at *vv.* 2 and 11 and the explanation of the significance of the Feet-washing given in *vv.* 7–10. And there is certainly much to be said for the view that this explanation is an insertion, interrupting as it does the natural sequence between the account of the act and the comment upon it at *vv.* 12 ff., and differing as it does from the latter, which is more in harmony with teaching elsewhere given in the Gospel.

Lastly, the lack of verisimilitude, which may be charged against the story of the prediction of the betrayal in *vv.* 21–30, may serve to shew that it could not have proceeded from an eye-witness, but not that it did not form part of the original Gospel, unless it is assumed that the Gospel in its original form was by an eye-witness.

Schwartz turns next to xx. 2–10, describing the race of Simon Peter and "the other disciple whom Jesus loved" to the tomb. This incident is regarded as an insertion both by him and Wellhausen on the ground that Mary Magdalene, who informed them that the tomb was empty, is standing weeping beside it when they have withdrawn, without our having been told of her return. This is an example of that pedantic kind of criticism, referred to above, which demands that every detail, however easily the reader can imagine it, shall be stated in so many words. Further, it should be observed that the words in *v.* 11, "But Mary stood without at the tomb weeping," could not have immediately followed "and seeth the stone taken away from the tomb." Whereas in their present position they follow reasonably well after the withdrawal of the disciples; for it can hardly be contended that a statement to the effect that she had returned was strictly required.

As to Schwartz's view[1] that the author of ch. xxi first identified the disciple who ran with Peter to the tomb, and that other disciple who introduced Peter into the high priest's house, with the disciple whom Jesus loved, it may be remarked that it would have been more natural for him to have indicated this interesting point about him on the earlier occasion instead of leaving his identity there dubious.

There remains the scene in which "the beloved disciple" appears at the foot of the Cross. With regard to this he is content to say that there is no place for him here if the flight of the disciples was (as he has argued) justified in the original Gospel, and if the two other narratives in which the beloved disciple is mentioned in our present Gospel did not belong to it. The "justification" for the flight of the disciples is, he holds, implied in the words addressed by Jesus to those who

[1] See above, p. 40.

seized Him at xviii. 8: "if therefore ye seek me, let these go their way." But it would be truer to say that if, as is assumed in the sequel, this request of Jesus was granted, flight was rendered unnecessary and the twelve may well have remained in Jerusalem, and there would be nothing to prevent the beloved disciple from standing by the Cross.

On the whole, then, the reasons given for thinking that the figure of the "disciple whom Jesus loved" was wanting in the earliest form of the Fourth Gospel appear to be insufficient.

Parenthetic comments. Let me next refer to the brief *parenthetic comments* in this Gospel, upon which, as we saw[1], Wendt lays stress, as also (it may be added) do Spitta and Bacon. Now it is of the nature of a comment that it is a reflection upon matter which has in some way come before him who makes it. No doubt it is conceivable that a writer might adopt the artifice of first putting into the mouth of another certain views or statements and of then drawing a moral therefrom *in propriâ personâ*; or that he might relate a story purely of his own invention, as though it had actually occurred, and then add observations upon it confessedly his own. But apart from the question whether a sincere writer would pursue this method, the process would in general be too cumbrous, and there would seldom be sufficient reason for employing it. Any differences that there may be in point of view between the comment and its context, such as those which Wendt insists on in certain cases, or want of harmony of any other kind, will, also, strengthen the conclusion that the author of the comment was not the author, at least in the same sense, of that on which he comments. But there is more to be considered as to the connexion between the comment and its context. The comment may have been originally nothing more than a marginal gloss upon a work substantially complete, which was subsequently introduced into the text; or it may be the remark of one who composed the whole work, largely out of previously existing material, and the form of that material and his own relation to it may (as I have already suggested) have been of different kinds. A somewhat careful examination of the parenthetic comments in the Fourth Gospel

[1] See p. 34 above.

is required in order to discover what information they supply in regard to the composition of the work. From the nature of the case such comments, even if they were made by the author who composed the context, would often be removable from it without disturbing the grammar, or logical sequence, of a sentence, or passage, and I think that critics have been tempted to use their knives too hastily by the facility of the operation in these cases.

It will be convenient to consider first those four instances of "similar misinterpretations" which Wendt brings forward. The earliest occurs at ii. 19 ff. After the challenge given by Jesus, " Destroy this temple etc.," and the retort of the Jews, " Forty and six years etc.," the explanation follows, " but he spake of the temple of his body." Yet the words, if spoken just after the cleansing of the temple cannot, it is said, have had this reference; and certainly it would seem more fitting to interpret them of the raising of a new spiritual temple, the Church which He would found. Be this, however, as it may, it does not seem difficult to imagine that even an Apostle who gave the saying of Jesus in the connexion in which he heard it spoken might afterwards have put upon it and connected with it a meaning which had been suggested to him by subsequent events and the thoughts of a later time. Still less is it hard to understand that one who was recording an incident and words which had been related to him should have misunderstood their significance. But, indeed, in the present instance, we must, I think, go further. It is not merely a question of what is possible. It is most probable that the explanation was added to the saying of Christ and the reply of the Jews in the first document in which the two latter were contained. Read the passage without that addition—as Spitta indeed leaves it in his reproduction of the original form of the Gospel—and mark how abruptly it terminates and how tempting it would be for any Christian writer, composing a work for edification, to seek to explain them.

The next comment in the group which Wendt instances is at vii. 38 f. where the gift of the Spirit after Jesus was glorified is treated as the fulfilment of the promise, " he that believeth on me, as the Scripture hath said, out of his belly shall flow

Parenthetic comments in the Fourth Gospel 59

rivers of living water." The third is that which connects the exaltation of Jesus, and His universally attractive power consequent thereupon, with His death by crucifixion (xii. 32 f.). It is argued that in these two instances as well as in the first the interpretation has the effect of narrowing the true import of the sayings. Upon this I would observe that, little as the point seems often to be realised, it may confidently be asserted to be characteristic of mystical thought, or at least of one form of it, that profound significance is seen in external acts and events. By the mystic they are regarded as sacramental. He often experiences the need of having something concrete to which to anchor his thought, lest he should be altogether lost in his sense of the vastness of spiritual realities.

I doubt, therefore, whether the three comments that have been noticed imply that the writer who made them stood in reality on a distinctly lower plane of thought than that of the teaching which he interprets. There is more ground for holding this in the remaining instance that Wendt gives, namely, xviii. 9. Here words which refer to Christ's protection of His disciples from spiritual dangers (xvii. 12) are applied to the request of Jesus addressed to those who came to arrest Him, that they would not seize His disciples along with Himself. But if lack of spiritual discernment is here shewn, this does not prove that the interpretation could not have proceeded from the evangelist. He may not have been able always to preserve the same level.

My difference from Wendt in regard to these comments is simply that they do not seem to me to shew collectively on the part of him who makes them such a want of appreciation of the teaching contained in the discourses that he could not be the writer who put the Gospel as a whole together, including the discourses. This does not preclude the possibility of distinguishing different degrees of spiritual depth and of primitiveness in different portions of the subject-matter. I proceed to discuss a few other comments, where various considerations arise.

At iv. 2 we have a correction of a statement about the action of Jesus. When it has been three times[1] said that Jesus

---
[1] iii. 22, 26, iv. 1.

baptized the qualification is added after the last of these "although Jesus himself baptized not, but his disciples." In this case it seems to me clear that we can trace the hand of a man who was revising a document that lay before him. A writer who thought it important that Jesus should not be supposed to have Himself baptized would, surely, if he had composed the whole account, have avoided saying so before. This would have been specially easy and natural, since here it would simply have been a question of moulding a narrative into the form which he believed represented the facts, not of altering sayings or pieces of discourse that had reached him. It seems probable, therefore, that the explanation at iv. 2 was a gloss upon the Gospel by a reader, or copyist, of it when it was virtually completed. The explanation at Jn iii. 24—"for John was not yet cast into prison"—may quite possibly have a similar origin. We can well imagine it to have been introduced with the object of placing the narrative in the context in its right chronological relation to the statement at Mk i. 14 and Mt. iv. 12. The case for supposing a mere gloss is not, however, so strong here as in the last instance. The manner in which the incidents in the contexts were related need not have been different according as the writer knew and remembered the Synoptic statement or did not do so, provided he believed them to have taken place before the commencement of the Public Ministry of Jesus in Galilee. Moreover, it is quite as natural to suppose that the evangelist of the Fourth Gospel would be aware of the statement of Mark, as that some later "glossator" would.

It will be suitable in this connexion to recall the explanation at xviii. 13, 14 as to who Annas was; but any further discussion of it may be deferred, as the whole passage in which it occurs must be considered later.

To return for a moment to the early chapters: the notes appended at ii. 11, and iv. 54, to the miracle in Cana and the healing of the royal official's son respectively, are by some held to have proceeded from the hand of a reviser who largely reshaped the Fourth Gospel. I can see no good reason for thinking that they are not remarks by a writer who determined from the first the main outlines of the work and embodied in it the greater part at least of its present contents. He, quite as well as a reviser, might have desired to explain why those two miracles had been chosen for mention.

The next instance to be examined is of special interest. At vi. 46, when Jesus has declared that those men who have listened to the Father's teaching and have been drawn by Him, will believe on Himself, and after He has quoted the words of the psalmist, "they shall all be taught of God," the remark follows which breaks the natural connexion between *vv.* 45 and 47, and which is at all events in a different vein from what precedes, "Not that any man hath seen the Father, save he which is from God, he hath seen the Father." It seems to me clear that we have here a "parenthetic comment" by one who is recording the discourse, but who feels that there is a danger lest the words of Jesus should be misunderstood, to the detriment of the truth that God can only be known through the Son. Is there a point of view from which this statement can be regarded as not really inconsistent with the preceding representation of the Father as Himself teaching and leading men? That is a problem for Christian thought to occupy itself upon. But in the present connexion we have only to observe that in the passage before us no hint is given as to how they may be reconciled. It is difficult not to suppose that if the man who made the comment had himself composed the discourse, or even had felt at liberty greatly to modify the material he had received, he would have expressed himself otherwise. But at the same time the thesis (so to call it) in *v.* 46 is insisted on again and again in the Gospel; so that there can be no reason for suggesting that he who is here anxious to safeguard it is other than the writer who has given form to the Gospel as a whole.

It has, perhaps, not generally been recognised that there is a parenthetic comment in the passage which we have just been considering. On the other hand, there is no question that the words at viii. 27, to which I now turn, are of the nature of a comment, or explanation. It may well seem a strange one. It is difficult to understand how when Jesus spoke of One who sent Him and declared that He uttered to the world what He had heard from Him, those who were addressed could be ignorant that the Father was meant. But the remark does not stand by itself. There are many references in the Gospel to the spiritual dulness of the Jews and of Jesus' own disciples, others of which, besides that just cited, strike one as exaggerated. Moreover, these remarks, crude as some of them may be in expression, emphasise the rejection of the Son of God by men, which is one of the leading thoughts of the Gospel. Here again, then, we should not be justified in making a distinction between the evangelist and some later interpolator.

I will mention two other possible instances of comments. In i. 14 the words καὶ ἐθεασάμεθα...παρὰ πατρός are by some held to be an interpolated comment. The clause that follows, πλήρης etc., appears to be an epithet agreeing with the nominative ὁ λόγος, but the connexion is rendered difficult by the intervening clause. But the thought in this clause is in entire accord with the purport of the Prologue generally; and without knowing better than we do what the feeling of the writer of the Prologue would be on the question of style we can hardly be justified in saying that the parenthesis must be another man's interpolation.

There is, again, a parenthetic comment in v. 15 if (with Westcott and Hort) we read ὁ εἰπών instead of ὃν εἶπον. With regard to the question whether in that case the remark must proceed from an interpolator similar considerations apply to those in the last example.

From these brief parenthetic comments I pass on to consider passages which may be held to consist of *reflections, added at the end of, or woven into, a recorded discourse.*

In Jn iii there are two paragraphs (*vv.* 13 (or 16)-21, and *vv.* 31-36) which have been, and I imagine still commonly are, regarded either as in reality, or as intended for, the concluding portions respectively of Our Lord's conversation with Nicodemus, and of a discourse by John the Baptist, but which several thoughtful commentators in the past[1] have held to be, as it were, meditations by the evangelist upon the words of Jesus and of John which he has given. There seems to be a

---

[1] E.g. see B. F. Westcott on *vv.* 16-21, and 31-36. He supposes the evangelist's own words in the former passage to begin at *v.* 16. Cp. also Westcott and Hort's text where a space is left before *v.* 16 and *v.* 31. It is surely evident, however, that the change of style begins at *v.* 13. See below, p. 171, n. 2.

Reflections added to reported discourses 63

change in the point of view marked (*a*) by the abandonment of the first person and the employment instead of descriptive phrases, "the son of man" etc., "he that is of the earth" etc., to designate Jesus and John respectively; (*b*) by differences in regard to the tenses used[1]. Further, the doctrinal teaching is of a more highly developed kind, such as is not likely to have been given at that early time, and which is specially out of character in the mouth of the Baptist. In the earlier of the two passages also the term μονογενής is employed, which is not elsewhere put into the mouth of Jesus, but is employed by the evangelist at i. 14 and 18, while it appears also at 1 Jn iv. 9, and not in any other place in the New Testament. It may be added that *v*. 13 appears clearly to assume that the Ascension has taken place already.

Those who have recognised these differences, and who have at the same time held that the Apostle John was the author of the Fourth Gospel, must have supposed that he had in his memory kept the conversations and discourses which he had heard distinct from his own later thoughts; that he wrote down, or dictated, the former as he remembered them, and that having done so he continued in a somewhat different style, and partly in a new vein, to dwell on the subjects suggested by the words of the Lord, and of the Baptist—no doubt without any intention of concealing the fact that he was now speaking in his own person, and also without being conscious of any necessity for indicating it in a formal manner.

If, on the other hand, we must not assume—and I have said that I do not myself think we can—that an immediate disciple of the Lord was the author of the Fourth Gospel, we must still suppose that someone who knew the discourse of Jesus as far as *v*. 12 inclusive, and of the Baptist as far as *v*. 30 inclusive, from having heard them reported, or who had them before him in writing, placed after each a continuation which was the fruit of his own meditation, or else derived by him

[1] Westcott (see his note on the section *vv*. 16-21) observes that the tenses ("loved," "were") in *v*. 19 "evidently mark a crisis accomplished, and belong to the position which St John occupied but not to that in which the Lord stood, when the revelation of His Person and Work had not been openly presented to the world." Again, on *v*. 33, he writes that "the aorists describe the later experience of Christian life."

from some different source. For it is extremely unlikely that if the whole of each passage from *v.* 3 to *v.* 21, and from *v.* 27 to *v.* 36 had been equally the composition of one person those changes in point of view and expression, to which reference has been made, would have occurred at and after *v.* 13 and *v.* 31 respectively.

There are passages in other discourses in the Fourth Gospel which stand in more or less marked contrast to, and are more or less easily separable from, their contexts. It is a question for consideration in all such cases whether there is or is not sufficient ground for supposing that an editor has added reflections of his own to, or has woven a passage from a different source into, a substratum. But I do not think that in any of these other instances, the signs point to such a conclusion so clearly as in the two that have just been considered.

Conglomerates. I pass on to consider three passages which may be described as *conglomerates*. The first of these is the series of sayings in regard to the spiritual harvest in iv. 35–38. Commentators have made various attempts to trace a consistent sequence of thought and one suitable to the time when, according to their present position in the Gospel, they were spoken, but without success. The first of these sayings (that in *v.* 35) suits the time and occasion admirably. The second also (that in *v.* 36) may well have been spoken in the same connexion. But if so "the reaper" must be Jesus Himself, since there is no hint of His disciples having been given any share in the work in Samaria. And in the latter clause of the verse "the sower" might be John the Baptist, part of whose ministry was exercised not far from, and possibly within, the borders of Samaria, so that it might well have had an influence on her inhabitants. The common joy of the sower and the reaper might then be compared with the joy of the friend of the bridegroom at hearing the bridegroom's voice (iii. 29). If it is thought that this interpretation limits too much the idea of the sower, the prophets of Israel in former ages may be included, and the joy to be shared with the reaper will be in the eternal world. But difficulties arise when we take *vv.* 37, 38 with the preceding. There seems to be no point in the words, "herein is the saying true, One soweth and another reapeth,"

Conglomerates

if taken with what precedes. How was this proverb illustrated by the common joy of the sower and the reaper? Moreover, it would harmonise ill with the leading ideas of the Fourth Gospel that a distinction between the work of the Christ and of His predecessors should be so strongly drawn. On the other hand, the saying in *v*. 37 fits in well with that in *v*. 38, where the disciples are forcibly reminded that the harvest, which it is their privilege to gather in, is due to the toil of others who were not permitted to see it. But there was not at the time of the visit to Samaria any act of Jesus to which the words, "I sent you to reap," could refer, according to the narrative either of the Fourth Gospel or the Synoptics. Moreover, as I have already indicated, the disciples were not employed to reap in Samaria on this occasion. It seems probable, therefore, that these different sayings were not all originally connected, but were subsequently brought together on account of their similarity of subject[1]. If this, however, is allowed it must still remain doubtful whether the third and fourth sayings, and possibly even the second, were added to the first where it now stands, or whether the whole little collection was made by the writer who composed the narrative generally, and was placed by him in the position which it now occupies in that narrative, or again was found by him ready-made.

The next instance of a possible "conglomerate" which I will consider is of a somewhat different kind. The interpretation which most naturally suggests itself of the parable, or allegory, in x. 1–6 is that which is given at *vv*. 11 ff., namely, that Jesus Himself is the Shepherd of the sheep. But in *vv*. 7–10 another interpretation is interposed; or (one is inclined rather to say) another, though kindred, allegory, with its interpretation, is inwoven. It does not seem likely that *vv*. 1–6 could originally have been thus dissevered from the more obvious application in *vv*. 11 ff. It seems more probable that two allegories, or two interpretations of the same allegory, which were not at first thus closely connected, had been combined in tradition, or in instruction given to the Christian assembly, or were so by the evangelist when writing his Gospel.

---

[1] For a couple of similar instances of "conglomerates" in St Luke, see vol. II of this work, p. 230.

Again, in xiii, *vv.* 6–10, and *vv.* 12–17 two wholly different lessons are founded upon the Feet-washing, while each ends up (last words of *v.* 10 and *v.* 11, and *vv.* 18, 19) with an allusion to the traitor. The explanation of their combination may, I think, be similar to that in the last case. Somewhat analogous to these last two instances would be such a combination of two variants to form a continuous passage as Wellhausen finds in i. 22–28, and 29–34[1]. But it seems to me doubtful whether these are really variants.

Seeming dislocations. I pass now to a class of phenomena in the Fourth Gospel which has on the whole attracted more attention even than any one of those which have been already discussed, namely, passages where the arrangement of the matter does not appear to correspond well with indications, given in the Gospel itself, of the sequence of events. Some students of the Gospel, who maintain that in other respects the present form of the Gospel is its original form, have, as we have seen, explained certain instances of this kind as due to *accidental* disarrangement. I have already given my reasons for dismissing this hypothesis[2].

As regards the hypothesis of *intentional* rearrangement to explain what seem to be dislocations, I think it may be at once said that it should be treated as subordinate to that of interpolation. Some motive for a change in the original order must be assigned, especially as *ex hypothesi* a worse order than that which the critic thinks he can restore has been the result. The introduction of fresh matter might render some recasting of the context into which it was introduced advisable, so that the very natural desire on the part of an editor to incorporate additional matter with which he was acquainted might induce him also to undertake the task of adapting thereto the form of the original document. It is difficult to suggest any other reason for a disturbance of the original order. If, therefore, a rearrangement is suggested, it will be suitable to ask at the same time whether there are signs of an interpolation, while it may be that an interpolation will by itself explain the apparently imperfect sequence, without our having to suppose any further disarrangement.

---

[1] See above, p. 38.   [2] See above, pp. 32 f.

Dislocations in the Fourth Gospel 67

We will first consider some points in regard to the sequence of events referred to in chs. v to vii. After ch. v has described a visit of Jesus to Jerusalem, and has concluded without any mention of His leaving it and returning to Galilee, the opening words of ch. vi appear abrupt and strange:—"After these things Jesus went away beyond the sea of Galilee, of Tiberias." This reference to the localities would be natural enough immediately after ch. iv when He was in Galilee. It has also been held that the words at vii. 1—"After these things Jesus walked in Galilee, for he would not walk in Judæa etc."—do not fit well with the narrative of ch. vi, when He was in Galilee.

It will be well, before we consider these points further, to refer also to the difficulties that are urged in regard to the position of the passage vii. 15–24. At *v.* 21 Jesus says, "I have done one work and ye all marvel," yet this "one work" was performed on the occasion of a previous visit to Jerusalem and in the interval the events related in ch. vi had occurred, as well as the stay in Galilee to which allusion is made in vii. 1. It is strange that the effect of that particular miracle should still be referred to. There seem to be also inconsistencies between the passage noted and its immediate context. At *v.* 20 "the multitude" treat the notion that there was a plot against the life of Jesus as a preposterous one; and yet at *v.* 25 "certain of the Jerusalemites" ask, "Is not this he whom they seek to kill?" Again, according to *v.* 31, it was not merely the "one work" which had made an impression, for "many from among the multitude believed on him," exclaiming "the Christ when he cometh, will he do more miracles than this man hath done?"

On the ground of these incongruities it has been held that the original position of the contents of ch. vi, or of such portions of it as are to be retained, was between chs. iv and v, and that of vii. 15–24 at the end of ch. v.

But in both cases and especially the former there are other considerations to be borne in mind. I have already urged that an interpolation is, generally speaking, more probable than a deliberate displacement. Further, although the transference of ch. vi to follow ch. iv would do away with the topographical difficulty at vi. 1, and also with that at vii. 1, if one really exists

5—2

there, about which more remains to be said, the order would in another respect be less satisfactory. For the account of the crisis in the work of Jesus in Galilee given in the latter part of ch. vi, if retained as part of the narrative and transposed with the rest, would come too early. Where it stands at present it is brought near to his final departure from Galilee. This is in itself more likely, and is certainly more in accord with the Synoptic outline, than that He should have thought it worth while to return there after that crisis had occurred and after a visit to Jerusalem. Accordingly, it seems necessary that this portion at least of ch. vi, if allowed to be part of the original Gospel, should be connected, as it is by Spitta, with the beginning of ch. vii.

It may be added that there are in the contents of ch. vi somewhat clear indications of the hand of a compiler, who may well not have been in such close contact with the facts as the writer of the rest of the Gospel. In the narratives of the Feeding of the Five Thousand and of the Walking on the Water the Synoptics have been far more closely followed than is usually the case in the Fourth Gospel. Moreover the discourse on the Bread of Life that follows has been connected with these narratives in a way that is not altogether happy[1]. The multitude that witnessed the miracle are brought back to hear that discourse in certain small boats (*vv.* 22–24) which after the miracle came to the place where it had been performed; the difficulty of conveying so vast a number in this manner is ignored. Again, it cannot but seem strange that those who had just seen so great a work should have been able to ask, "What then doest thou for a sign that we may see and believe thee?" (*v.* 30).

Nevertheless, it is certainly not impossible that the abrupt introduction of the narrative in the early part of ch. vi, and the defects to which I have referred in the connexion between it and the discourse that is given afterwards, may be due to the writer of the rest of the Gospel, who was more concerned to illustrate certain great beliefs than to narrate events with historical precision. And in particular in view of the fact that in the Gospel generally the centre of interest was Jerusalem

---

[1] Cp. reference to Wellhausen on this subject, above, p. 39.

Dislocations in the Fourth Gospel 69

and Judæa, it appears to me that the statement at vii. 1, "After these things Jesus walked in Galilee," may quite naturally bear the meaning that Jesus *continued* to walk in Galilee, instead of departing for Jerusalem whither He might have been supposed to be in haste to return. On the whole I am disposed to think that the contents of ch. vi, or a portion thereof, may have been interpolated in the original Gospel.

If ch. vi is an interpolation, its introduction might have accidentally caused the omission of some matter at the end of ch. v for which the interpolator desired subsequently to find a place; and this may be the history of the present position of the passage vii. 15–24. But this passage might also have been an account of the attitude of the people in Jerusalem to Jesus when He appeared there at the time of the Feast of Tabernacles, parallel to that which stands in the context, and known either to an editor, or to the original writer, which may have been woven in with the latter. And even the discrepancies which there appear to be between them are capable of reasonable explanation, if we suppose that "the Jerusalemites" and portions of the multitude gathered together for the feast from other places held different views, and possessed different degrees of knowledge as to the intentions of the rulers.

I pass to the conclusion of the Public Ministry of Jesus. In ch. xii after He has apparently pronounced His last judgment openly upon the Jewish people, and we have been told that He "went away and hid himself from them," and some reflections have been added upon the ending of that day of opportunity which had been granted to the Jews, through the Ministry of the Christ among them, another address of Jesus upon the subject of His Mission is appended, which is introduced by the words "Jesus cried and said." This final summing up by Jesus Himself of the results of His Ministry is a very impressive one; and I do not think that many readers are either disturbed, or misled, by the fact that we have been informed just before that He had already withdrawn. Instinctively they refer this last utterance to a time before that. Nevertheless, the actual position of these last words spoken by Jesus to the Jewish nation may, perhaps, be most easily understood, if they had not been handed down as part of the preceding discourses, but in some distinct source, from which they were here taken subsequently to the composition of the Gospel as a whole.

Yet, again, in chs. xiii–xvii, the arrangement of the matter calls for explanation. In the closing verses of ch. xiv Jesus appears to be taking leave of His disciples, and the passage ends with the words "Arise, let us go hence." But the farewell discourse in its present form does not end here. Chs. xv and xvi contain matter of the same kind and largely on the same themes as the latter part of ch. xiii and in ch. xiv; and finally we have the great prayer of ch. xvii; immediately after which at xviii. 1 we read, "When Jesus had spoken these words, he went forth with his disciples beyond the brook Kidron." Those who hold that the Gospel as we have it (as amended on textual evidence) has not been altered from its original form explain the phenomena which I have indicated in one of the two following ways. They suppose either (1) that the contents of xv–xvii were spoken after Jesus and His disciples had left the supper chamber; or (2) that only the first part of the proposal in xiv. 31 was at that moment carried into effect, but not the second; that is to say, that the party rose from the supper table, but stood lingering in the room till after the prayer in ch. xvii. With regard to the former suggestion it must, I think, be said that it would be most unnatural that words so intimate as those in chs. xv and xvi, and still more that the prayer of ch. xvii, should be spoken *en route*, either as the little company walked, or at any point on the city-side of the Kidron. The second explanation is at first sight less open to objection. Nevertheless, it would have been more natural that if the discourse was thus continued while they were standing in the room instead of sitting—a wholly immaterial point—the words "Arise etc." should have been omitted. It should, also, be noticed that the transition to the allegory at the beginning of ch. xv is somewhat abrupt.

To meet, or lessen, these difficulties it has been proposed that xiii. 33–xiv. 31, or whatever parts of this section are held to be original, should be placed after chs. xiii–xvii. Here again improvements in the sequence of thought cannot be secured by this rearrangement alone, apart from omissions. For example, the questions of Peter at xiii. 36 and Philip at xiv. 15 could

Dislocations in the Fourth Gospel 71

hardly have been asked after the teaching of xvi. 5 ff. had been given. Again, no suitable place can be found for the prayer of ch. xvii in the middle of the discourses.

To me it seems more probable that the resumption of the discourse after xiv. 31 is to be explained on the supposition that either the original writer of the Gospel had access to material preserved in a fragmentary form, all of which could not be arranged in a perfectly self-consistent manner, but of which he was unwilling to lose any portion; or that a copyist soon afterwards, belonging to the same circle, and who had some matter at his disposal of the same character as that in the Gospel, and which gave in fact a parallel account of the same farewell discourse, was anxious to include it.

It is to be added that there appears to be a certain difference in the doctrinal point of view between xiii. 31–xiv. 31 and xv, xvi. In the second of these the Holy Spirit takes somewhat more definitely for a time the place of Christ on His visible withdrawal, instead of mediating His continued spiritual presence[1]; and the expectation of a speedy return of Christ visibly, and not merely inwardly to each individual believer, is more clearly indicated in the latter piece than in the former[2].

The last passage which I will notice is Jn xviii. 12–27. The difficulties in this narrative are a subject familiar to students of the Gospel. The most serious is that after Caiaphas has been stated to have been "high priest that year" (v. 13), "the palace of the ἀρχιερεύς" (v. 15) should naturally mean Caiaphas' palace, and, the ἀρχιερεύς who in the sequel examined Jesus should similarly be Caiaphas. Yet this would not be consistent with the statement that those who arrested Jesus brought Him "to Annas first" (v. 13) who did not send Him to Caiaphas till after that preliminary examination (v. 24). The title of ἀρχιερεύς was given, as we know from the Synoptic Gospels[3] and the Acts[4] and Josephus, to other members of the high-priestly family besides the high priest himself, and it might with special meaning be used of Annas who had held that office, and who probably still possessed much influence when sons of

---

[1] Cp. xiv. 12–28 with xv. 26, xvi. 7–15.
[2] Cp. xiii. 36, xiv. 2–7, with xvi. 16–33.
[3] Mt. ii. 4, xx. 18 etc. [4] Acts iv. 1 etc.

his and his son-in-law were put in his place. But it is certainly strange that he should be designated by this title in the present passage where just before it had been used of the actual high priest.

On account of this confusion, or at all events lack of lucidity, it has been held that the original narrative has been tampered with. There are supposed to be other indications of this in the fact that the account of Simon Peter's denials is interrupted at *v.* 18, and resumed again, after Jesus had already been sent to Caiaphas, with the words " Now Simon Peter was standing and warming himself."

The whole matter contained in this passage is arranged in the Sinaitic Syriac in a way to afford a clear and connected narrative. The order of verses there is 13, 24, 14, 15, 19–23, 16–18, 25 ff. and Mr C. W. Turner thinks that he has found some support for this arrangement of the text in an old Latin MS., Codex E, or the Palatine MS.[1] But the evidence which he produces appears to be of a very doubtful kind. And surely it is most probable that this arrangement is the work of someone who wished to harmonise the account of the trial of Jesus in the Fourth Gospel with that in Mark and Matthew. It is impossible to explain how that arrangement of the text, if it had been the original one, should have given way to that which we find in all other MSS. and Versions.

The chief difficulty of the passage will be removed if we may suppose either that (1) the parenthetical reference to Caiaphas (*vv.* 13, 14), or (2) the mention of Annas (*vv.* 12 and 13*a*, and 24), is an addition to the original narrative. Of these hypotheses I prefer the first. To the other criticism of the narrative which I mentioned I am unable to attach great importance. If, as we may well imagine to have been the case, Annas and Caiaphas occupied different portions of a range of buildings round a common court-yard, and Simon Peter was standing by a fire somewhere in that court-yard, he would have been near the place where Jesus was being tried in each of the trials referred to; while the division of the account of his own fall into two parts might be intended to give an impression of the duration of the ordeal to which he was exposed.

---

[1] See *Journal of Theo. Studies* for Oct. 1900, pp. 141 f.

Dislocations in the Fourth Gospel 73

The examination in which we have been engaged has not been exhaustive. But I have discussed the passages in regard to which the case against their having formed part of the original structure of the Gospel seems to me strongest, and others on which critics of the analytical school have laid special stress. The result of the inquiry seems to me to be that the structure of the Fourth Gospel is somewhat looser than was commonly supposed before the analytical critics urged their views; that in a few instances editorial remarks have been introduced and sayings added in a manner that was inappropriate to the context; and that there has been at least one considerable insertion after the Gospel was first put forth; but that in the main the features of the Gospel are most consistent with the view that herein a great Christian teacher has put together what he had been accustomed to teach orally in divers parts, setting forth the whole in accordance with the grand outlines of his own conception of the Gospel.

THEORIES AS TO ACCIDENTAL TRANSPOSITIONS OF CERTAIN PASSAGES IN THE FOURTH GOSPEL

As long ago as 1871 Archdeacon Norris suggested that the contents of ch. vi had been accidentally transposed from before ch. v to its present position (see *Journal of Philology*, vol. III). In 1893 Spitta, in vol. I of his *Zur Geschichte und Literatur d. Urchristentums*, put forward a theory that this and certain other displacements of the subject-matter of the Fourth Gospel, which he believed he could trace, were due to disarrangements of the pages of a papyrus-roll. He argued that either (1) the pages of the roll had come apart through the failure of the matter with which they were fastened to adhere, or (2) the pages had been written upon before they were pasted together; and in either case that they were not arranged throughout in the right order in the copy from which our text is derived (pp. 182 ff.). In proof of this theory he shews that the passages which on internal grounds need to be transposed are multiples of a certain unit of length, or in one case that unit of length itself, which he takes to be the contents of a page of the roll. He obtains his unit from a comparison of the length of xiii. 31*b*–xiv. 31 with that of chs. xv, xvi, which should,

74 *Theories as to accidental displacements*

he holds, be inverted in order to give a satisfactory order. The former contains very approximately $4 \times 18\frac{1}{2}$, the latter $6 \times 18\frac{1}{2}$, lines of Westcott and Hort's small Gk. Test. Therefore $18\frac{1}{2}$ lines of this edition represents the average contents of a page of the papyrus-roll from which the Fourth Gospel as we have it was derived. Similarly he finds that ch. vi, which should be placed before ch. v, contains seven such pages, and vii. 15–24, which should stand between vii. 52 and viii. 12, forms one such page. That passage having been accidentally removed to an earlier place the space here left was filled with the *Pericope de adultera*. [Spitta, *ib.* p. 197. According to him also, the 33rd of the papyrus-roll ends with ch. vii and the *Pericope de adult.* in the text of the oldest witness *Codex Bezæ* occupies a page, p. 198.] But in order that the transposed pages might be removed accidentally from the point where they were originally it would be necessary that a new page should have begun there. Spitta argues that it is probable that the second half of the Gospel, extending from xiii. 1, would in the original have been begun on a new page and xiii. 1–31*a* would have filled $3 \times 18\frac{1}{2}$ lines of W.H. (p. 185). He also calculates that a page (the 21st) ended at v. 47, to which ch. vi was transferred (*ib.*). There is one instance in which he is unable to shew that a page ended at the point at which a page which properly belonged elsewhere was placed, viz., at vii. 14. The introduction here of vii. 15–24 Spitta attributes to the perplexity of the transcriber where to place it.

F. Warburton Lewis, in his *Disarrangements in the Fourth Gospel*, 1910, employs Spitta's "key," with a useful modification. He points out that in order for our present chs. v and vi to have been accidentally transposed ch. v must have filled a certain number of pages as well as ch. vi, and he finds that though five is not a multiple of $18\frac{1}{2}$ of W.H.'s lines it is of about half this amount, say 9·3 lines. This accordingly should be taken for the unit. With this unit he is of course able to explain all the transpositions for which Spitta argues[1], and he also notes one more, iii. 31–36, of the length only of his own unit.

It may be observed that while for the theory of accidental transposition of chs. v and vi it is necessary that the matter in ch. v should, as Lewis argues, have filled a certain number of pages, it would also be necessary that, as Spitta calculates, the matter from the beginning of the Gospel down to the end of ch. v should have occupied a certain number of pages.

---

[1] Lewis, however, introduces chs. xv, xvi after xiii. 32, not as Spitta does after xiii. 31*a* (*ib.* 40–5). Lewis does not concern himself with the question whether xiii. 32 would end a page.

Lewis does not (I think) deal with the difficulty at vii. 14 which Spitta notices, and explains independently of the theory.

It is no doubt curious that the relative lengths of the passages which it is desired to transpose should correspond so approximately in the way that has been described. But it may be questioned whether the correspondence is not even too close. For in the most carefully written MS. there would be likely to be greater differences between the contents of the pages than in a printed work. This consideration shews that the test used is necessarily a precarious one. Further it would be strange that a disarrangement arising in the way suggested should not have been discovered and corrected. It was usual to revise copies of ancient MSS. before the task of preparing them for use was complete.

Some reasons of a broader kind for dismissing the hypothesis of accidental displacements have been given above, pp. 32 f.

REARRANGEMENTS IN TATIAN'S *DIATESSARON*

Prof. Bacon has suggested[1] that the rearrangement in Syr. Sin. (see above, p. 72) of the account in the Fourth Gospel of Simon Peter's denials, together with some of the rearrangements in Tatian's *Harmony* in which he gives an order more like that which some critics believe to be the original one, is due to acquaintance with "extra-canonical sources" in which an earlier form of "Johannine material" had been preserved. The foundation for this supposition seems to me but slender. There is but one instance in Syr. Sin. and here Tatian follows the order in the Fourth Gospel as we have it. So he does in several other cases where it has been argued that the original order must have been different, e.g. he gives *vv*. 13–24 of ch. vii between *vv*. 1–12 and 25 ff. and chs. xiii–xvii in the same order as in our Fourth Gospel. His chief transpositions are that he introduces the contents of ch. vi before the greater part of chs. iv and v, places the visit to Samaria, iv. 4–45, after the visit to Tyre and Sidon and return through Decapolis to Galilee (Mk vii. 24–37), transfers ii. 13–iii. 21 (the cleansing of the temple in Fourth Gospel etc.) to the last part of the history, and places xii. 42–50 before xii. 36*b*–41. It is not necessary to attribute great acumen to Tatian in order that he might be able to make these changes, if he did not know an older form that retained signs of it. His reasons

[1] See *American Journal of Theology* for 1900, pp. 770 ff. and cp. *Fourth Gospel*, pp. 521 ff.

for the course he has pursued in each instance appear to lie on the surface and to correspond with his plan as a whole. It will be sufficient if, after indicating what that plan is, I refer to the two chief transpositions. Tatian did not shrink from taking far greater liberties with the arrangement of each of the Gospels than modern Harmonists have ventured to do. He did not feel bound, as they commonly have held themselves to be, to assume that the chronology of each was right and consequently to assume that, when they could not bring accounts in the different Gospels into line, they referred to different events. Further, while in the case of events narrated in all four, he commonly prefers John's account to that of the others, and supplements it only from them with additional details, he is on the whole most influenced by the Synoptic Gospels in his general outline, and this very naturally, because their outline is simpler and appears to be more continuous. Accordingly, after giving the preliminary matter from St John, he takes up the Synoptic narrative of the Galilean Ministry and follows it down to the Feeding of the Five Thousand, and here having a parallel in St John he uses that Gospel for it and for the discourse thereby suggested, and then turns back to ch. v. But he also makes a still greater transposition from identifying the Cleansing of the Temple in Jn ii with that placed in the Synoptic Gospels among the events of the Last Visit to Jerusalem. With it he naturally removes also to that time the other occurrences related in St John as belonging to the same visit.

CHAPTER III

THE PLACE OF THE FOURTH GOSPEL IN THE JOHANNINE LITERATURE

THE relations between the Fourth Gospel and other writings in the New Testament which by tradition have been attributed to John the son of Zebedee have a bearing on questions regarding the origin of the Gospel, and we must therefore to a certain extent examine those writings[1].

THE APOCALYPSE OF JOHN

The questions as to the composition of the Apocalypse —its unity, or successive revisions, or compilation from various sources—are far too intricate and difficult to be fully discussed as a mere subsection in a volume the main subject of which is the Fourth Gospel. Certain observations, however, must be made as to the phenomena which the book presents, in order that we may estimate rightly the value and purport of the indications it affords as to its actual or professed author. When we examine the book with a view to ascertaining its structure, we get the impression—so it seems to me—that its visions which were either taken from different writings, or orally communicated at different times, and which are in part independent of one another, have been finally put together by an editor who had a general plan in his mind, so that he has imparted a measure of order to the whole, but who has not so modified his material in every case as to remove all inconsistencies.

We are entitled to look for a chronological arrangement, a series of events leading up to the end, in the vision that extends from ch. iv onwards. Such an arrangement is most in accord with the spirit of Apocalyptic literature, and it is suggested by the machinery (so to speak) of the vision, the successive seal-openings, and the successive trumpet-blasts

[1] It will not be necessary for our purpose to include an examination of the Apocryphal *Acts of John*.

which announce new occurrences. After the seventh trumpet-blast also the connexion is preserved to a still later point through the temple in heaven becoming the centre of action from which angels, one after another, go forth to execute the Divine Will (xi. 19, xiv. 15, 17, xv. 5 ff., xvi. 1, 17). Moreover this chronological sequence which we expect to find we may also trace in the subject-matter of the successive scenes, conformably with the most probable date of the book, provided we are allowed to assume that in certain of the earlier ones, events which were already past are represented as future. If the notion that any past events should be so treated, especially in connexion with the claim of " John " to be the Seer, appears to any of my readers objectionable, it must for the moment suffice for me to reply that in the present instance the various indications can best be explained thus, and that such a treatment of past and contemporary events is common in Jewish Apocalypses. We will, then, suppose that the calamities foretold through the opening of the first six seals and down to the sixth trumpet-blast (ix. 13) after the opening of the seventh seal are those which *preceded* the Fall of Jerusalem, and correspond with those contemplated in the " Little Apocalypse " which has been embodied in the Synoptic Gospels, and was no doubt widely known in substance, if not in actual form, when the Johannine Apocalypse was given to the world. Further, the commission given to the seer a little after the point just mentioned plainly presupposes that the temple at Jerusalem and its courts are still standing (xi. 1, 2). Its object seems to be, in preparation for an approaching devastation, to preserve the knowledge of what was most precious in the system under which the ancient people of God had lived. Then follows the witness of the believers in Jesus in the sinful city of Jerusalem.

After ch. xi a new vista opens, and we are permitted to have a view of a conflict in heaven which was to have a counterpart on earth. The subject of the earthly conflict, that of the Church with the World-power, as represented by the Roman State, occupies xii. 13–xix. This had in point of fact barely begun when the first period of the Church's history, terminated by the Fall of Jerusalem, was drawing to a close.

Structure of the Apocalypse 79

A spirit of hostility on the part of the State, the reasons for which were as yet obscure, manifested itself in Nero's persecution, but it came to be more clearly defined and declared twenty years or more later under Domitian, the *Nero redivivus*, to whom reference is made at xiii. 1–3, 12, and xvii. 1–14, according to the most probable interpretation of those passages. Here the vision is concerned with things contemporary as before it has been with things that were past; after this it passes to things still future, to the eagerly expected doom on Rome, the Millennial Reign of Christ, the Last Judgment and the final ushering in of a New World.

There is then, broadly speaking, an orderly arrangement in the Apocalypse of St John, and separate portions are also well compacted. Nevertheless, a lack of natural connexion is to be noted at some points. The description in vi. 12–17 seems to suit the very eve of the Last Judgment, if it is not already the end of this world. The sealing of those who were to be saved through and out of the great tribulation, instead of coming after this as it does in ch. vii, should, one thinks, have been mentioned before this. And even the calamities which are seen to befall after the seventh seal has been opened, when the first six trumpets sound (viii and ix), are not so appalling, or indicative of the end of the present world.

Later in the book we are again faced with a similar difficulty. We might have supposed that when He Who is "like unto a son of man" has appeared and has with His sharp sickle reaped the harvest of the earth which is over-ripe (xiv. 14–17) nothing would remain to be done of the same kind. Yet immediately afterwards an angel appears who proceeds again with a sickle to gather the vintage of the earth and to cast the grapes into the winepress of the wrath of God. And still after this seven angels appear having bowls full of the last plagues.

Less significant, but not unworthy of notice, is the fact that when the seventh of the angels holding bowls pours out the contents of his bowl the judgment on Babylon takes place (xvi. 17–21). Yet immediately afterwards one of these angels bids the seer come and behold the judgment on Babylon, which is now described at much greater length and in a different form (xvii, xviii). This reads like an independent vision, though it is not inappropriately placed here as a fuller explanation of that mystery.

It may, also, be observed that the point of view of the seer changes in the middle of the book without any explanation being given of the change. At iv. 1 ff. he is bidden to come up through a door opened in heaven, and in heaven he witnesses the breaking of the seven seals. Yet afterwards when at x. 1 he beholds an angel descending from heaven, and generally in the remainder of the book, we must suppose his position to be on earth.

These inconsistencies suggest compilation. Moreover, in addition to the inconsistency between allusions from which we might infer that Domitian was already reigning and the treatment of the Fall of Jerusalem as still future, we have also an inconsistency, though not quite such an obvious one, between some allusions in the three prefatory chapters and this relation in time to the Fall of Jerusalem. The seer was an exile in Patmos; now we do not know of any state-conducted persecution in the reign of Nero outside of Rome to account for this. This exile of an eminent Christian from Ephesus, or some other city in the province of Asia, would be far more likely to have taken place under Domitian. Again, various observations in the Epistles to the Seven Churches —that to Ephesus having lost her first love, that to a martyrdom in the past at Pergamum, that to the lukewarmness of Laodicea—shew that these churches had been in existence for some while, and this is the general impression as to all the churches which the Epistles to them give. Moreover, of five out of the seven churches we hear nothing in connexion with the work of St Paul. Although, therefore, a date for these Epistles before A.D. 70 is possible, a somewhat later one seems more suitable.

Now it is surely less likely that one who had himself passed through all the experiences should have fallen into these chronological inconsistencies, or disregarded them as immaterial, than that they should have arisen through editing, or be the work of a writer who was in whole or in part devising a setting for the visions he recorded.

This conclusion will affect our view of the evidence

Date and Authorship of the Apocalypse

afforded by the book as to the person of the seer John, who appears in it. To consider then the authorship first in connexion with the Domitianic date of the book. Although tradition assigns the book to the son of Zebedee, and also favours placing its composition near the end of the reign of Domitian, the age which he must then have attained—over eighty, even if we suppose him to have been as young as twenty at the time of the Crucifixion—makes it improbable that he could have been in a full sense the author. But if the putting together of the whole is from another hand, or if his authority is merely assumed, the case is altered. Again, it has been urged that one of the twelve would not be likely to refer to the twelve in the manner that the Apocalypse does. But such a vision might have been introduced among visions received from him or attributed to him without its having been perceived that it did not altogether correspond with what he might be expected to have written. If the visions of the Apocalypse were not only (as must almost necessarily have been the case) seen at different times, but some of them also by a different person from the seer of the original series, and the whole collection was made by a different hand, difficulties in the book itself in the way of regarding the John who speaks at i. 1 f. and xxii. 8 as the Apostle are removed. Further, the case for connecting the same John with the composition of the Gospel is in one respect simplified. On account of wide differences in style and thought between the Apocalypse and the Fourth Gospel, students in recent times who desired to adhere to the traditional view of the *authorship* of both writings felt constrained to depart from the traditional view of the *date* of the Apocalypse—the latter part of the reign of Domitian—and to place its composition soon after the death of Nero, in order to allow a sufficient interval for the author of the Apocalypse to acquire that greater accuracy in the use of the Greek language which is shewn in the Gospel, and also to reach that new point of view doctrinally which we meet with there. The view that the Apocalypse was composed circ. A.D. 70 by John, the son of Zebedee, also found advocates in the Tübingen School, though they denied the authenticity of the Fourth Gospel. But the tendency of modern criticism has been to revert to the reign of Domitian as the time of the composition of the Apocalypse. If this is right, as it appears to be, the ground is cut from under the feet of those who would attribute both it and the Gospel to the same author, in the usual sense of the word author. But obviously the differences between the two writings do not weigh to the same extent, or it may be at all, against an identity, not of authorship, but only of the principal seer whose visions were recorded in the Apocalypse with the revered teacher whose testimony and instruction were made use of in the composition of the Gospel by a disciple, a different man from the editor of the Apocalypse.

But in addition to the question of the date of the Apocalypse, and its bearing upon the possibility of this work and the Fourth Gospel having had the same author, we have the fact of the connexion of the John of the Apocalypse with Asia Minor. Among those who reject the commonly received tradition in regard to the residence of John the son of Zebedee in Asia Minor in his later years, some hold it to be necessary to explain how the story grew up, and they suppose it to have been due to confusion of the Apostle with some other eminent John who did reside in Asia Minor. This John they generally suppose to have been John the Elder mentioned by Papias, and they also unnaturally identify him with the exile of Patmos[1]. I have already discussed this subject to some extent in vol. I of this work[2], and it will be most convenient for me to add what seems to be necessary in regard to it at the end of the present chapter, in connexion with the title of the Elder in the Address of 2 and 3 John, and in the next

---

[1] In vol. I, p. 163 n., a number of writers are referred to who reject the Ephesine residence of John the son of Zebedee, some only of whom adopt the explanation of the growth of the legend referred to in the text. One of these, Bousset, has gone over the ground again in two articles in *Theol. Rundschau* for 1905, pp. 225 ff., 277 ff. His position remains the same as before, except that he reduces to smaller proportions than apparently he supposed before the amount of information derived from "the John of Asia Minor," which was embodied in the Fourth Gospel. See *ib.* p. 290. Von Soden is another comparatively recent writer who has adopted to a considerable extent the same line as to "the John of Asia Minor and his part in the different Johannine writings." See *Urchristliche Literaturgeschichte*, 1905, pp. 213 ff.

[2] See pp. 163 f., 168 ff., 231, 2.

The First Epistle of John

chapter[1]. I would only here lay stress on the fact that this assignment of the authorship of the Apocalypse to John the Elder is purely a hypothesis. Indeed documentary evidence is somewhat adverse to it. Eusebius suggested that this John might have been the author, but it is clear that he has no evidence to go upon. And undoubtedly if Papias had stated it Eusebius would have supported himself by his testimony; and it is also probable that if it had been the case Papias would have known it and would have referred to it.

THE FIRST EPISTLE OF JOHN

The First Epistle is written in the name of a group of persons (*vv.* 1–5), much as a group is referred to in the Prologue to the Fourth Gospel (i. 14), or as a group—a different one—gives at the end (xxi. 24) its attestation as to the authorship and the veracity of the record. But we cannot assume that the group in the Epistle is the same as either of these others. We must consider later what can be gathered on this point. We may, however, at least suppose that they were persons held in esteem among their fellow-Christians, and that one among them, who had taken up his pen to write, and who at i. 7 etc. uses the first person singular and exhorts in a tone of authority, was the most eminent man in the Church of the city from which he writes; and we may further, without much fear of contradiction, take that city to have been either Ephesus or some other place of importance in Proconsular Asia.

It has been commonly held in the past, and is still held by not a few critics, that quite apart from the attribution of the First Epistle as well as the Fourth Gospel to the Apostle John in the New Testament Canon, the close resemblances between these two writings supply amply sufficient ground for believing them to be by the same author[2]. On the other hand a considerable number of critics have of late years contended on the ground of differences between the two writings that

---

[1] See below, pp. 108 ff.
[2] I may name among recent writers the following: Jülicher, *Einleit.* 6th edition, pp. 212 ff.; Baumgarten in *Die Schriften d. Neutest.* by J. Weiss, p. 862; Harnack in *Zeitschr. f. Theol. u. Kirche*, 1892, p. 193, n. 1; A. E. Brooke in *The Johannine Epistles*, International Crit. Com., 1912, Introduction.

they are from different hands[1] and that the resemblances are due to the two writers having belonged to the same school of Christian thought, and—since that of itself hardly seems sufficient to account for the extent and character of the resemblances—to one writer having been acquainted with and used the work of the other. Commonly, at least by those who hold the two writers to have been different, the Gospel has been regarded as the earlier work, while the writer of the Epistle has been supposed to have made use of his knowledge of it; but it has also recently been argued that the evangelist came after and was in a sense the disciple of the author of the Epistle. It will be gathered even from the statement already made that the two questions of order in time of composition and of identity or difference of authorship are likely to be closely connected, since on the assumption of different authorship dependence is apparently involved with order; and in point of fact I believe it will be found that the force of the arguments for difference of authorship depends in large part upon the Epistle being held to be the later work, while an opposite view of the order of composition suits better with the writer being the same.

That being so, it will be well before going farther to examine the contention that the Epistle contains certain express allusions to the Gospel; and, moreover, that in various other passages of the Epistle acquaintance with the Gospel is presupposed. In ch. i. 1, 3, 5, and iv. 14, reference is made to that which the writer and those whom he associates with himself in his address have seen and heard and "declare" or "testify." Since no statements of the kind are to be found in the Epistle itself we must, it is said, look to the Fourth Gospel for them. But, surely, the reference may equally well, or even more naturally, be to the testimony which this group of witnesses habitually bore. Again, some adherents of the view that the Epistle was written either some time after the Gospel, or to accompany it, have taken the aorist ἔγραψα at ii. 14 following upon the pre-

---

[1] I will name H. J. Holtzmann, *Das Problem d. ersten johanneischen Briefes in seinen Verhältniss zum Evangelium* in *Jahrb. f. Prot. Theol.* 1881, 1882 (a series of four very important articles). Schmiedel, *Der erste Johannesbrief* in *Religionsgesch. Volksbücher*, p. 32; von Soden, *Neutest. Lit. Geschichte*, pp. 224, 229.

of John in point of date and authorship 85

sent γράφω in *v.* 13, as an allusion to the Fourth Gospel. But there is nothing in the classification here of the persons addressed, or the reasons given for addressing them, which recalls the form and contents of the Fourth Gospel. If the purpose mentioned had been that stated in ch. v. 13, there would have been more reason for supposing a reference to the Gospel. But in that passage the motive in question is that which there was for writing the Epistle. Critics who deny identity of authorship cannot of course so understand ἔγραψα.

As regards those cases where it cannot be pretended that an earlier work is actually indicated, but where it is alleged that there is a covert reference to the Gospel[1], it may, I believe, be confidently maintained that no more need in point of fact be assumed than that the readers and hearers for whom the Epistle was intended should have previously received oral instruction similar in substance with the substance of much of the teaching in the Fourth Gospel. In certain cases where a thought found in the Gospel is more concisely expressed in the Epistle it is argued that for the latter to be intelligible the fuller exposition in the former would have to be borne in mind. I do not think that in any of the instances that are given[2] the language in the Epistle is more obscure than in the Gospel; but, be this as it may, the brief affirmations in the Epistle may have summarised teaching with which the readers have become familiar otherwise than through the Fourth Gospel. It should be remembered also that the great majority of those addressed in the Epistle would not possess copies of the Gospel, even if it was already written, and could know it only through having heard it read. They could not be trusted to be able clearly to recall particular passages of it, or to turn to them in order to refresh their memory of them[3].

[1] "Zu constatiren ist die Unverständlichkeit mancher abbreviirten Formeln des Briefes ohne das Evangelium. Es seid namentlich Stellen wie ii. 2 (=Joh xi. 52); 23 (=Joh. xv. 23, 24); 27 (=Joh. xiv. 26); iii. 8 (=Joh. viii. 44); iv. 6 (=Joh. xiii. 47); v. 12 (=Joh. iii. 36); 14 (=Joh. xiv. 13, 14) in welchen man nicht bloss die kürzere, sondern auch die reifere, jedenfalls die spätere Form wahrzunehmen glaubt." Holtzmann, *ib.* VII, p. 703.

[2] See note 1 above.

[3] One might almost imagine those who employ such an argument as that mentioned above to be thinking of the readers of the Epistle as each holding in his hands a modern bible with marginal references.

The priority of the Gospel cannot then be learned from its being referred to, or presupposed, in the Epistle. So far as evidence of that compact and definite kind is concerned the question of the order of composition of the two writings remains open. For solving it the only means available are of the same kind as those for solving the problem of identity or difference of authorship. The same kind of facts, largely the same facts, must be considered in their bearing upon each question, namely the characteristics of the two writings, their resemblances and differences in phraseology and type of thought, in style and the expression of particular sentiments. And we must make up our minds what interpretation of the facts seems on the whole to afford the most probable answer not for one of these questions only but for both[1]. Obviously therefore it will be most convenient to keep both questions more or less before our minds throughout our inquiry, and not to come to a final decision in regard to either till we reach the close of it.

We will turn first to consider various resemblances, some more some less close, in particular ideas and in phraseology. If a proof of identity of authorship is forthcoming at all, it will of course be provided from the resemblances between the two writings. But it will be allowed that we cannot declare for it on the ground of resemblances taken by themselves before we have also considered the differences. The resemblances therefore must not only be carefully scrutinised, but we shall do well to consider how they should be explained, in case we should be constrained by other evidence to assume different authors.

Some of the resemblances might I think be quite naturally accounted for by the two writers belonging, or having belonged, to the same Christian circle.

Such are the recurrence in both writings of the following words and phrases: "seeing and testifying" (1 Jn iv. 14 =

---

[1] I am sorry to differ from my friend and colleague, Dr Brooke, on the connexion between the two questions of priority and authorship. *Ib.* p. xix. Holtzmann in part admits it. All the more, I think, he would have done better not to decide for the priority of the Gospel, as he has done in the first article of his series, and thenceforward to assume it. He should have reserved his conclusion on the question of priority as well as that on the authorship till after that further investigation of the relations of the Epistle and Gospel which he carries out in the three remaining articles.

Jn iii. 11, 32; xix. 35); "the fulfilment of joy" (1 Jn i. 4 = Jn xv. 11; xvi. 24; xvii. 13); "doing the truth" (1 Jn i. 6 = Jn. iii. 21); "keeping his commandments" (1 Jn ii. 3, 5 = Jn xiv. 21); "abiding in him" (1 Jn iii. 24 = Jn xv. 4).

Again, in some instances one can well imagine that a *logion* of Jesus, at first separately repeated, has been included in a piece of discourse in the Gospel, and has independently suggested an exhortation or reflection to the writer of the Epistle. We may have a case of this at Jn viii. 12 and 1 Jn i. 6, 7, ii. 6; also at Jn xv. 13 ff. and 1 Jn iii. 14–16. Other examples might be given.

At Jn ix. 31 we have what, from its form and from its being put in the mouth of a Jew, appears to have been a common Jewish sentiment; at 1 Jn iii. 22 an application of it is made to Christians, and at Jn xv. 7, 16, xvi. 23, a Christian application of it of a more specific kind. Again, at Jn xi. 9 we probably have a proverb, and there is a spiritual application of it both at xii. 35, and at 1 Jn ii. 11; but in the former case it is a warning to the Jews not to let slip the opportunity afforded them by the presence of Christ in their midst, in the latter to Christians not to fail in love to the brethren.

Identical phrases occur, but in a different connexion, one quite as natural and effective in the Epistle as in the Gospel. Thus at Jn v. 24 we read "He that heareth my word and believeth on him that sent me...*hath passed out of death into life*," and at 1 Jn iii. 14, "We know that we *have passed out of death into life*, because we love the brethren." Again, the reflection that "*No man hath seen God at any time*" receives at Jn i. 18 the addition, "the only begotten Son, which is in the bosom of the Father, he hath declared him," and at 1 Jn iv. 12, 20, "if we love one another God dwelleth in us." Even as to 1 Jn v. 13 and Jn xx. 31, closely similar as these are, it may be pointed out that in the inverse order of the clauses there is a subtle adaptation to the difference between the two in purpose. In the Gospel the object is to supply the grounds for believing that Jesus is the Christ, upon which the possession of life will follow; in the Epistle it is to make those who do believe in Him more fully aware of the fact that as a consequence they possess eternal life.

These divers applications of the same sayings, or phrases, can be better explained by supposing that both writers (if different) found them in the comparatively plastic source of oral teaching than by regarding one as dependent upon the composition of the other.

The different employment of παράκλητος in the Epistle (ii. 1) as a description of the Son, in the Gospel (xiv. 16 etc.) of the Spirit, is specially suggestive owing to the addition of the epithet ἄλλος in the latter. It is thus plainly implied there, too, that the Son also was a παράκλητος, and this, taken with the passage in the Epistle, is an indication that the title was in point of fact already used of Him.

Once more, there are cases in which an individual application is made in the Gospel of some principle which is more broadly stated in the Epistle. Thus at 1 Jn iii. 10 the writer insists that "he who loves not his brother is not of God," while at Jn viii. 42 Jesus says to the Jews "if God was your Father ye would love me." At 1 Jn ii. 11 the writer declares that "he that hateth his brother is in the darkness, and walketh in the darkness and knoweth not whither he goeth," while at Jn xii. 35 Jesus exhorts the Jews to walk in the light while they still for a short while have the light among them, lest the darkness should overtake them, because "he that walketh in darkness knoweth not whither he goeth." At 1 Jn v. 4 we have the assertion, "whatsoever is begotten of God overcometh the world," and at Jn xvi. 33 Jesus says in regard to Himself "I have overcome the world." So also at 1 Jn iv. 5 the writer says of the false teachers, "they are of the world: therefore speak they as of the world," and at Jn iii. 31 it is said with reference to the contrast between John the Baptist and Christ, "he that is of the earth is of the earth, and of the earth he speaketh"—"earth" being used and not "world," because John could not be said to be "of the world." Now we cannot suppose that in these instances the ideas in the Epistle were extracted from the special applications of them in the Gospel. In reality they belonged to the system of thought represented in both writings, and they are likely to have been apprehended as broadly true before any special applications were made.

But that system of thought was a distinct and remarkable

one, and in all probability took shape in the mind of some one man and gained a hold under his influence. Any other Christian teacher who thought and taught similarly would have been dependent in some way on the teaching of his predecessor. He might have been accustomed to hear him orally; but familiarity on his part with anything which that predecessor had written would also be probable, and would help to account for the resemblances noted.

There are besides some passages where the resemblance between the Epistle and Gospel extends to several connected sentences. Here especially direct literary dependence on one side or the other suggests itself, *always on the assumption of difference of authorship*. I refer especially to the following:

1 Jn iii. 10–12, 15 = Jn viii. 41–44;
1 Jn iv. 9, 14–16a = Jn iii. 16–18;
1 Jn v. 9–12 = Jn v. 32–37a, and viii. 17, 18.

Moreover, even in these passages it would not be necessary to suppose an actual purpose and effort to imitate. The memory of what had been written mingling with the second writer's own reflections and teaching would suffice to lead to the reproduction of the lines of argument, as well as of individual expressions.

The most natural explanation of the resemblances we have been reviewing taken by themselves would seem to me to be that the two writings proceeded from the same man. But at the same time a dependence such as I have endeavoured to describe would I think have been quite possible, and must be assumed if, after due consideration of all the facts and their apparent significance, it seems to be most probable that the two writings were by different authors.

But if there was dependence on which side was it? At least one recent critic holds that the Epistle and Gospel proceeded from different authors and that the Gospel was the later—he is of opinion considerably later—written by the "more advanced" thinker and teacher[1]. As to the greater development of the theology in the Gospel, there would be general agreement; and on a close comparison of the two works we shall find that there are good grounds for this

[1] Von Soden, *ib.* p. 225.

view. Probably also many would agree as to the signs of greater intellectual grasp. Holtzmann characterises it as greater "originality[1]." Now there would be no reason why a second thinker and teacher should not have arisen in a school of Christian thought who was greater than its chief originator. Origen was greater than Clement, and yet it is less probable that the author of a work shewing relatively to another work the kind of superiority noted should have borrowed from that other, than that the borrowing should have been on the other side. Consequently the view that the authors were not the same can be best adjusted with the precedence of the Gospel in the date of composition.

This is all that can be admitted with respect to the bearing on the questions which we have to decide of the "originality" of the evangelist, or his intellectual powers in whatever manner they should be characterised. If it can be shewn on general grounds that the writers were not the same so that there must have been dependence, it is more likely to have been on the part of the author of the Epistle. But there is nothing surely in the difference of mental quality shewn in the two writings which might not be the result of greater maturity of mind, when the Gospel was written, in the man who had at an earlier time written the Epistle. Holtzmann, indeed, on the ground of the "originality" shewn by the fourth evangelist argues that "if he twice took up the pen he could not have been merely in a position to copy himself[2]." I cannot but agree with Dr Brooke[3] that to find the author of the Gospel in a certain sense repeating himself—dwelling continually on a few leading ideas, placing them in slightly varying lights—is what we should expect from reading the Fourth Gospel. It is to be added that those leading ideas receive in the Epistle distinct and forcible illustration, and that it contains some profound thoughts to which there is in the Gospel no strict counterpart[4].

It has, however, also been contended that the fourth evangelist cannot have been the author of the Epistle for a precisely opposite reason from that considered above,—not because if he had been he would have abstained from repeating

---

[1] *Ib.* VII, p. 702, cp. Brooke, *ib.* p. xxiii. [2] *Ib.* VIII, p. 134.
[3] *Ib.* p. x. [4] E.g. 1 Jn iii, 23, iv. 8.

himself, but because he would have done so where he has not. "A number of important expressions," says Prof. Schmiedel[1], "occurs only in the Epistle, though the inducement to use them might well have occurred in the Gospel, too, if they had been part of the writer's currency." A different view of the actual relations between the two writings from that of Holtzmann is here implied; and more justice is done to the independent value of the Epistle. Nevertheless, this argument, also, appears to be inconclusive. Even a writer who was prone to dwell frequently on the same themes, and who did not fear to employ again expressions he had made use of before, if they suited his purpose, might very naturally have failed after an interval to recall them at the moment of writing, or if he recalled them to find a place for them in a work of a different character conceived on a different plan.

We will proceed now to a more comprehensive comparison between the two writings with the special object of noting differences rather than resemblances, and estimating their significance. A careful study has been made of grammatical usages in the two writings[2]. In the construction of sentences and other points of grammar there is on the whole great similarity. Among the instances of it that can be given there are some, as Dr Brooke truly suggests, which could not be easily imitated.

The differences that are commonly noted under this head are not numerous. I will mention those of them which seem to me to be important. The preposition παρά is used seven times after ἀκούειν, thrice after λαμβάνειν, once each after αἰτεῖν and πυνθάνεσθαι in the Gospel; in particular ἀκούειν παρὰ τοῦ πατρός, or τοῦ θεοῦ may be reckoned as characteristic. In the Epistle ἀπό, never used in the Gospel with any of these verbs, is used with all of them, παρά never; οὐ μή occurs seventeen times in the Gospel, not once in the Epistle; μέν is used eight times in the Gospel, not at all in the Epistle. These differences—and I do not know of any others which are of equal significance—ought not to count for much in an estimate of the probabilities for and against identity of authorship. Even the

[1] *Ib.* p. 32.
[2] E.g. see Holtzmann, *ib.* VIII, pp. 135 ff. and Brooke, *ib.* pp. ii ff., xi ff.

style of a writer, the usual forms of his sentences and his vocabulary, may vary in greater or less degree, owing to the influences under which he may have come in the interval between the composition of two writings, the suggestions which his mind has received, and the action of memory. So far as the instances mentioned have any force they tell in favour of the view that if the evangelist was also the author of the Epistle he wrote the Epistle first, for they shew more familiarity with ordinary Greek idiom[1].

From grammatical usages we will pass to a study of the subject-matter with the object especially of noting any respects in which the theological point of view and teaching of the Epistle are to be distinguished from those of the Gospel.

That we may judge fairly it will be important that we should first make clear to ourselves what the aim of the Epistle was. It will be remembered that it contains no names of persons or places, no allusions that have a strictly local character. It was probably intended for Christian brethren in more than one place, and has, therefore, naturally taken the form of a homily rather than of a letter. It has been said to have been addressed to the whole of Christendom[2]. But there is nothing in the writer's language which suggests that he imagined for himself such a widely extended circle of readers as this. His mode of address and the character of the subject-matter imply rather that he was writing for those who were personally acquainted with him, and whose spiritual needs and dangers he knew; and this might well be if they were the members of Christian communities which he had from time to time visited, in a district in the Western part of Asia Minor.

One object certainly which the writer has very much at heart is to guard those whom he addresses against the false teaching of certain men who had formerly belonged to the

---

[1] Holtzmann, *ib.* p. 137, notes that ὅτε occurs 22 times in the Gospel, not once in the Epistle. But it is natural that there should be indications of time in a narrative, and that they should not be required in a homily. He also observes that ἐκεῖνος and αὐτός are frequently used in the Gospel after a noun or participle with the article. In the Epistle this construction is not found, but the emphatic use of the personal pronouns is common. Here again the difference may be accounted for by the character of the work.

[2] So Pfleiderer, *Primitive Christianity*, IV, p. 154.

of John in point of date and authorship

Church, but had separated themselves from it[1]. At the same time, we ought not to regard this object as the primary one, if we would judge rightly of the writer's temper, and of his teaching as a whole. It is misleading to call this writing a *Streitschrift*—a controversial work—as some critics do[2]. The writer's principal aim is the purely practical and religious one of deepening in the hearts of his brethren true spiritual faith in God and Christ, and promoting amongst them mutual love and holiness of living. The false teaching was one influence which endangered their Christian integrity, but it is not likely that it was the only one, or that the writer would have been blind to others, or less solicitous to warn against them[3]. It should be remembered also that even those false teachers who are most definitely referred to may very likely not all have put forth precisely the same theories. Christians living in the cities of Proconsular Asia near the end of the first, or in the early part of the second, century would be exposed to a variety of temptations both speculative and moral. It is unwise, therefore, as some writers on the Epistle seem inclined to do, to take every warning and exhortation therein as implying a charge against a certain well-defined body of false teachers. The situation was most probably a confused one, owing to a mixture of elements in the Christian communities addressed, and divers currents of opinion by which they were affected. And this confusion is naturally reflected in a certain vagueness in the impression conveyed by the Epistle, as to the precise errors which the writer desired to combat.

When, however, all due allowance has been made for this uncertainty, it remains sufficiently clear that the false views most distinctly referred to were of a Gnostic kind[4]. We have allusions to those who valued highly a speculative knowledge of God, but who did not strive to conform their conduct to a

---

[1] ii. 19.   [2] So Pfleiderer, *ib.*; and v. Soden, *ib.* p. 191.
[3] On the importance of not losing sight of the pastoral aim, cp. Brooke, p. xxx.
[4] Wurm (*Bibl. Stud.* VIII, 1903) maintains that the heretical teachers in view in 1 Jn did not hold Gnostic doctrines of any kind, and were simply Jews or Judaisers. Clemen, *Zeitsch. f. N. T. Wiss.* 1905, pp. 271 ff. agrees with Wurm that they were not Docetæ or Cerinthians; but he differs from him as to the nature of their errors. The remarks in the text will shew why I cannot accept the conclusions of these writers.

truly Christian standard (iv. 7, 8). Moreover there were false prophets—it is reasonable to suppose that in part at least they were the same men as those condemned on other grounds—who, professing to speak "in the spirit," denied that Christ had come in the flesh (iv. 2), though it does not appear whether they taught the purely Docetic doctrine that Jesus was a mere phantom, or that a heavenly being, the Christ, had for a time occupied the body of Jesus of Nazareth but had withdrawn before the Crucifixion[1]. In an earlier passage reference is made in more general terms to those who denied that "Jesus is the Christ" (ii. 22). This description would fit those Jews who held that Jesus was a great and true prophet, but did not allow Him to be more than this. Very likely it was meant that they should be included in it. But in view of the reference later in the Epistle we must suppose that those who taught Docetic, or quasi-Docetic, doctrine, were equally and it may be principally in mind. For both classes, the Cross of Jesus was undoubtedly the great stumbling block. Express allusions to teachers who corrupted the Christian Faith would have been wholly inconsistent with historical propriety in the Gospel. Nevertheless the strong assertion of the doctrine of the Incarnation in the Prologue, and under other forms in the Gospel generally, may have been in part called forth by the necessity for counteracting Docetic error.

Again, there may be a reference to Gnostic pretensions in several passages both in the First Epistle and Gospel which treat of *knowing*[2] God. In all of those in the Epistle a note of warning may be perceived. Right conduct, and above all love shewn in deeds, are given as a practical test of the possession of true knowledge (1 Jn ii. 3–6, iii. 6, 16–20, iv. 7, 8, 13). Another test insisted on is the conformity of any supposed knowledge with the Faith as it has been held from the begin-

---

[1] One or other of these views must surely be indicated by the emphatic ἐν σαρκὶ ἐληλυθότα at 1 Jn iv. 2, in spite of what Clemen writes, *ib.* p. 274. I lay no stress on 2 Jn. 7, because of the ambiguous force of the pres. ἐρχόμενον.

[2] It is characteristic of the writer both of the Fourth Gospel and First Epistle of John that in these great matters of the Spirit, he prefers verbs to nouns. Though γινώσκειν occurs frequently in the Johannine writings, γνῶσις never does. Similarly while πιστεύειν is used repeatedly in both Gospel and Epistle, πίστις occurs only at 1 Jn v. 4.

ning, and is preached by its accredited representatives (1 Jn iv. 2, 6, v. 20). In the Gospel where it is declared that the Jews do not know God, the Gnostics can hardly be in view, since the religious attitude of Jews generally was very different from theirs; but the Gnostics would be included in the wider statements at i. 10 and xvii. 25 as to the world's ignorance of God. On the other hand in those sayings in which in the Gospel it is implied that the knowledge of God is itself and in what it involves the greatest of gifts that can be bestowed on man, we may, perhaps, discern an intention to shew that an aspiration which had given rise to Gnosticism could be satisfied in connexion with genuine Christian teaching (xiv. 7, 17, xvii. 3). Further, it has been maintained that in expressions about the subjection of this world to the Evil One (Jn xii. 31, xiv. 30, xvi. 11, 1 Jn v. 19), or which refer to men who are his offspring (Jn viii. 46, 47, 1 Jn iii. 8, 10), or who are "of the things below" or "of the world" (Jn viii. 23, 1 Jn iv. 5), which closely correspond in each writing[1], the writer shews an actual infection of his mind by Gnostic dualism. The most convenient point for considering whether this is the case will be when we are endeavouring to picture the environment in which the Fourth Gospel was produced, and for that purpose have to determine the type of Gnosticism to which the various indications we have noted point. For the present we are concerned only with the relations between the First Epistle and the Gospel, and it will suffice to observe that the Gnosticism of the existence of which each gives evidence appears to be substantially of the same kind, and that in their attitude to it there is only this shade of difference, that in the Epistle the writer almost confines himself to guarding his readers against false knowledge, while in the Gospel we have a vision of a true knowledge as penetrating and comprehensive as that which the Gnostic professed to be able to communicate. This difference may be supposed to spring from fuller reflection, shewn in the Gospel;

---

[1] In the use of terms there is a slight difference. ὁ ἄρχων τ. κόσμου τούτου occurs three times in the Gospel (xii. 31, xiv. 30, xvi. 11), but not at all in the Epistle. ὁ πονηρός is used once in the Gospel (xvii. 15), but five times in the Epistle (ii. 13, 14, iii. 12, v. 18, 19). ἐκ τῶν κάτω occurs only at Jn viii. 23, but ἐκ τ. κόσμου is plainly equivalent to it.

or it may be attributed to the hardening effect of longer opposition, shewn in the Epistle. I incline myself to the former view, as the more probable. But there are more marked differences between the two writings in the character of their teaching than the one which has just been noticed[1]. The main themes of the Gospel are indeed those of the Epistle also—the Incarnation of the Son of God (i. 1, 2, ii. 22, iii. 8, iv. 9), and the witness borne to Him (i. 2, iv. 14, v. 6 ff.)—the gift of eternal life (i. 2, ii. 25, iii. 14 f., v. 11 ff.)—a new, Divine birth (ii. 29, iii. 9, iv. 7, v. 1 ff.)—the inward guidance and pledge of the Spirit (ii. 27, iii. 24)—the opposition between light and darkness, the world and God, Christ and the devil (i. 5, ii. 8 ff., 15 ff., iii. 1, 8, 13, iv. 4 f., v. 4, 19)—the love of God (ii. 5, iii. 1, 16, iv. 7 ff., v. 3), and the love which Christians should shew to one another (ii. 10, iii. 10 ff., iv. 7 f., 11 ff., 20 f., v. 1 f.).

Nevertheless, there are special features in the teaching of the Epistle, and they have on the whole a common character. There is less precision in the conception of the Person of Christ and of His relation to the Father and to men in the Epistle than in the Gospel. We are met by this difference on comparing the opening verses of the former (*vv.* 1–4) with the Prologue to the latter (*vv.* 1–14). Though there is a general resemblance between the ideas in each, it is undeniable that in the Prologue to the Gospel there is decidedly greater fulness and exactness of doctrinal statement. The "word" in the Epistle, instead of bearing a signification derived from philosophy, is used, as it commonly had been in Christian preaching and teaching[2], in a phrase denoting the Gospel-message. And in the introductory passage of the Epistle as a whole there is a simpler appeal to the fact of contact with the Divine in Jesus Christ apart from any consequences that this might appear to have when it had become a subject for theological reflection. The idea that a personal distinction within the Godhead is implied in the coming forth of the Divine Life, in such wise that it had been felt and had become known, is not

---

[1] In connexion with the following comparison of the theology of the First Epistle with that of the Fourth Gospel, I would refer especially to the treatment of the subject by Holtzmann, *ib.* VIII, pp. 133 and 139–152, which has been of special assistance to me. [2] See note at end of chap. on 1 Jn i. 1–4.

enunciated as it is in the Prologue to the Gospel, or even suggested. Reference is also only made to the manifestation of this life in Jesus Christ, not to its presence in Human History generally and in Creation. And the thought that Christ is the Life, to which there are parallels in the Pauline Epistles (e.g. Col. iii. 4), is not developed into His being also the Light of men as at Jn i. 4, 9 (cp. iii. 19, viii. 12); in the Epistle God is the Light. Whether or not, on a broad consideration of all the evidence, we are to conclude that the composition of the Epistle was later or earlier than that of the Gospel, the thought at all events in the opening verses of the Epistle now before us is logically prior to that in the Prologue to the Gospel.

A different view of the relation between the ideas in the two passages has, indeed, frequently been taken[1]. It has been held that, in order that the statements in the Epistle might be rightly understood, a conception of the Logos-doctrine, as it is set forth in the Prologue to the Gospel, would be required, and that consequently both writer and readers must be assumed to have been already familiar with that conception. I cannot but think that those who argue thus are unduly influenced by the thought of later ages about the Person of Christ, and that they fail to place themselves at the historical point of view, the point of view of the time when the dogmatic conception of the Person of Jesus Christ was in the first stages of its formation, and when the question of "personality," as we understand it, did not loom so large before men's minds as it did afterwards.

To proceed to another point; the doctrine that Christ is the one true mediator, the means of communication between God and man, which is insisted on so strongly in the Gospel, is not brought out with the same clearness in the Epistle. At

---

[1] See A. E. Brooke, p. xx. Cp. Holtzmann, *ib.* p. 704, and writers there cited. Also VIII, p. 139, where he writes, "Mit demselben Rechte, womit die Vertheidiger der Priorität des Briefes hier die Logoslehre erst im Werden begriffen finden kann man sie auch unter der entgegengesetzten Voraussetzung im Zustande der Auflösung begriffen antreffen." But surely this does not hold. In the first place, there is no true analysis; several elements do not appear. And further it would be much more natural that the writer should give the doctrine as he knew it, at the stage of development which it had reached, than that he should set himself to resolve the doctrine as he knew it, in order to give it in a less exact form.

1 Jn. v. 20*a*, indeed, it is said that, "we know that the Son of God is come, and hath given us an understanding, that we know him that is true." The thought is also suggested by the latter part of the same verse and by ch. ii. 24, that if we abide in Christ we abide in God. It is also asserted at ch. ii. 22, 23, that he who believes in Jesus Christ possesses the Father, has, that is to say, a right knowledge of Him, and is accepted of Him. But plainly none of these passages, which are those most deserving of consideration in the present connexion, state the doctrine that Jesus Christ is the revealer of, and means of access to, the Father with the absoluteness and definiteness of Jn i. 18, xiv. 6, 9, or declare Him to be God's vicegerent in government and judgment as do Jn iii. 3, 5, and v. 22; or state the believer's dependence on Christ with the breadth of xv. 5. With the first of these passages where the affirmation "no man hath seen God at any time" is followed by the explanation, "the only begotten Son, which is in the bosom of the Father, he hath declared him," we may contrast 1 Jn iv. 12, where likewise it is said, "No man hath beheld God at any time," but without any addition as to the revealer, while the thought in the sequel is that through having love in our hearts we know God. Again, while in the Gospel the disciples are assured that their prayers will be answered if offered in the name of the Son (xiv. 13 f. and xvi. 23); in the Epistle the simpler conviction is expressed that God will hear us if we ask in accordance with His Will (v. 14).

To speak generally; while there are passages in the Epistle which refer to the mission of the Son from the Father and the special work of the Son (1 Jn iv. 9, 10, 14, ii. 1), the parts of the Father and the Son in man's salvation are not throughout so consistently differentiated as in the Fourth Gospel. The Father and the Son are mentioned together without any distinction being made as to the relation in which the believer stands to each (i. 3, ii. 24; the instance most nearly parallel in the Gospel appears to be at xiv. 1). The writer passes from the one to the other without marking the transition (iii. 2), or otherwise fails to make plain which is intended.

Again, he introduces indifferently the one or the other in

similar connexions; thus he speaks, as the Gospel does, of abiding in Christ (ii. 5 f., 27 f.) but also of abiding in God and of His abiding in us (iii. 24, iv. 12 ff.), to which there is in the Gospel no parallel; he refers like the Gospel (xiii. 34, xiv. 15, 21, xv. 10, 12) to the commandments of Christ (ii. 3 f.) but also to the commandments of God (iii. 22 ff., iv. 19 ff., v. 2 f.). He also derives the new birth from Christ in one passage (ii. 29), as well as from God (iv. 7, v. 1, 4, 18), which latter is more in accord with the usual language of the Fourth Gospel[1] and of the New Testament generally.

On the other hand, the atoning efficacy of the death of Christ is more emphasised in the Epistle than in the Gospel. In the latter it is taught in the words of the Baptist at i. 29, but not distinctly elsewhere. 1 Jn iii. 5 may well be founded upon a reminiscence of the words of the Baptist. But in the Epistle we are, also, told that "the blood of Jesus God's Son cleanses us from all sin" (i. 7); that Jesus Christ is "the propitiation for our sins, and not for ours only but also for the whole world" (ii. 2, and cp. iv. 10); and in close connexion with these statements, that "if we confess our sins, God is faithful and just to forgive us our sins and to cleanse us from all unrighteousness." For parallels we should have to turn to the Pauline Epistles and the Ep. to the Hebrews, or to Apoc. i. 5, and v. 9, rather than to the Fourth Gospel. In the latter the blood of Christ is referred to only as spiritual drink (vi. 53 etc.), that is, His death is viewed as a condition for the appropriation of His Life. The word $\dot{\alpha}\phi\iota\acute{\epsilon}\nu\alpha\iota$ is used of the remission of sins in the Fourth Gospel only at xx. 23, where it is a question of their remission by the disciples of Christ through His authority; while the word $\kappa\alpha\theta\alpha\rho\acute{\iota}\zeta\epsilon\iota\nu$ does not occur there. Again, at Jn xi. 52, which in part resembles 1 Jn ii. 2, the thought is that through His death Christ would "gather together into one the children of God who are scattered abroad," not that His death "made atonement for the sins of the whole world." Lastly, in the Fourth Gospel the Cross is represented as the means of Christ's glorification (iii. 14, viii. 28, xii. 32, 34),

---

[1] The Fourth Gospel speaks of being "of God" (viii. 47); also of being "born from above" and "of the Spirit" (iii. 3, 5 etc.). At the same time the Incarnate Son confers "the right to become children of God" (i. 12).

a thought which is not found in the Epistle, or elsewhere in the New Testament.

The teaching concerning the Holy Spirit is substantially the same in the Gospel and the Epistle[1]. The title ὁ παράκλητος is, however, not given to the Spirit in the latter, but to the Son (ii). On the other hand τὸ χρίσμα is not used in the Gospel, nor indeed is it elsewhere in the New Testament; but the verb χρίειν is, at 2 Cor. i. 21, with the same connotation. τὸ χρίσμα indicates the gift of spiritual enlightenment, individually bestowed, as a permanent possession (so long as it is not forfeited by neglect); at the same time it may contain a reference to the laying-on of hands. Again, the use of πνεῦμα in the Epistle at iv. 1 ff. is the same as at 1 Cor. xii. 3, 2 Thess. ii. 2, 1 Tim. iv. 1, a sense in which it is not found in the Gospel.

Once more the expectation of the Second Coming of Christ in its ordinary form, which in the Gospel is to a great extent over-shadowed by other thoughts, is prominent in the Epistle. The term παρουσία to describe it, which is used so frequently in St Matthew, the Pauline Epistles, James, 2 Peter, but is absent from the Fourth Gospel, occurs at 1 Jn ii. 28. Moreover, φανεροῦν, used always in the Gospel of the manifestation of the Son of God while on earth, and so used also at 1 Jn i. 2, iii. 5, 8, is applied in the Epistle besides to His reappearing (ii. 28, iii. 2), as it is at Col. iii. 4, 1 Pet. v. 4. The term παρρησία is also here used in a technical sense, so to speak, to denote a privilege belonging to the Christian now (iii. 21, v. 14) which he must seek to retain at the day of judgment (ii. 28, iv. 17). With the former of these applications of the word we have parallels at Eph. iii. 12, Heb. iv. 16, x. 19, 35, and with the latter there is one at Heb. iii. 6; but neither is found in the Fourth Gospel.

These differences between the Gospel and the Epistle may, perhaps, *in part* be due simply to the different aim and form of the two writings, the one purporting to be a narrative, which in its framework of history gave Christ's own view of His relation to, and mission from, the Father; the other a directly

---

[1] Cp. 1 Jn iii. 24, iv. 13 with Jn vii. 39, xiv. 17; 1 Jn v. 6 with Jn xvi. 8 ff.; 1 Jn ii. 27 with Jn xiv. 26, xvi. 13.

hortatory address. It would be natural that, for instance, in the latter, the subtler aspects of the Atonement and of the promised Coming of Christ dwelt on in the Gospel, should be passed over, and that more prominence should be given to aspects of these great beliefs which were specially fitted to stir the emotions. But this in itself alone will not suffice fully to explain the contrast between the two writings in respect to their teaching.

We must beware, however, of exaggerating the contrast. There is no actual inconsistency between the teaching given in the two works. The features in the Epistle which we have noticed afford no ground for connecting it with the middle of the second century rather than its beginning, or than the end of the preceding century. It is misleading to apply to this type of thought the name "Monarchian" as Holtzmann does. There may be in the First Epistle of St John lack of consistency, or there may be silence, with respect to beliefs which Monarchians denied. But vagueness of thought and silence more or less complete are one thing, and either affirmation, or formulated opposition, is another[1]. What we may rightly say as to the First Epistle is that it is in closer agreement than the Gospel with a type of thought which was both earlier than that specially represented in the Gospel, and also lasted on in various quarters after the appearance of the latter. The difference in question is at least sufficiently marked to put out of court the idea suggested by Lightfoot[2], and also by Ebrard[3], that the Epistle was, as it were, *l'envoy* to the Gospel, that is to say, that it was written by the evangelist himself to accompany the Gospel and to commend it to the attention of the Church. For it is most unlikely that this difference would appear in two writings composed by the same writer about the same time and intended to be circulated together.

From the character of the difference it seems natural to assume that the Epistle was the earlier work. By some it has been maintained that the author, though he had either himself

[1] I agree with Dr Brooke, pp. xvii ff. that there is not a "fundamental difference of conception between them."
[2] *Biblical Essays*, p. 198.
[3] *Com. on 1 Ep. Jn.*, Eng. trans. p. 25.

written the Gospel, or was thoroughly familiar with it and reproduced many of its thoughts and much of its language, purposely accommodated himself in a measure to ideas of Christian truth which were somewhat simpler and were more widely held than those therein contained. Now that there should have been such an adaptation on the part of the writer is specially unlikely if he was the evangelist himself[1]. We are thinking of a generation when thought and belief were peculiarly earnest and intense; and assuredly the thought and belief of the author of the Fourth Gospel were so. He would have been anxious to speak fully his own mind, more particularly in a writing in which he was in some respects more free than in the Gospel to communicate his own thoughts. Moreover, what motive could he have for withholding his most advanced teaching from believers whom he could address in the words of 1 Jn ii. 20, "Ye have an unction from the Holy One, and ye know all things"?

It would be less difficult to understand that in a writing by a different man—who, though he belonged to the same circle as the author of the Fourth Gospel, and though he was acquainted with that work, might not have felt so deeply the importance of all its distinctive ideas as the evangelist himself must have done—some of those ideas might not reappear. He might have fallen back more or less unconsciously on a form of Christian belief which was familiar to him before he read the Gospel, and which would seem to him sufficiently exact in an Epistle which was mainly hortatory. Yet even for a successor who was a lesser man it would be more natural that he should give expression to the more advanced theology. Actual doctrines would in point of fact have been precisely what he could seize, and would probably be anxious to convey.

My conclusion then is that the First Epistle of St John is from the same hand as the Gospel, and that it was written earlier. Difficulties connected with the supposition that the author is the same appear only when the Gospel is held to be

---

[1] I can claim Holtzmann's support for this view, *ib.* VIII, p. 152. On the other hand Dr Brooke, who holds that the Epistle and Gospel are by the same writer, also makes the Epistle later.

the earlier writing. And there is nothing to constrain us to assign this order to them. Indeed the differences between them in the main point to the opposite one[1].

There is finally a consideration of a more general kind in favour of identity of authorship. It is an old Aristotelian maxim that in the investigation of Nature *causæ non sunt multiplicandæ præter necessitatem*. And surely in like manner in the endeavour to understand human phenomena in obscure periods of history more great unknown personalities should not be imagined than necessary. The reason, however, for making this our rule in the latter sphere is somewhat different from what it is in the other. In Natural Science we do so because observation and inquiry have shewn the unity of Nature, so that the apparent cause in one case may be traced up into some other. In obscure periods of history the reason is that if indeed there were various remarkable men living and working they might have been expected to give more distinct proofs of their existence. To speak particularly of the instance before us; the respective individualities of two men, the one the author of the Epistle, the other of the Gospel, would have shewn themselves in more, and more strikingly distinct, traits than we have here. Men capable of producing either of these writings are not made, still less do they in life continue to be, so much alike in their modes of thought and speech, however strong their sympathy with one another, and however much one may have come under the influence of the other.

THE SECOND AND THIRD EPISTLES OF JOHN

It remains that we should consider whether the mode of address in the two minor Epistles attributed to John, together with the contents and character of the letters themselves, serves in any way either to define, or further to complicate, the problem of the authorship of the Fourth Gospel.

[1] For the view here maintained, combining the identity of the authorship of the First Epistle and Gospel and the priority of the Epistle, compare Huther in the Introduction to his Commentary on the First Epistle of Jn in 3rd edition of Meyer's *Commentary*, 1868; also an admirably clear and concise statement by Aug. Sabatier in Lichtenberger's *Encycl. des Sciences Religieuses*, VIII, pp. 178 ff.

The two letters have commonly been held to be by the same writer and there is strong reason for believing it. They are connected by the same description of himself, ὁ πρεσβύ-τερος, used by the writer; the concluding verses in both (2 Jn 12, 13, 3 Jn 13-15) are almost identical; and there are other expressions which are the same in each, one of which does not occur elsewhere[1]. The writer of each must have been a genuine correspondent of the persons addressed, and known to them. This is evident from the personal references so patent in 3 John, and to be found also (as we shall see) in 2 John. It is most improbable, therefore, that one could have been written imitatively of the other. The writer was a man of spiritual authority among Christians—though in the church to a member of which he wrote the Third Epistle, it was resisted by a man whom he does not charge with heresy, but only with the "love of being first." This is somewhat strange if the Elder was the commanding figure in the Church that some critics have imagined him to have been. We have also no means of determining the extent of the region over which his influence extended.

There are plain indications in 2 John that by "the elect lady," to whom it is addressed, it is not an individual Christian woman that is intended, as has sometimes been supposed, but also that he is not addressing the Christian Church as a whole, but some particular Church, and moreover that his object was not merely to compose a letter to a particular church which the Church in any place might take as if it were addressed to herself, so as virtually to make it a letter to the whole Church[2]. If he had not had the actual condition of some one Church in view there would be no meaning in his declaring that all who knew the truth loved her children (v. 1), which, considering the errors that were widespread, was plainly a testimonial to their orthodoxy; nor again could he have expressed his joy that he has found some of her children walking in truth (v. 4). Nor would there be point in his appeal

---

[1] ἐν ἀληθείᾳ περιπατεῖν, 2 Jn 4, and 3 Jn 4. The latter of these, however, inserts the def. art. before ἀληθείᾳ. In both Jn and 1 Jn we have περιπατεῖν ἐν τῇ σκοτίᾳ and in the latter also ἐν τῷ φωτί.

[2] This is asserted by Pfleiderer, *Primitive Christianity*, IV, p. 154.

addressed to a particular Church 105

to those addressed that they should not lose that which had been wrought by the writer, and it may be also by fellow-labourers of his in the work of evangelisation and of building up the Church (*v.* 8)[1], for he could not claim to have laboured in every place nor could he suitably have held out the prospect of a visit from himself (*v.* 12), except in a definite instance. Moreover, as the Elder describes the Church of the place from which he writes as "thine elect sister" (*v.* 13), so also "the elect lady" to whom he writes must be the Church of a particular place. It has been thought by some that it may have been the Church of which the Gaius of the Third Epistle was a member and that it is the previous letter to which allusion is made at 3 Jn 9a[2].

It remains that we should consider what probability there is that the Elder who was the writer of these two letters was also the author of any of the other "Johannine" writings, and then see whether the effect of combining the conclusions so obtained from the writings themselves with the references to the Elder John by Papias should be to influence in any way our attitude to the traditions about the later life of the Apostle John.

First as to the writer of 2 and 3 John being the author of the Apocalypse. We might, I think, have expected to meet in 2 John with some traits common to it and the Epistles to the Seven Churches if they had had the same author; but there are none. And with the great subject of the Apocalypse there is at most one point of contact (in 2 Jn 7) where the deceivers are mentioned who have gone forth into the world playing the part of Antichrist in that they do not confess Ἰησοῦν Χριστὸν ἐρχόμενον ἐν σαρκί. The present participle here is to be compared with ἐληλυθότα at 1 Jn iv. 2. Moreover it has been suggested that by the use of the present tense the Incarnation is taken out of all connexion with time. I myself, however, find it easier to understand the words as expressing the belief that the Christ was on the point of reappearing[3]. There cannot be said to be a case for identity of

---

[1] ἵνα μὴ ἀπολέσητε ἃ ἠργασάμεθα, ἀλλὰ μισθὸν πλήρη ἀπολάβητε.

[2] E.g. see Harnack, *Texte u. Untersuch.* XV, Heft 3.

[3] Brooke, who gives the former interpretation adds in a note, "there is, how-

authorship between the Apocalypse and 2 and 3 John on the ground of the matter and style of the writings. There is no close correspondence in thought and language between even the one eschatological passage in the two latter and the former[1].

The two short Epistles and the First Epistle and the Gospel have the following points in common, which at least on a cursory inspection are impressive.

(1) The prominence of ἀλήθεια and ἡ ἀλήθεια. Some of the verbs used with it are the same : γινώσκειν τὴν ἀλήθειαν, 2 Jn 1 = Jn viii. 32, and cp. 1 Jn ii. 21. ἀγαπᾶν ἐν ἀληθείᾳ, 2 Jn 1 = 1 Jn iii. 18.

ἀλήθεια and ἡ ἀλήθεια are, however, almost as common in the Pauline as in the Johannine writings. It should also be noted that ἡ ἀλήθεια is personified in 3 Jn 8 and 12 in a manner that is peculiar to this Epistle.

(2) μένειν at 2 Jn 2, 9 (bis); a favourite word in the Fourth Gospel and the First Epistle, in similar connexions, Jn v. 38, viii. 31 etc., 1 Jn ii. 10, 14 etc.

(3) The commandment to love not a new, but to Christians an old commandment, 2 Jn 5 = 1 Jn ii 7. Cp. Jn xiii. 34, xv. 12.

(4) ἀπ' ἀρχῆς, 2 Jn 5, 6 = 1 Jn ii. 7, 24, iii. 11. Cp. also Jn xv. 27 and xvi. 4.

(5) The stress laid on keeping the Divine Commandments, 2 Jn 6 = 1 Jn ii. 3, 4, iii. 22, 24, v. 2, 3, and cp. Jn xiv. 21, xv. 10.

(6) ἡ διδαχὴ τοῦ Χριστοῦ, 2 Jn 9 (bis), 10, cp. Jn vii. 16, 17, xviii. 19.

(7) θεὸν οὐκ ἔχειν, ἔχειν τὸν πατέρα καὶ τὸν υἱόν, 2 Jn 9 = 1 Jn ii. 22, 23.

(8) There are men who are going about doing the work of Antichrist, 2 Jn 7 = 1 Jn ii. 18, 22.

(9) The article of belief at 2 Jn 7 and 1 Jn iv. 2.

(10) ἵνα ἡ χαρὰ ἡμῶν πεπληρωμένη ᾖ, 2 Jn 12 = 1 Jn i. 4.

(11) ὁ ἀγαθοποιῶν ἐκ τοῦ θεοῦ ἐστίν· ὁ κακοποιῶν οὐχ ἑώρακεν τὸν θεόν, 3 Jn 11. ἀγαθοποιεῖν and κακοποιεῖν do not occur in the Fourth Gospel and 1 Jn, but the sentiment and in other respects the expression are closely similar to 1 Jn iii. 6, 10.

But when we go on to notice not only the difference between

ever, much to be said for the simpler interpretation of ἐρχόμενον which refers it to the future manifestation of the Parousia, cf. *Ep. Barn.* VI. 9, ἐλπίσατε ἐπὶ τὸν ἐν σαρκὶ μέλλοντα φανεροῦσθαι ὑμῖν Ἰησοῦν. But in 2 Jn 7 teaching of a Gnostic type may be condemned which denied any true manifestation of the Son of God in the flesh." *Ib.* p. 175."

[1] Cf. Bousset, *Theol. Rundschau*, 1905, pp. 277 f.

as of other writings attributed to John 107

the Fourth Gospel and First Epistle and these two short Epistles from the latter in intensity of spiritual emotion and power, but also the marked absence of ideas and expressions which belong to what was most vital in the mode of thought and theology of the former, grave doubts arise as to whether the writer can be the same man. There is no mention in 2 and 3 John of the Spirit. Nor is there any reference to the believer's communion with and life in and through Jesus Christ; nor of the revelation of the Father through Him; nor of any aspect of His Atonement for sin; nor of the New Birth. In the Second Epistle stress is laid only on being loyal to an orthodox, anti-Docetic Creed and on keeping the commandments of God and of Christ, without any indication of the true source of the Christian's strength for doing so. In the Third Epistle the only allusion even to Jesus Christ is in the mention of those who have gone forth "on behalf of the Name"; the actual words "Jesus," "Christ," or "the Son," do not occur. Again, among characteristic Johannine words which are wanting I may name $ζωή$, $φῶς$, $αἰώνιος$, $πιστεύειν$. Another difference is that in the First Epistle the author appeals to the spiritual illumination of his readers (ii. 21, 22); and that he associates himself habitually with other believers as regards the dangers and the privileges of the Christian life, the aims which all must set before themselves, the tests which all must apply to themselves (e.g. i. 6, ii. 1, 5, 6, iii. 1 ff., 14, iv. 9). In the Second and Third Epistles they stand over against him and he addresses them as from another level. When every allowance is made for the shortness of these Epistles it is not credible that the author of the Fourth Gospel and First Epistle of St John should have written the Third Epistle to an esteemed Christian friend, who was his child in the Faith, without any allusion to the deeper experiences of the Christian life. How different in this respect is St Paul's Ep. to Philemon, another brief letter, equally occupied with external incidents. Still less is it conceivable that the author of the First Epistle and the Gospel should have written a letter, however brief, to a Christian Church, as the Second Epistle is, in which he did not seek to remind them of those spiritual mysteries. No! the resemblances which there are between 2 and 3 Jn and on the other hand 1 Jn and the

Fourth Gospel are such as could be due to imitation, or which might be of the number of the ideas and expressions current in the Church of a particular region. They are for the most part of a superficial kind as compared with those characteristics which are wanting, some of which must have appeared if the writer had been the same[1].

We must now finally take account of Papias' references to the Elder John. I still find it impossible, as when I discussed these and Eusebius' comments thereon in my first volume, (1) to suppose that Papias has in mind only one John, and that he means the son of Zebedee alike when he mentions John in the enumeration of members of the twelve, and when just afterwards he speaks of the Elder John[2]; (2) to admit that the notion of there having been two Johns *in Asia* is "baseless[3]," and that the only John who was ever prominent in the Church there was "the Elder John."

Papias does not in point of fact in the fragments preserved to us mention the residence of either John in Asia. He is referring to reports made to him of what some of the twelve, and two other disciples of the Lord, Aristion and the Elder John, declared. The only difference that he makes in speaking of what was stated to be the testimony of the two last is that he uses of them the present tense—"what they say." This seems to shew that these two were alive when their words were reported, while the others were so no longer.

The grounds for believing that John the son of Zebedee had lived in Asia are those which have been examined in vol. I, and which, as to a couple of points, I must examine further in the next chapter. The residence of the Elder John in Asia may be regarded as a thing not in itself improbable, and it is not an unreasonable suggestion that he was "the Elder" of 2 and 3 John. This description was evidently for a time commonly used of those who still survived from among the first

---

[1] Pfleiderer, *ib.* p. 164, E. Schwartz and Jülicher, *Einleit.* p. 218, who all hold that 2 and 3 Jn are by a different author from 1 Jn, have founded their opinion upon some other considerations, which are not, however, to my own mind so convincing as the one in the text.

[2] See further note at end of this chapter on Dom J. Chapman's Essay.

[3] Bousset starts from this point in his exposition of his theory in *Offenbar. Joh.* pp. 36 ff., *Encycl. Bibl.* I. 198, and *Theol. Rundschau* for 1905.

John the Elder

generation of Christian believers, when men who belonged to it were fast disappearing. If in some Church, or little group of Churches, there was one such man remaining, and he was also their most revered spiritual guide and teacher, he might well have borne and used the title—whether he was Papias' John the Elder or not, and whether or not it was given to him in the whole of Western Asia. Nevertheless, we will proceed on the assumption that John the Elder was the writer of 2 and 3 John for which, because of his adopting the name "the Elder," there is in reality more ground than for regarding him as the author of the Apocalypse. Would, then, the fact that this other John did reside in Asia weaken the force of the testimony to the Asiatic residence of the Apostle John, by suggesting that the tradition concerning the latter had grown up through confusion with a different person of the same name? It is to be observed, first, that this theory labours under the difficulty that he must have been a man of considerable eminence in order to lend traits to the Apostle, while the more eminent he was the more difficult it is to suppose that he could, in the memory of the Church, have been telescoped into him. If besides writing 2 and 3 John he had been the author of the other Johannine writings, and in addition one of the last surviving personal followers of Jesus, he could hardly have failed to make such a mark on the Church in Asia that he could not have been forgotten, or confused with an Apostle who had never been in that same region. But so far as we can form any well-grounded idea of the extent of his authority and influence and personal calibre from what Papias tells us about him, and from the character and contents of 2 and 3 John[1], the ecclesiastical writers of half a century or more, or even of a few years, after his death, whose writings have survived, might well have had no occasion to mention him.

[1] Bousset, who supposes the Elder John to be the author of the Apocalypse, but not of 2 and 3 Jn, says, *ib.* p. 232, that "the man who could write as he does to the Seven Churches of Asia, must in relation to them have played an altogether specially preeminent rôle." Surely there is nothing whatever in those Epistles to shew this. All the warnings, exhortations etc. are put into the mouth of Christ. Anyone who felt deeply convinced that the Churches needed them, and that he was inspired to utter them as from Christ, could have done the like.

JOHN THE PRESBYTER AND THE FOURTH GOSPEL, BY DOM J. CHAPMAN, O.S.B.

I take this opportunity of writing a few words in reply to my friend Dom J. Chapman's Essay on this subject, published in 1911. His thesis is that Eusebius (*H.E.* III. 39) wrongly supposed Papias to refer to two Johns, and that there was never but one John of note in the Church in Asia, namely the son of Zebedee who was of the number of the twelve. I do not think that Dom Chapman supplies any stronger reasons for taking this view than those succinctly stated by Dr Salmon in his article on "John the Presbyter" in *Dict. of Christ. Biography*, III, pp. 400 f. But for coming to a conclusion on the subject, it is convenient to have before one a fuller discussion of it, such as Dom Chapman's. I still believe Eusebius' interpretation of the words of Papias to be the natural one. Even apart from the oddness of John being mentioned the second time, with a new designation, if he was the same person as the Apostle already named and also of his being placed the second time after Aristion, Papias would surely have considered the reports by his informants as to what they had themselves heard the Apostle John say, who when he met with them was still alive to be appealed to, as of greater value than what they had only learned of his words at second-hand. He should accordingly have laid more stress on those first-hand reports, by noticing them first. Further, if Papias had himself been "a hearer of John (the Apostle)," he could hardly have been satisfied only to allude to this fact, as Dom Chapman supposes that he does, in the general statement, ὅσα παρὰ τῶν πρεσβυτέρων ἔμαθον, thus including the Apostle in the same class with men of altogether inferior authority. With regard to Irenæus' statement that Papias was "a hearer of John, a companion of Polycarp" (*Adv. Hær.* v. 33, 34), it should be observed that it does not appear on what ground he states this. There is nothing to shew that Papias himself said as much. Irenæus may have known it as a tradition, or have inferred it, rightly or wrongly, from the words of Papias, or of someone else about him. And if Papias had in reality been a hearer of the author of the Fourth Gospel, we might surely have expected that some pieces of teaching worthy of such a teacher would have been preserved by him, and cited by Irenæus or Eusebius. Dom Chapman holds it to be certain (p. 51) that Papias knew the

John the Elder

Apostle John, simply on the ground of the testimony of Justin that the latter saw the Apocalypse in Asia, and of Irenæus that he resided there till the days of Trajan. But, in the first place, if we accept as convincing (as I do) the evidence for the Ephesine residence of John, it does not follow that we can be confident as to the soundness of every item of the tradition, such as the length of his life. Some exaggeration as to this would be very natural. And further we know little about the life of Papias except that he was bishop of Hierapolis. He may not have been born, or have spent his youth, at Hierapolis, but somewhere much further off from John's place of residence. Moreover, even if we suppose that he wrote his *Expositions* as early as A.D. 130, the date selected by Salmon, it is probable that he would only have been a child of 8 to 12 at the beginning of the reign of Trajan, and not able to undertake a journey for the sake of seeing the last of the Apostles.

Whether Papias himself was a hearer of John the Presbyter is a matter of much less importance. I argued, vol. I, p. 169, that though Eusebius holds that he was, his ground for doing so is somewhat uncertain, because after stating it as a fact, he proceeds ὀνομαστὶ γοῦν πολλάκις αὐτῶν μνημονεύσας etc. I rendered γοῦν "at any rate," and Dom Chapman says it should be rendered "in fact," and thinks that thus the point of my argument is turned[1]. To me it does not seem to make much difference whether it is rendered "at any rate" or "in fact." The *fact* on which Eusebius relies for proving that Papias was a hearer of the Elder John is that he several times mentions him by name and gives traditions derived from him. But obviously that does not prove it.

[1] Pp. 28 f.

CHAPTER IV

THE ATTRIBUTION OF THE AUTHORSHIP OF THE GOSPEL TO JOHN THE SON OF ZEBEDEE

THE external evidence in regard to the authorship of the Fourth Gospel was discussed by me at considerable length in vol. I of the present work, because it appeared to me best to treat it as part of the general subject of the reception of the fourfold Gospel in the Church. The conclusion at which I arrived was that while the evidence is fully sufficient to establish the fact of John's residence in Proconsular Asia and also of some connexion between the contents of the Gospel and his testimony and teaching, it is not such as to prove that the composition of the Gospel must have been his work. To decide the question what his connexion with the work was, it is necessary to take account of evidence of other kinds. It will be my aim in this chapter to carry the examination of this question of authorship a few steps further, by discussing certain statements in the Gospel itself which more or less clearly bear upon it.

But before I pass on to do this I shall here seize the opportunity of repairing certain omissions in the discussions in my first volume.

(1) First, let me notice certain additional arguments which have been adduced for rejecting the widely-received tradition as to the Ephesine residence of John the son of Zebedee.

THE ALLEGED MARTYRDOM OF JOHN THE SON OF ZEBEDEE BY THE JEWS

In my first volume I considered the statement by Georgius Hamartolus, and in a fragment discovered by de Boor, that, according to Papias, John and James, the sons of Zebedee, were both put to death by the Jews, and I do not desire now to add anything on this particular portion of the evidence alleged for the death of John in Palestine[1]. But since the time

---

[1] See vol. I (1903), pp. 166f. Dr L. Jackson in *The Problem of the Fourth Gospel*, pp. 143f., speaks of the statement of Georgius H., and the fragment in the collection of extracts discovered by de Boor as confirming one another. He has not considered the probability that both are derived from the same source, Philip of Side, who has been proved to be a bungler.

Evidence opposed to Asiatic tradition

that I there wrote a good deal of stress has been laid on some items of evidence seeming to support that view, to which, comparatively speaking, little attention had been directed before; mainly the two following: (*a*) the fact that a Calendar in Syriac, transcribed in A.D. 412, which gives "the names of confessors and victors and the days on which they gained their crowns," has on Dec. 27, "John and James the Apostles, at Jerusalem"; (*b*) the saying addressed to both the sons of Zebedee, "Ye shall indeed drink of the cup that I drink of, and be baptized with the baptism that I am baptized with" (Mk x. 39, Mt. xx. 23)[1].

(*a*) *The Syriac Martyrology*[2].

In judging of the significance of the evidence of the Syriac Martyrology, the most important point to note is that the first

---

[1] Wellhausen in his commentary on *Mark*, 1904, treated this saying as a prediction framed *ex eventu*, based upon the double martyrdom of the two brothers.

[2] This Syriac Martyrology was first published by the late Dr Wm Wright, Arabic Professor at Cambridge, in the *Jour. of Sacred Lit.* for 1866, vol. VIII (new series), pp. 45 and 423 ff. There is an important examination of it by L. Duchesne in an essay on *Les Sources du Martyrologie Hiéronymien* pub. in *Mélanges d'Archéologie et d'Histoire* of the *École Française de Rome* for 1885, pp. 121-137. Further, in the *Acta Sanctorum Novembris* (Supplement, 1894), Tom. II, p. 1, pp. iii ff., he has given in parallel columns the Syriac Martyrology freshly collated, a translation of it into Greek and the entries of the Hieronymian Calendar so far as they correspond therewith. The same vol. contains also the whole Hieronymian Calendar edited by de Rossi and Duchesne from different MSS.; but Duchesne does not discuss its statement in respect to John and James. Erbes, so far as I am aware, was the first to use this statement to confirm that attributed to Papias. He touched upon it, *Zeitschr. f. Kirchengesch.* 1901, pp. 200 ff. (The main object of this article was to shew that Peter also was crucified at Jerusalem.) He also examined the Syriac Martyrology elaborately in three articles on *Das syrische Martyrologium und der Weihnachtsfestkreis*, *ib.* 1904, pp. 329 ff. and 1905, pp. 1 ff. and pp. 463 ff. Finally, he returned to the subject in an article on "Der Apostel Johannes und der Jünger, welcher an der Brust des Herrn lag," *ib.* 1912, pp. 199 ff. Prof. Burkitt, again, appeals to this Syriac Calendar as testifying to a "Catholic tradition," which is reflected in the position of St John's Day even in our own Calendar, and which is in reality different from that which has been commonly supposed to be the universal tradition of the Church about the later years of St John. (See *The Gospel History and its Transmission* for 1906, pp. 252 ff.) On the other side see an article in the *Irish Church Quarterly* for Jan. 1908, on "The Traditions as to the Death of John the Son of Zebedee" by Dr J. H. Bernard, now Provost of Trinity College, Dublin.

part of it seems clearly to be an abridged rendering of a Greek Calendar, which represented the usage of the Church in the eastern portion of the Roman Empire. The Syriac MS. was made in A.D. 412, probably at Edessa. It consists of two parts; the first contains martyrs of the Roman Empire arranged according to months and days, beginning from Dec. 26; the second the saints of Babylonia and Persia, according to their ecclesiastical status, bishops, priests, deacons, without regard to the Calendar, and without any indication of their anniversaries[1]. The first part concludes with the note, "here end the confessors of the West," i.e. west of the eastern boundary of the Empire. The second part is evidently a sort of appendix, and its form suggests that a regular calendar had not yet been established for the Church in those regions. The fact that the first part, just indicated, is concerned with martyrs belonging to the Greek-speaking portion of the Church, would of itself make it highly probable that the Syriac is a translation from Greek; but this is confirmed by the close correspondence, for the saints of all this portion of the Church, between the Hieronymian Calendar of the Latin West and the Syriac. Further, a comparison between these two shews plainly that the Syriac was an abridgment of a Greek original to which both go back[2]. And the reproduction substantially of this Greek original in the Hieronymian Calendar shews that it represented the prevailing practice of the Greek-speaking Church.

From a study of the names included and the manner in which certain provinces of the Empire are described Duchesne infers that the date of the Greek original of the Syriac was at least not much after, and perhaps before, A.D. 363 (i.e. the death of Julian)[3]; while Erbes assigns it to circ. A.D. 340[4]. Nicomedia is held to be the place where it saw the light[5].

Now, in the first place, the fact itself that the Syriac is an abridgment, and moreover one that has evidently been care-

---

[1] Duchesne, *Mélanges*, *ib.* pp. 121 f.
[2] See Duchesne, *ib.* pp. 122–6. Erbes also (*ib.* 1904, p. 337) admits that the Syriac Calendar was abridged from a Greek one, which the original of the Hieronymian closely resembled. It is not clear that Duchesne means to maintain more in spite of Erbes' criticism, *ib.* p. 355.
[3] *Ib.* p. 129.   [4] *Ib.* 1904, p. 376, and 1912, p. 199.
[5] Duchesne, *ib.* pp. 134 f., Erbes, *ib.*

Evidence opposed to Asiatic tradition 115

lessly executed[1], must detract from its value as a witness in regard to the point at present before us. It is not unreasonable to suppose that in such an abridgment some indication that the fate of James was not to be attributed to John has been obliterated[2].

If we examine throughout the entries in which the Hieronymian and Syriac calendars correspond, we find indeed very few instances in which any similar error could have arisen in the Syriac, because there are very few in which the commemorations of saints in different places occur on the same day. But there are a few, and in the case of one of this small number, namely that for the 5th of April, we have just such a compression leading to error in the Syriac Calendar as I have supposed that there is at Dec. 27. There in the Syriac we have, "At Alexandria, Claudianus and Didymus"; while in the Hieronymian it is "At Nicomedia, of Claudianus....In Alexandria of Didymus, presbyter[3]."

But, further, the strong probability that the identification of John's end with that of James is due to the carelessness of the Syriac translator, or to some other accidental error, is established by considering what the intention of the Greek Calendar is likely to have been in view of the known beliefs of the portion of the Church to which it belonged. If the Syriac Martyrology were itself an original, it might well be supposed

[1] The Syriac abridger has jumped from June 5 to July 6, and transferred the entries belonging to July to June; see Erbes, *ib.* 1904, p. 338. A smaller instance of carelessness will be given below.

[2] The entry in the Hieronymian Cal. at Dec. 27 is: "Adsumptio" (or in other MSS. "depositio" or "dormitio") "S. Johannis evangelistæ apud Ephesum et ordinatio episcopatus S. Jacobi fratris Domini qui ab apostolis primus ex Judæis Hierosolymis est episcopus ordinatus." Most probably the entry in the Greek original of the Syriac did not differ from the latter so much as this.

In the Armenian Calendar the entry for Dec. 28 (the festivals of the Sons of Zebedee and of Peter and Paul have here been inverted) is "The festival of the holy sons of thunder, James and John." In the ancient *Kalendarium Carthaginense* (printed in Append. to Ruinart's *Acta Martyrum*), we have the following entry for Dec. 27, "Sancti Joannis Baptistæ et Jacobi Apostoli quem Herodes occidit." Here, no doubt, "Baptistæ" has been substituted for "Evangelistæ," owing to the similarity between the Baptist's fate and that of John. But it should be observed that it is stated only in the case of James. At the same time we see the kind of confusion through which the story of the death of John the evangelist in Palestine might have arisen.

[3] See *Acta SS. Nov.* pp. liii ff., also *Mélanges*, p. 123.

that in its notice of St John, it preserved a piece of ancient tradition concerning him, which it had received from the Church of Palestine, and which differed from that which had gained currency in the great Greek-speaking Church. But it is practically impossible that the custom of the Church as to St John's commemoration in this portion of the Church should have been determined by a tradition different from that which we know to have been generally accepted there from the latter part of the second century onwards. There must, then, have been some other reason for his having been assigned the place which he occupies in the Calendar than the idea that he had suffered martyrdom. We might feel sure of this if we possessed no specific notice in any early writer giving us ground for thinking so. But in point of fact we have such notices in the sermon preached in 379 by Gregory of Nyssa on the death of Basil of Cæsarea[1], and in an earlier *Laudatio S. Stephani*[2]. In both he implies that the place of the commemorations of Peter and Paul and James, no less than John, so near that of the Nativity, was due primarily to their being Apostles. He does not suggest that they were commemorated then because through martyrdom they were born into a heavenly world as Christ was born into this one—not surely a natural association of ideas. But even if the claims of Peter, Paul and James to the positions given them in the Calendar rested on their having endured martyrdom—and no doubt this added to their lustre, and Gregory refers to the different kinds of death by which they glorified God—it would not follow that the reason for placing the commemoration of John where it stands should be precisely of the same nature. It was suitable to associate him with his brother James, and his eminence among the Twelve and as an evangelist justified it, and his sufferings for Christ's sake and faithful witness throughout a long life could also be called to mind, as they are by Gregory[3].

[1] Migne, *Patr. Gr.* xlvi, col. 789.   [2] *Ib.* col. 725.
[3] Cp. on this subject Bp Bernard, *ib.* pp. 64 ff. Erbes, *ib.* 1912, p. 200, discounts Gregory's testimony on the ground that he wrote 40 years after the composition of the Calendar; but views do not alter rapidly on a matter of that kind. In point of fact, however, we do not really need anybody's testimony as to what a calendar framed and generally accepted in the Greek Church in the earlier half of the fourth century can have meant. Clearly it should be interpreted by the long-established and well-known tradition of the Church.

A similar broad conception of suffering for, and witnessing to, the cause of truth seems to afford the most natural explanation of the reference of Aphraates, in a passage near the close of his homily on Persecution, to James and John as having both of them "followed Christ." The preceding part of the homily is mainly taken up with comparisons between Old Testament saints and Jesus on the ground that they were persecuted as He was, though the great majority of those whom he so compares with Him did not undergo a violent death[1]. Even apart from this, since Aphraates is not known to have held a different view of the course and end of John's career from the usual one, the presumption surely is that he held the usual one.

(b) *The prediction at Mk* x. 39, *Mt. xx.* 23[2].

There is something fascinating in the notion that one can discover evidence of an almost forgotten fact of history in a saying, the true meaning of which has long passed unnoticed. But this must not be allowed to bias the judgment. It must be observed that it is a common characteristic of predictions concerning the future to allow considerable latitude of interpretation. And when the time for fulfilment came their terms were not rigorously scrutinised to see that they exactly fitted all the circumstances of the case, or cases to which they were applied. That surely is admittedly true of the oracles of classical antiquity. But there is an instance precisely to the point in the saying of Jesus to Simon Peter recorded at Jn xxi. 18: "when thou shalt be old, thou shalt stretch forth thy hands, and another shall gird thee, and carry thee whither thou wouldest not," which is followed by the comment, "Now this he

---

[1] "Moses was persecuted and Jesus was persecuted"; "Elijah was persecuted and Jesus was persecuted"; "Elishah was persecuted and Jesus was persecuted"; "Daniel was persecuted and Jesus was persecuted" etc.
    The Syriac Homilies of Aphraates were edited by Prof. A. Wright, 1869. There is a translation of them in *Texte u. Untersuch.* 1st series, III, and also in *Nicene and Post-Nicene Fathers*, XII.

[2] Wellhausen in his *Evang. Marci* (1904), p. 99, and *Evang. Jo.* (1908), p. 119, and p. 120, n. 1; E. Schwartz, *Ueber den Tod der Söhne Zebedai* in *Abhandlungen d. Göttingen Gesell. Wiss.* B. VII, no. 5, 1904; *Nachrichten*, 1907, pp. 266 ff.; Erbeş, *ib.* for 1901, p. 204, and for 1912, pp. 196 ff.; Bacon, *Fourth Gospel*, 1910, pp. 127 ff.; L. Jackson, *ib.* pp. 142 f., 148 f.

spake, signifying by what manner of death he should die." But the description in the saying does not (as commentators allow) specially suit crucifixion, and indeed it does not clearly suggest any manner of *death* at all. It would, for example, fit deportation into exile.

It appears to me, therefore, perfectly legitimate to suppose that the image of "drinking the cup" and "being baptized with the baptism" of Christ was from the first understood differently in the case of the two brothers, and that a long life of faithful service, with the self-abnegation and suffering which it involved, was reasonably held to be a fulfilment of the prediction in the case of John.

Schwartz contends, and apparently Wellhausen agrees with him, that from the saying in question it must be inferred, not merely that both sons of Zebedee were martyred, but that the martyrdom of John took place at the same time as that of James, namely, in A.D. 43 or 44, the date which is to be gathered from Acts xii, the testimony of which work he accepts in this case.

I will take this point first.

Schwartz writes: "If one deals seriously with the demand of the sons of Zebedee for the two places of honour on the right and the left of the returning Messiah, then it is not merely impossible to avoid the conclusion that they both died as martyrs, but the sitting on both sides is only comprehensible and clear, if in point of fact they left the earth at the same time and together; finally, I do not know how that whole claim could have been framed, if they were not the first, and did not for a considerable time remain the only ones who 'took up their Cross[1].'"

In this passage Schwartz does not only require that the description of the prospect lying before James and John should be rigorously interpreted in precisely the same sense for both, but he misinterprets. For (1) they were not promised the two seats on the right and left hands respectively, but warned not to expect them, and (2) it is impossible to see why, even if the request for these two seats had been granted, this should involve their dying at the same, or approximately the same, time. This will appear plainly unnecessary if it is remembered that

[1] *Ib.* p. 4.

Evidence opposed to Asiatic tradition

the desire attributed to them was not that they should have these places on Christ's right and left in heaven on their own departure from earth, but that they should have them in the Messiah's kingdom on His return to earth, after a period which had not elapsed even at the close of the Apostolic Age.

But, further, the theory that John suffered martyrdom at the same time as his brother James, or at any time early in the Apostolic Age, is confronted with two objections which to most minds will seem fatal to it, namely, that the Acts is silent about it and that in Gal. ii. 9 a John, who must in all likelihood be held to be the Apostle bearing that name, is mentioned as a "pillar" of the Church at Jerusalem several years after his brother's death. With regard to the silence of Acts about any persons martyred along with James, Wellhausen admits that it strikes one as remarkable. And he adds that "one can scarcely avoid suspecting that Luke has here suppressed some names; perhaps only a single one[1]." Surely one may say that a theory is in bad case when its supporters have to avail themselves of such a supposition as this. The defence is no stronger in regard to the notice in Gal. ii. 9. Schwartz is ready with the suggestion that the John intended was John Mark. It is nothing to him that the notices of Mark in Acts (from which he has taken the fact of the martyrdom of James) are wholly incompatible with his having occupied such a position, and that no other statement or allusion has come down to us which renders it even remotely probable.

Erbes[2] and Bacon[3] both find it impossible, in view of the silence of Acts and the notice in Gal. ii. 9, to accept the theory that John died at the same time as his brother James. Bacon supposes him to have been among the "certain others" to whom Josephus alludes as having been put to death by the high priest Ananus along with James "the brother of Jesus," on the charge of being "transgressors of the law[4]." To help out this hypothesis Prof. Bacon observes that "we are not compelled to understand Mk x. 39 in the sense of a *simultaneous* martyrdom of the two brethren. That conception

[1] *Götting. Nachrichten* for 1907, p. 9, n. 2. The "single one" is presumably a cryptic reference to John.
[2] *Ztschr. f. Kirchgesch.* 1912, p. 196.   [3] *Ib.* p. 144.
[4] *Antiqu.* xx, ch. 9, § 1.

might quite as easily be based on the confusion so frequent in early Christian writers between James the brother of John and James the brother of the Lord." Prof. Bacon, I think, forgets that, though the two eminent persons named James might sometimes be confused two or three centuries after their deaths, it is not the same thing to suppose the confusion to have occurred, as he does, early enough for the saying under discussion to have been embodied in Mark's Gospel, i.e. at furthest not more than ten or twelve years after the death of James the Lord's brother, when the events in question were fresh in the recollection of a very large number of members of the Church[1].

But, further, while it is not difficult to understand that the Jewish historian might have passed over the name of the Christian Apostle and have mentioned only the resident leader of the Church in Jerusalem, it is to be remembered that we have also in Eusebius[2] a long account of the martyrdom of James, quoted from the early Jewish Christian writer Hegesippus, and that it is almost inconceivable that he should not in the same context have mentioned the Apostle John, if he was one of those who suffered martyrdom at the same time, or that Eusebius should have suppressed any reference to this[3].

Erbes[4] thinks it possible that the death of John took place in A.D. 62 at the time fixed, also, for the death of James, the brother of the Lord, in Josephus. But he prefers to place it a few years later, because he holds that John did reside for a time at Ephesus and lead the Church there, probably from A.D. 62-6, after which, according to Erbes, he returned to Palestine, and was one of those whom the Roman procurator Albinus put to death, when about to be superseded in his office. But there is nothing in Josephus' notice of this action on the part of Albinus to suggest that the executions had anything to do with religion, or that they were designed to please the Jews on that account[5].

---

[1] It may be noted, too, that there seems to be some confusion in Prof. Bacon's own argument. For he first of all tells us that the saying does not require that both deaths should be simultaneous, and then explains it by supposing that the death of John was simultaneous with the death of a James, but another one.

[2] *H.E.* II. 23.

[3] See further below, p. 122, on the silence of Eusebius.

[4] *Ib.* pp. 204 ff.   [5] See Joseph. *ib.* § 5.

Preponderance on side of Asiatic tradition

Any further considerations that appear to be needed for forming a judgment upon the particular points which I have discussed in the preceding pages may be most conveniently included in the few concluding remarks that I will now make, on the whole subject of the residence of John the son of Zebedee in Asia.

We have here, as in many questions of fact that are brought into the law-courts, or come before us in daily life, a case where there is a conflict of evidence, and where we must choose between the testimony of different witnesses, according to the value which seems to belong to each, owing to the circumstances in which it is given, or for other reasons. In support of an *alibi* we have an oracular saying in St Mark and St Matthew which is supposed to imply it; an entry in a Syriac Martyrology in which the deaths of James and John are jointly mentioned; the allegation that Papias had referred to the death of John at the hands of the Jews. We have examined these items of evidence and have found the interpretation put upon the first of them to be a very questionable one, and the second and third to be very untrustworthy. On the same side, however, it is to be added that there is silence about the Apostle John in one or two early writers, more particularly in the Epp. of Ignatius, where we might have expected him to have been mentioned if he resided for some time in Asia[1].

On the other side we have the statements of Irenæus[2] that Polycarp at whose feet he himself sat in boyhood spoke of his intercourse with John, by whom (it is generally admitted) he means the son of Zebedee. The clearest and fullest of these are contained in a letter addressed to one who had been a fellow-hearer of Polycarp with himself, but who was some years older. He is expostulating with him on his falling into heresy

---

[1] See this discussed, vol. I, pp. 19 ff., 165 f., 235 ff. I may mention here the strange statement in the Apocryphal Acts of Andrew in respect to the fields of labour assigned to different Apostles: καὶ ἐκληρώθη Πέτρος τὴν περιτομήν· Ἰάκωβος καὶ Ἰωάννης τὴν ἀνατολήν· Φίλιππος τὰς πόλεις τῆς Σαμαρίας καὶ τὴν Ἀσίαν. Bonnet, *Act. Apost. Apocr.*

This, if it is inconsistent with the Ephesian residence of John, is equally, if not more, inconsistent with the early martyrdom in Palestine of James and John.

[2] See on these which are here simply recalled to mind the discussion in vol. I, pp. 213 ff.

and appeals to him by their common memories of Polycarp's teaching and references to the Apostle John, and so challenges contradiction[1]. There is other evidence which is, to my mind, even stronger. The Quartodecimans of Asia, in the middle of the second century and later, defended their practice in regard to the observance of Easter by claiming that in this they followed the example of John who had resided amongst them. Is it possible that none of their opponents in the Church of Rome, who were anxious to suppress the Quartodeciman custom, would have discovered that there was another tradition about John's end still to be found in other parts of the Church, which convicted the Ephesine one of being a recent invention, or that no one in their interest would have produced the statement which Papias' book is said to have contained? The conditions, then, under which the statements that John the Apostle resided in Asia were made, were such as to lead to their disproof, if they were untrue. Nor was it only at Rome, and in connexion with this particular controversy, that the other (supposed) account of John's end would be preferred. Everywhere except in Asia the interest and sympathy of Christians would be enlisted on its side. According to it the glory of martyrdom belonged to John; why should he be deprived of this? And in particular would the Church of Palestine have consented to forgo its right to include among its own glories the name of one of the chief Apostles? And why should Eusebius, who was bishop of a see in Palestine, and very learned in all the literature and traditions of the Church at large, not have referred to it?

If the total—or almost total—suppression which must have taken place of the fact of John's martyrdom in Palestine is compared with the silence in regard to the Ephesine residence in some quarters where one might have expected it to be mentioned, it will be seen how much greater are the difficulties created by the former supposition[2].

[1] For other witnesses see *ib*. pp. 228 ff.
[2] The very critics who at times press the argument from silence unduly, usually ignore it altogether in the case of this supposed substitution of one tradition for another. It is to the credit of E. Schwartz that he has attempted to offer an explanation. But I am not aware that his theory has been accepted by anyone.

(2) Another point on which I desire to add some observations to those in my first volume is *the silence of Irenæus, the Muratorian Fragment, and Eusebius as to any early recognition of the authenticity of the Gospel according to St John.*

I there considered broadly the significance for the history of the reception of the Fourth Gospel of the appearance in the latter part of the second century of the Alogi, as a set of people who rejected the authority of that Gospel, and yet did not differ in their doctrinal beliefs in any definite manner from the majority of orthodox Christians and were not formally excommunicated. (See vol. I, pp. 198-212, 235, 242 f.) I do not feel it necessary to add anything on that general question to what I there said. I contended that this phenomenon does not shew that the authenticity of the Fourth Gospel either was not at that time, or had only recently come to be, generally believed; but I also observed that "the conception of the Fourfold Gospel had not as yet acquired that firm hold on the mind of every professing Christian, which only clear and positive definition and a prescription of some generations could give." My only doubt, in reviewing what I then wrote, is as to whether this last explanation even is needed. For we have an instance that seems to shew that it is not, in the rise in recent times of a sect which believes that Lord Bacon wrote plays which for nearly three centuries have universally been, and by the great majority of critical students still are, believed to have been by William Shakespeare. But of one aspect of the subject I did not treat, viz. the question what the contemporaries of the Alogi who condemned them might have been expected to say, but did not say, about the origin of the Fourth Gospel. I ought not to have passed this over; for Corssen had directed marked attention to it[1]. Stress has also since been laid upon it by Loisy[2], and by B. W. Bacon[3].

[1] First in his able essay, *Monarchianische Prologe zu den vier Evangelien* in *Texte u. Untersuch.* Bd. 15, 1897, pp. 104-6, and later in his article, *Warum ist das Vierte Evangelium für ein Werk des Apostels Johannes erklärt worden?* in *Zeitschrift f. d. Neutest. Theol.* 1901, p. 222.

[2] *Le Quatrième Évangile*, 1903, pp. 22 f.

[3] *The Fourth Gospel in Research and Debate*, 1910, p. 84.

First, let us consider Irenæus. The most recent writer is the most emphatic. "Irenæus was fighting," says Prof. Bacon, "with every available weapon, but chiefly the weapon of Apostolic tradition in Asia, against those wretched men who wish to set aside that aspect (of the fourfold tradition) which is presented by John's Gospel." From such language as this it might be supposed that Irenæus' treatise was directed primarily against these "impugners of the Fourth Gospel," or that they were at least among those whom he had clearly marked out as a school against which he was arguing. But as a matter of fact his treatise is directed against the Valentinians (especially one sect of them), and other Gnostic Schools, with whom the Alogi had nothing in common, either doctrinally, or in their attitude to the Fourth Gospel, which the chief Gnostic Schools accepted as by the Apostle John. And except in the few lines to which Prof. Bacon refers there is not in the whole of Irenæus' treatise any mention of them, nor any trace that he is thinking of them. In another passage shortly before (ch. xi. 1) in which Irenæus is comparing the beginnings of the several Gospels, he says that John intended by his commencement to teach that there was "one God Who made all things through His Word," and so to confound the false teaching of Cerinthus, and of the still earlier Nicolaitans and of those who had followed them. He gives not the slightest indication that those to whom he refers afterwards as rejecting the Fourth Gospel were included among those whom he has here in his mind. When he speaks of them, he says that their objection to that Gospel lay in the promise that it contained of the sending of the Paraclete. It is, indeed, not improbable that both the name *Alogi* and the accusation that they were opposed to the doctrine of the Logos were the invention of Epiphanius, nearly two centuries later[1].

Again, Irenæus, in his fifth book appeals to the Apocalypse and to traditions handed down by disciples of John, in support of Millenarian teaching. He makes no allusion to the Alogi though the Alogi, as we know of them through later writers, rejected the Apocalypse as well as the Fourth Gospel. It is undoubtedly the Gnostic dislike to Millenarian doctrine that

[1] See vol. I of this work, p. 203.

Lack of early defence of Fourth Gospel

Irenæus is combating, and he does it by appealing to the authority of him who was acknowledged to be the beloved disciple and the fourth evangelist.

Turning to the passage where the solitary reference to "the impugners of the Fourth Gospel" occurs, what do we find? In the same context he mentions Marcion who "rejecting the whole Gospel, nay, rather cutting himself off from the Gospel, boasts that he has a part of the Gospel." He also speaks of the Valentinians, who acknowledge all the Gospels, but who by allegorising them read into them a meaning contrary to the Apostolic tradition preserved in the Church, and also have writings of their own to which they give the preference. Shortly before he has spoken of the Ebionites who acknowledge only the Gospel according to St Matthew, and of Marcion who uses an expurgated Luke. In mentioning some who deny the authenticity of the Fourth Gospel, he does but complete his review of the misbelievers who acknowledge either more or fewer Gospels than the Church. And if to "the impugners of the Fourth Gospel" he devotes a few more lines than to any of the others except the Valentinians, it is to be observed that what he dwells upon is not their rejection of it, but that which he held to be the motive thereof, their refusal to recognise the reality of those spiritual gifts in which was to be seen the fulfilment of Christ's promise, recorded in the Gospel according to St John, that He would send another Paraclete[1].

Corssen and Loisy know better than to make any sweeping statements about Irenæus' treatise like that of Prof. Bacon quoted above. Nevertheless, they imply that the existence of

[1] The words between inverted commas given as a quotation from Irenæus in the passage cited above from Prof. Bacon are an abbreviation of Irenæus, and an abbreviation which does not give an accurate impression of what he actually wrote. He does not lay the *chief* stress on the rejection of the Gospel according to St John by the persons in question, but on their hostility to the gifts bestowed by the Spirit, whose coming was promised in that Gospel. It is on account of this that he calls them "truly miserable." Prof. Bacon, however, himself gives the passage of Irenæus at length, pp. 240 ff. In the same context he recognises the fact that Irenæus "makes no single reference in all his voluminous writings save this one" to the Alogi. But he says not a word there that justifies his assertion in this earlier place that "Irenæus was fighting with every available weapon...against those wretched men."

the Alogi supplied a motive which must have induced Irenæus to cite any specific piece of information that he knew of in the works of Papias, or any other ancient writer, regarding the composition of the Fourth Gospel. I cannot but think that, owing to their own preoccupation with the Johannine problem, they attribute to Irenæus' reference to a set of people who rejected the Gospel according to St John an amount and a kind of significance which there is no reason to think it had for him. For clearly we are not entitled to assume that the class of persons to whom he alludes were already in his day even of so much consequence as they seem to have been twenty years later at Rome; still less that among those whom he expected his treatise to reach they were numerous or influential enough to make it necessary for him to spend much time over them. The known facts are decidedly adverse to such a supposition.

Another mistake that is made relates to Irenæus' method. Prof. Bacon falls into it. He informs us "that the pre-Eusebian age was almost as familiar as we with the higher criticism in *both* its forms, *historical* as well as literary," and goes on to instance Irenæus (p. 81, and see further quotations given below, pp. 128 ff.). I could wish that Prof. Bacon had given some illustrations of this characteristic of Irenæus. I confess that to me this notion of Irenæus being a "higher critic" is an exceedingly strange and unsuitable one. I do not know where he has given us a taste of his quality in this character. The fact is, surely, that his idea of the way to maintain the truth is altogether different. He asserts what is generally believed in the Church. Opinions may differ as to the reliance that should be placed on this common belief when all the circumstances of its history, all the safeguards against error that there may, or may not, have been, are taken into account. But at all events the chief significance of Irenæus in connexion with the history of the Canon of the New Testament is that he is a witness to the common belief. And the same is true of other ecclesiastical writers a few years later than himself. M. Loisy states this justly enough in regard to Hippolytus as well as Irenæus. "Il (Hippolyte) ne paraît pas avoir employé l'argument d'authenticité tel que le comprennent les théologiens modernes.

En cela il n'a fait que suivre Irénée, qui ne songe pas à confondre les Aloges par le témoignage exprès des personnes qui avaient connu Jean et qui auraient dû savoir dans quelles conditions son livre avait paru" (p. 22, and see further, pp. 25–8). Yet even M. Loisy shews that he hardly realises how natural it was for Irenæus to content himself with declaring the common belief of the Church, when he infers (as he does) from the appeal which Irenæus makes to it that he had no more specific knowledge to rely upon. On the contrary, it would seem to him unnecessary to produce the testimony of individuals just because the common belief had so much weight with himself, and would be the most effective argument he could use with multitudes of other men.

The same wrong assumption about a kind of proof that Irenæus must have felt to be desirable, if only he could have supplied it, appears to underlie (I think) Corssen's treatment of Irenæus' statements about the several Gospels. That about St John is quite as full and precise as are those about St Matthew and St Mark, fuller than that about St Luke. Corssen is content to believe that the two former were probably taken from Papias, although Irenæus does not say so; and yet he argues that, if he derived his information about John either from that source or from any other ancient witness, he must have given his reference[1]. I have already observed above that there is no good reason for thinking that Irenæus would have felt it incumbent upon him to contend for the authenticity of the Fourth Gospel more than for the others. But even if he did, would he have thought the mention of a passage in Papias' book the most effective way of doing so? One may sometimes appear to weaken a statement which one desires to see accepted as matter of common knowledge and beyond question by simply giving one or two references for it, and this would have been the case still more in that age than in the present.

I pass from Irenæus to the *Muratorian Fragment on the Canon*. It is held that in this document traces of the controversy with the Alogi are discernible; and M. Loisy argues that if the writer of it could have confronted these people with

---

[1] *Monarch. Prol.* pp. 110 ff.

any clear historical proof of its authenticity, such as "for instance that of an official communication from the Church of Ephesus to the Church of Rome at a stated time," he would certainly have produced it. I think that the polemical purpose of the *Muratorian Fragment* is not clear enough to justify the inference that such an episode must have been mentioned in it. I do not, however, imagine that there had been any official communication on the subject. In some way or other we should probably have heard of it, if there had. But apart from any formal authentication of this kind, there might be a large amount of good testimony to the apostolical authority of the Gospel, of a kind that could not conveniently be given in a list of Canonical books, or any compendious statement.

Prof. Bacon regards not only the *Muratorian Fragment*, but the whole series of lists of Canonical books and brief introductions to the several Gospels coming to us from the two centuries following, as signs of a conflict that was going on over the Fourth Gospel throughout a considerable portion of that period and interprets thereby the significance of "the silence of Eusebius." "Had Lightfoot," he writes, "been able to foresee the light which the closing decade of the nineteenth century would throw upon the debates of the second and third regarding the trustworthiness and authority of the Gospel narrative, he would hardly have defined it as the 'main object' of Eusebius in regard to the four gospels merely to 'preserve any anecdotes which he may have found illustrating the circumstances under which they were written.' He would have realised that the pre-Eusebian age was almost as familiar as we with the higher criticism in *both* its forms, *historical* as well as literary. He would thus have appreciated that the 'statements concerning' the gospels in both Irenæus and Eusebius are only links in a long chain of prologues, or *argumenta*, by which writers of both *orthodox and heretical* circles endeavoured to establish the apostolicity of their traditions of the Lord's life and teaching. Of these we have had one example in the *argumentum* already cited....The famous Muratorian Fragment now stands forth in its true light as one more link in this chain...."

Lack of early defence of Fourth Gospel

" He (Eusebius) had the example of two centuries of effort to *authenticate the Gospel record*, and both he and his predecessors give evidence of having searched their authorities with almost the diligence of a modern critic for anything that might tend to prove its close connexion with the Apostles. To imagine, therefore, that Eusebius would remit the search in such a work as *Papias*, still more to suggest that 'Eusebius would be more likely than not to omit' a statement of Papias, such as Lightfoot assumes, is to betray a conception of the external evidence and what it signifies impossible to impute in our day to a scholar of Lightfoot's eminence.

"This, then, is the outcome of a full generation of research on the point in question....Modern discovery forces us to look upon the silence of *both* Irenæus and Eusebius as highly significant....

"Both Irenæus and Eusebius had the little five-chaptered treatise of Papias open before them and would eagerly search every nook and corner of the work for any statement directly connecting the Gospel with the Apostle, in fact *anything of the kind* reported by the *argumenta*[1]."

(The italics throughout are Prof. Bacon's.)

I believe that the "discovery" that during the third and early years of the fourth century the authenticity of the Gospel according to St John was still in debate and that we have evidence of a series of efforts during this time to "authenticate the Gospel record" is purely Prof. Bacon's own. I had imagined, at any rate, till I read his book that students of the early history of the Canon of the New Testament were agreed, that from the close of the second century onwards the authority of the four Gospels—grounded in the case of the first and fourth on supposed authorship by Apostles, in that of the second and third on the relation in which the writers stood to Apostles—was fully acknowledged in the Church throughout the Græco-Latin world. M. Loisy, who will not be accused of conservative bias, or of having failed to take account of recent critical work, writes as follows:—"Le quatrième Évangile, d'après l'opinion commune des critiques et la tradition elle-même, n'a pas été composé avant la fin du premier

[1] *Ib.* pp. 81 ff.

siècle: à partir du troisième, son histoire n'a plus d'obscurités ; il est universellement accepté comme livre canonique et comme œuvre de l'apôtre Jean, et aucun doute n'a été soulevé à cet égard jusqu'à la fin du xviiie siècle[1]." And again, "A cette date (A.D. 160–80), l'Évangile est répandu dans toute l'Église et partout reçu comme une œuvre apostolique, non obstant des protestations isolées qui, autant qu'on en peut maintenant juger, ne trouvent pas d'écho[2]." Though Prof. Bacon recognises, in commencing his remarks on Lightfoot's treatment of "the silence of Eusebius," that Lightfoot justly pointed out the "fundamental distinction" made by Eusebius between "disputed" or "spurious" and "acknowledged" writings, he himself completely ignores this fact afterwards. He apparently does not perceive that his own picture of "two centuries of effort (extending to the time of Eusebius) to authenticate the gospel record" is in flat contradiction with Eusebius' own inclusion of the Gospel among the "acknowledged" writings. He also ignores the fact that if the Gospels were still in debate he should have noticed not only accounts of the composition of the Gospels, but also citations from them, as in the case of the "disputed" writings, which plainly he does not do[3].

[1] *Le Quatrième Évangile*, p. 2.
[2] *Ib.* p. 18. See also pp. 25–8, and 30, n. 2.
[3] I will add here remarks on a couple of other points in Prof. Bacon's arguments. The reader will have noticed in a passage from Prof. Bacon given above his confident assertion that "both Irenæus and Eusebius had the little five-chaptered treatise of Papias open before them." The treatise in question consisted (as Eusebius tells us) of five "books" (βιβλία, not "chapters," κεφάλαια), each of which in the time of Irenæus, and probably also of Eusebius, would be contained in a separate *roll*. We may also assume that it was no easier to find any particular passage in them that you wished to refer to than in most other books of the period (see vol. I of this work, pp. 122–5, note on "The form of ancient books as affecting habits of quotation"). Further, while it is most probable that Eusebius had a copy of Papias' *Expositions* at hand in the library of the Church at Cæsarea, it is decidedly improbable that Irenæus had one with him in Gaul. For two very striking instances of the rarity of books in ancient times, see Bigg, *Origins*, pp. 164 f.

Efforts of imagination applied to history, which give life to the circumstances and conditions of a distant time, are a very fine thing and necessary for the true historian, but they need to be controlled by attention to what we do know about those times, and the sphere for their exercise will be found far more in realising differences of other times from our own than in transferring present conditions to the past. It would perhaps be superfluous to comment on such obvious instances of a false kind of imagination applied to history as these of the "little five-chaptered book," and Irenæus and Eusebius as "higher critics," were it not that in more

Lack of early defence of Fourth Gospel 131

Corssen, in his later article referred to above, states the question in regard to the "silence of Eusebius" in a way that brings out clearly the one point about which there seems really to be some room for difference of opinion. "It has been said," he writes, "that the silence of Eusebius proves nothing, because he does not collect any testimonies to writings, which seemed to him indisputable. But the matter does not stand so The question is not here about a testimony for the genuineness of the Gospel, but for the circumstances of its origin, which for Eusebius must have been quite as interesting as the Elder John's account about Matthew and Mark[1]." It is not easy to judge precisely what would be "interesting" to Eusebius, or to those for whom he wrote. I can imagine that, for instance, if he had found in Papias, even given on the authority of the Elder John, merely the statement of Irenæus that "last of all John put forth his Gospel while dwelling in Ephesus," he might have regarded this as a fact so well known that it was unnecessary to repeat it, deeply interesting though it would have been to us at the present day to know that it was made by Papias. On the other hand, the principles which guided Mark in his composition, and the limitations under which he wrote, placed the statement about him in an altogether different category; while even the brief statement about Matthew may have seemed fresh and worthy of being recorded on account of the unusual

subtle ways it has often been a source of error in speculations about early Christian times.

I may take this opportunity of referring to a statement of Prof. Bacon's on pp. 171, 172. "Eusebius informs us," he writes, "—on what authority he does not say—that 'the age immediately succeeding that of the Apostles' was distinguished by many attempts to deliver the gospel in writing to the Churches throughout the world." From Prof. Bacon's rendering of Eusebius and from the sequel in which he speaks of "the multiplication of Gospels," he evidently understands Eusebius to refer to the putting forth of other Gospels besides those accepted in the Church. But this is not what Eusebius speaks of here (III. 37). What he says is that in the generation following the Apostles there were still many who, having distributed their goods, went forth on long journeys and performed the work of evangelists, being zealous to preach Christ to those who as yet had not at all heard the word of faith, and to deliver to them the writing of the divine Gospels—τὴν τῶν θείων εὐαγγελίων παραδιδόναι γραφήν. For Eusebius "the divine Gospels" were unquestionably the four received by the Church. He represents these "evangelists"—missionaries, not writers, throughout the chapter—as not only preaching the word, but disseminating copies of the four Gospels, or of one or other of them.

[1] *Warum ist das vierte Evangelium etc.* p. 222.

9—2

expression "he composed the oracles," and the reference to a time when "every one rendered them (from the original) as he was able." The force of the tradition as to the authorship of the Fourth Gospel does not, therefore, appear to be substantially impaired, because Irenæus and other writers did not make the sort of reply to the Alogi which modern methods of historical criticism would have suggested.

I abide, then, by the conclusion reached in my first volume. The external evidence for the Johannine authorship of the Fourth Gospel must be held to have real weight. In all probability it would be generally accepted as decisive, if there were no reasons for doubt arising from features in the contents of the Gospel. But plainly even if these are such as to render it improbable that the son of Zebedee could himself have been the author, it may still be quite conceivable that the author had personal contact with him and relied in greater or less degree upon his testimony. The question whether the phenomena of the Gospel on the whole favour this view will have to be considered. If they are found to do so, we shall in adopting it be able (I believe) to do justice to the external evidence. That evidence is not of a kind to preclude the possibility that one who had been a teacher of the actual author of the Gospel, a witness whose testimony was embodied in it, might in the common estimate of the Church have been transformed into its author. But the fact of such a connexion between the Apostle and the Gospel would explain the belief of early times. There has been and still is inclination on the part of many critics to pay too little respect to widespread traditions. This has been a natural reaction from the habit of accepting them in their entirety without question; but it may be expected that a more balanced view of their value will yet be taken.

We may now turn to indications in the Fourth Gospel itself. It will be convenient to begin from the statement in xxi. 24, which affords a natural transition from evidence commonly reckoned as "external," seeing that—as being an addition to the original work—it partakes itself of the character of external evidence.

The notice appended to the Gospel

The statement with regard to the authorship of the Gospel made at xxi. 24, and in connexion therewith the other references made in the Gospel to "the beloved disciple."

In ch. II we saw that not only v. 24 but probably the whole of ch. xxi is an addition by a different hand from that of the author of chs. i–xx, and that if so we have an indication of the time within which the statement in v. 24 was made. For the question to which a reply is furnished in the verses preceding is one which would be most likely to arise at no great distance of time—say not more than a decade or two—after the death of the disciple referred to. But, however this may be, it will scarcely be disputed that we have here the earliest statement that we possess with regard to the authorship of the Gospel, and that it could not reasonably be placed later than the middle of the second century. It is also pretty evident that the author of the statement, and those associated with him in making it, believed "the beloved disciple" to be a real person, and indeed had a particular person in mind, whom they held to be designated by this description where it occurs in the preceding chapters. For their object is to furnish a guarantee of the truth of the facts related in the work which they desired to circulate.

This statement, then, is one of considerable importance, but we have still to examine its precise effect. The "beloved disciple" is declared (*a*) to be "the disciple that beareth witness of these things."

If (as there is reason to think) it was made after that disciple's death the present participle must be intended to convey the idea that the testimony enshrined in the book is a living testimony. This is quite a natural use of the present. The things in regard to which his testimony was given would strictly speaking be those in the preceding book, if the whole Appendix was by a later hand; but these additional incidents might have been derived from him without its being thought necessary to specify the fact. But (*b*) it is further said of the disciple in question that "he wrote these things." "These things" can here at any rate only refer to the preceding twenty chapters, if the Appendix was added after his death. What is the exact meaning and force to be assigned to this statement? We observe first a certain want of precision therein; he says "these things" and not "this book." Further, the words "and wrote these things" seem to be added to "beareth witness concerning these things" as a kind of afterthought. Most prominence at all events is given to his having borne witness. From the position and form of this reference to writing, it is not unfair to infer that there may have been some uncertainty in the mind of the framer of the statement as to the extent to which it was to be attributed to the same disciple. Moreover, in view of the less rigorous notions which then prevailed as to authorship and its rights than those to which we are accustomed, the part played by an eminent witness and teacher in the composition of the Gospel might, after the lapse of a few years and when his death had already occurred, easily be exaggerated even by the comparatively well-informed who did not intend to deceive.

In the statement, then, of xxi. 24, taken as a whole and with its context we have, as it appears to me, evidence of considerable strength in favour, if not of the authorship in the strict sense of chs. i–xx by one of the immediate disciples of Christ, yet of his oral testimony and teaching having been a source from which more or less directly its contents were derived.

We must, however, examine the view of those critics who, while they admit, as most would, that the author of the statement in xxi. 24 supposed "the beloved disciple" to be a real person, yet hold that in point of fact an ideal figure merely is in the body of the Gospel intended to be represented under that description, and that in short it indicates the perfect disciple, one who possesses true spiritual discernment and rightly understands the Master's teaching, and is therefore the special object of His love. There is something attractive in this theory, and it is natural that it should appeal powerfully to those who have persuaded themselves that the whole Gospel is pervaded by symbolism. Nevertheless, there are objections to it which appear to me to be fatal.

1. Let it be borne in mind that the evangelist must have had readers in view, and that he cannot have been indifferent to the manner in which expressions used by him would be understood. The generality of readers would suppose him to be referring to some particular person when he spoke of "the

The disciple "whom Jesus loved"

disciple whom Jesus loved," or of "another disciple," or of one who "saw and bare record," in the same contexts with others whose names he gave. Readers who were not yet converts to the faith, for whom it is probable that the book was in part intended, might be satisfied not to inquire after the name of the disciple designated by these periphrases. But the work could not have been kept back from the members of the Church in the place where it was produced. Nor can it be supposed that they would have been educated up to the point of recognising that a type not an individual was in the writer's mind. They would certainly, as they knew something of the Gospel history, have inquired whether this was one of the characters of whom they had already been told, or some other. And that they would do so must surely have been foreseen.

2. If the beloved disciple were a fictitious character and the purpose of his being introduced were to teach what is the right attitude of mind towards the Gospel, he should have appeared at more points in the Gospel than he does. A writer who was not restrained by consideration for historical fact might have been expected to carry out his plans consistently. There are certainly other points in the narrative where it might have been conveniently arranged that he should play his part. At places where an anonymous disciple is mentioned and the same person is supposed to have been intended, it should have been made evident that this was the case, and more use should have been made of his appearance on the stage. Above all, the words attributed to Simon Peter at vi. 68, "Lord, to whom shall we go? thou hast the words of eternal life?" should have been put into the mouth of the disciple of special insight.

3. The scenes in which the beloved disciple appears along with Simon Peter may conceivably be intended to raise him to a position of authority equal, or even in some respects superior, to that of Peter among the original witnesses to the facts of the Gospel and teachers of the Christian faith, though I myself consider this view of them to have been at the least very much exaggerated. But what I would now point out is that these scenes are not fitted to suggest, as it is alleged that they do, the inferiority of the original Jewish disciples, represented by Peter, to those of a later generation who possessed higher spiritual

knowledge, and who though they had not seen yet believed. Not only does the beloved disciple belong to the first band of followers, but various details in the scenes are plainly incompatible with the part he is supposed to fill. Loisy argues that at the Last Supper only the beloved disciple was admitted fully to his Master's confidence and entered into His purpose to allow Himself to be betrayed. If the disciple had not understood this to be the will of Jesus, he must, Loisy contends, after the intimation he had received, have intervened to thwart Judas in the execution of his plan. But the unsuspecting reader would, I think, imagine that, when the beloved disciple had obtained the information for which Peter asked, he would communicate it to Peter; therefore care should have been taken to guard against this supposition, if it was important in connexion with the rôle of the beloved disciple that he alone should have known who the traitor was. But, further, the full comprehension of the traitor's plan and of the Lord's mind in regard to it, which M. Loisy attributes to the beloved disciple, is irreconcilable with the remark later on in the narrative, "Now no man at the table knew for what intent he spake this unto him," when Jesus had said to Judas, "What thou doest do quickly." The definite manner in which the traitor is pointed out according to the Fourth Gospel makes its account of the announcement by Jesus at the Last Supper in regard to the betrayal harder to understand than the corresponding accounts in the Synoptics. If it is thought worth while to try to explain the failure on the part of all those present to understand the Lord's words to Judas, after the intimation that had been given that he would be the traitor, it may be suggested that they had not been told how soon or in what manner Judas would prove himself the traitor. But the one point to be noted here is that no exception is made as regards the general want of comprehension, in favour of the beloved disciple.

Again, in the account of the visit of Peter and the beloved disciple to the tomb in which Jesus had been laid, if the beloved disciple, as is affirmed, represents disciples of that later generation who "have not seen and yet have believed," the emphasis with which the narrator declares that "he *saw* and believed," is surely most inappropriate. The meaning is plain from the

The disciple "whom Jesus loved"   137

context; the disciple saw with the eyes of the body the empty tomb and the carefully arranged grave-clothes, and he drew from these signs the right inference. We have in short here fact and the discerning interpretation of fact, both of which were held to be of such immense importance by the writer of the Gospel. And those who were in immediate contact with the facts of the Gospel were necessarily the original disciples. Such were both Simon Peter and the beloved disciple, and the authority of the latter as well as of the former was founded on this.

So in regard to the incident of piercing the side of Jesus after His death, where the disciple referred to as present is generally supposed to be, and is probably, the same. The two-fold stream of blood and water is evidently regarded by the evangelist as full of doctrinal significance, but this significance lends importance to the testimony borne to the alleged facts.

There are two other incidents in which a disciple appears whose name is not given. It has been usual in both of these for those who uphold the Johannine authorship to suppose that John the son of Zebedee is referred to; and the critics whose theory we are now examining in like manner suppose the ideal beloved disciple to be meant. Whether the identification of the anonymous disciple in either, or both, of these instances with the beloved disciple is justified or not shall be considered later. Our concern with them now is only—on the supposition that it is—to consider their bearing on the theory that the beloved disciple is an imaginary character. In the earlier incident it is held to be significant that he becomes acquainted with Jesus before Simon Peter, which is supposed to shew that he was accounted superior to him. But his companion in the visit to Jesus is Andrew to whom more prominence is given in the narrative. He then, also, and still more, must be superior to Simon; and further there can be no ground for asserting that the unnamed disciple represents a class which is on a higher level than the whole class of original disciples. So at least it will seem, I think, to most minds, though the slightness of the notice accorded to the unnamed disciple is itself supposed to be full of meaning.

"He gives in his adhesion," it is said, "in silence—in spirit[1]." It must be admitted that this explanation shews an ingenuity which can be daunted by no difficulties. But shall I be using too strong a word if I call such reasoning puerile?

There remains the reference to a disciple "known to the high priest" who obtained admission for Simon Peter into the high priest's house. Here, again, it is said, Simon Peter is placed in a position of inferiority; he is dependent upon the good offices of the other disciple. But how does such dependence as this imply spiritual inferiority? And in what way can acquaintance with the Jewish high priest—which is the one trait by which the unnamed disciple is here described—indicate superiority in Christian enlightenment? Again, we are told that this disciple known to the high priest is mentioned because it was a matter of importance that at least one disciple of Jesus should have been present at the trial—I presume, in order that he might relate what happened. But if the narrator regarded that as important, why did he not make it evident that this disciple, after he had brought Peter into the court-yard where the servants were, himself passed into the room where the trial was proceeding, though even so it might be asked how those who "had not seen and yet believed" were typified by one whose rôle on this occasion, as on some others, it was to be a witness of the facts?

4. Lastly, if the evangelist intended under the figure of the anonymous disciple to represent a class of disciples, to which he himself belonged, who were superior in spiritual enlightenment to the original disciples, this idea should be borne out by the other and plainer teaching of the Gospel. Instead of this, the promise of the Spirit Who should guide into all the truth, and other similar promises, are made to the Twelve. So again, the notion, that in the scene in which Jesus commits His mother to the care of the beloved disciple His mother typifies the body of early Jewish believers who are to receive fuller instruction, cannot be supported out of other parts of the Gospel. Yet surely a writer who set store by such a

---

[1] "André reconnaît en Jésus le Messie. L'autre ne dit rien. Il adhère en silence, en esprit." J. Réville. *Le Quatrième Évangile*, p. 317. The words are quoted by Loisy, p. 127, where he himself adopts this explanation.

thought would not have been satisfied to hint at it so obscurely.

The theory, then, that "the beloved disciple" is an imaginary character is not supported by solid and self-consistent reasoning. If it is allowed that a real person is meant the difficulties to be met will depend on the answer to be given to the question whether he was the actual author of the Gospel, or a witness to whom the author appeals. There are—apart from the statement at xxi. 24, which has already been discussed—two passages to be considered in this connexion, namely, the declaration in the Prologue, "we beheld his glory"; and the reference in the narrative of the Crucifixion to the witness who vouched for the flow of both water and blood from the pierced side.

It will be convenient to take the latter first as the points there raised are more nearly allied to those in the preceding discussion. This witness is not described as "the beloved disciple," who (as we are told a few verses before) took charge of the mother of Jesus, presumably without waiting till the soldiers came to ascertain whether the victims were dead, and whose return has not been mentioned. It is, however, commonly assumed that this disciple is meant; and it is probable that the man who penned xxi. 24 regarded him as the same in view of the stress that is laid both here and there on the bearing of testimony. As every one who has taken any interest in the problem of the authorship of the Fourth Gospel is aware, the force of the preposition ἐκεῖνος at xix. 35—ἐκεῖνος οἶδεν ὅτι ἀληθῆ λέγει—has been the subject of much controversy. The arguments that have been urged, whether on the one side or the other, do not appear to me to be very convincing. On the one hand it does not seem impossible, or unlikely, as has been alleged, that the witness should refer to himself as "that man," and should solemnly re-affirm the truth of his testimony. Moreover, he alone, strictly speaking, could know that he knew; in other words, could be quite sure that he had correctly observed and reported what happened. But, on the other hand, if the witness was also the evangelist he was at that moment *writing* the true things, whereas "*saith* true things" may at least equally well, if not more naturally, convey the idea that he was in the habit of saying them. I think, too, that someone who was impressed by his evident feeling of certainty might well declare on his behalf, "he knoweth that he saith true things." The "true things" are in any case a fact, or facts, of special significance, and more particularly, if not solely, the incident that has just been mentioned. The record as a whole, the written Gospel, does not come into view. The present tense, however, still deserves attention. According to the ordinary usage of language it would imply that at the time of the composition of the work the witness alluded to was alive and wont to speak as reported. Yet I do not think that an isolated expression such as this should be pressed to prove that the work was written within the life-time of the disciple in question, apart from a general review of probabilities.

It is well known that those who hold that this disciple was himself the author, and was John the son of Zebedee, attribute the absence of his name from the Gospel to modesty. And when it is urged that the character of the references in which he would have been understood to indicate himself are not consistent with this trait, they reply that he dwelt on the favour shewn him by Christ not from pride, but in a spirit of humble thankfulness. This is, perhaps, a possible explanation, but I do not find it an easy one to accept.

On the other hand, the use in the Gospel of the title "the beloved disciple," and the inclusion therein of what we there find related of him, cause no difficulty if he was not himself the author. If the scholars of some teacher, who was himself an immediate disciple of the Lord, or the members of a portion of the Church in which he had lived, had learned to look upon him as a man of exceptional spiritual insight, and if they had gathered that this trait had begun to manifest itself very early, and that he had been regarded by Christ with peculiar favour and affection, it would not be strange that he should have been described as "the disciple whom Jesus loved," or that incidents should have been told of him which illustrated his unusual quickness of spiritual perception.

It remains to consider a declaration in the Prologue which is of greater significance, since it appears to be a claim by the writer of the Gospel himself to personal knowledge of Jesus Christ while He was on earth: "The Word became flesh and dwelt among us and we beheld his glory." Whatever the inference as to the authorship of the Gospel which these words permit us to draw may be, the attempt to explain them as referring solely to spiritual vision is surely a mistaken one. The theme of the whole passage plainly is, that the Divine glory was manifested in a human life, and that it had been perceived through contact with that life while it was being lived on earth. The use of the aorist "we beheld," its occurrence in direct connexion with the statement that "the Word became flesh and dwelt among us," the remark shortly afterwards in a particular instance that Jesus "manifested his glory and his disciples believed on him" (ii. 11), render it impossible to suppose that the revelation of the glory of Jesus which is meant was independent of a knowledge of Him through ordinary human intercourse. This view of the meaning of the words is confirmed by 1 Jn i. 1–3, which leaves no doubt as to the part played by the bodily organs in the reception of the revelation, while the anti-Docetic character of the whole Epistle gives point to it. The difference of position also between the witnesses and the general body of Christians addressed in the Epistle is very clearly marked[1].

In support of the notion that the perception intended was of a purely spiritual kind, such as believers of any generation may have, the words at Jn i. 16 are indeed adduced, "of his fulness have we all received and grace for grace." But this statement is by no means equivalent to that at *v.* 14 and the introduction of the word "all" marks the difference. Here the reference undoubtedly is to an experience which all true Christians share, whereas at *v.* 14 it is to the original experience from which all the subsequent life of the Church had flowed. The later experience served to confirm, but could not take the place of, the testimony borne to the other.

But there is a chronological difficulty to be faced in con-

---

[1] Both Holtzmann, *Hand. Kom. Briefe d. Joh.* p. 328, and Loisy, *Quatrième Évang.* p. 187, recognise that the expressions in question, according to their natural meaning, refer to ocular testimony. But having made the admission, each—it is not unfair to say—runs away from it.

nexion with this claim to personal knowledge of the facts of the Gospel made in the Johannine Gospel and First Epistle. It is generally agreed that the Fourth Gospel, owing to its character, cannot have been composed earlier than the last decade of the first century, and this is the traditional time for it. The First Epistle, we have seen, should be placed earlier, but it may have been earlier only by a few years. Now if John the son of Zebedee was but a youth when he was attracted to Jesus, we must suppose him to have been eighty, or nearly that, in A.D. 90. Moreover, a difficulty arises in connexion with the use of the first person plural, more particularly where in the Epistle it occurs in a verb in the present tense. When the writer speaks in the past tense of what he and others had seen he might be alluding to an experience which he had shared with a body of persons of whom he was the sole survivor. But when he says "we declare" he seems to imply that there were others besides himself still on earth who could give, and were in the habit of giving, this testimony. But it is unlikely that there should have been at that date several survivors of the original band of disciples, of whom we have assumed John to have been the youngest, or one of the youngest.

The question for us then is what interpretation of the words under consideration will best take account of their natural force on the one hand, and on the other hand of the meaning which they are likely to have had at the probable date of the composition of the writings in which they occur. Reasonably to justify their use we must, I think, at least suppose that the writer, if not old enough to have been an actual follower of Jesus in the days of His Ministry, could yet regard himself and a few compeers as belonging to the generation then fast disappearing in which the great revelation had been made. They knew well, from personal knowledge, what the original disciples had declared from the earliest days of the preaching of the Christian faith, and felt entitled to unite themselves with them and to speak in their name; and some instances of personal contact with Jesus might be included among the reminiscences of their own childhood. In any attempt, therefore, to estimate the value from a historical point of view of the evidence afforded by the Johannine writings as to Christian

The disciple known to the high priest 143

origins, justice must be done to the appeal they contain to certain external facts, which are regarded as the medium of Divine revelation, and it must be borne in mind that he who makes it was one of a little band who, if not of the number of the chief personal followers of the Lord while on earth, had been in close touch with them, and knew well what the beliefs of the Christian Church had been from the beginning.

Thus far we have been engaged in discussing the question whether it is to be inferred from references in the Fourth Gospel that an immediate disciple of Jesus was the author, or at least in greater or less degree the authority for its contents. It remains that we should consider whether any of these references favour the view that he was some other disciple than the son of Zebedee.

It has been commonly assumed—as I have already observed —that the anonymous disciple who obtained admission for Simon Peter to the high priest's palace was the beloved disciple of whom we have heard just before in the account of the Last Supper. By some of those who make this assumption it has not unnaturally been pointed out that it is very unlikely that John the son of Zebedee, a Galilean fisherman, would have been "known to the high priest" and would have had influence with members of his household. They have accordingly suggested that the beloved disciple was a Jerusalemite, of higher social rank than most of, if not indeed all, the Twelve. But I would ask whether it is likely that if the disciple who introduced Simon Peter into the high priest's palace was indeed one who had figured so prominently in an incident related shortly before, he would here simply be described as "another." I would also observe that a writer, whose habit of mind it suits to refer to a particular disciple without naming him at least in the case of "the disciple whom Jesus loved," might well do so in some other cases also. It seems to me that supporters of the traditional view of "the beloved disciple" have been led to identify the disciple who introduced Simon Peter into the high priest's palace with him from a desire to fill in as much as possible their picture of him; and that other writers have followed suit without sufficiently considering the question. It is more probable that the unnamed disciple at xviii. 15 was one of that number among the upper classes, several times referred to in the Fourth Gospel, who believed in Jesus but did not belong to the innermost group of His disciples[1].

The statement at xix. 27 that after Jesus had commended His mother to the care of the disciple whom He loved, "from that hour the disciple took her unto his own home," has also been held to indicate that his home was in Jerusalem. But the Greek εἰς τὰ ἴδια does not suggest some particular house, as the rendering of our English versions seems to do. The meaning of the original would surely be fairly given if we were to say, using a different English expression in which the word "home" also occurs, that "from that time the mother of Jesus made her home with that disciple"—that is to say, wherever for the time being his home might be.

It might be somewhat easier to reconcile some phenomena of the Gospel—the prominence given in it to the Ministry of Jesus in Jerusalem and comparative silence about that in Galilee, and the signs of acquaintance with Hellenistic thought —if the author was a Jerusalemite, and a man who from comparatively early years might have been brought under Hellenic influences. But as regards the former of these points, it would not be strange that any Jew should learn to appreciate the special significance belonging to the visits of Jesus to Jerusalem, while the incidents connected therewith would be frequently recalled to the mind of John during his continued residence in the holy city in the early years of the Church there, of which the allusion in the Ep. to the Galatians, as well as in the Acts of the Apostles, affords evidence. That the signs of the influence of Hellenic thought in the Gospel would be more natural in the case of a beloved disciple about whom there is nothing supposed to be known, except that he was a Jerusalemite of the upper classes, is a very precarious hypothesis. Moreover any difficulty that can be felt on the score of these signs is greatly lessened, as regards the son of Zebedee, or any other immediate follower of Christ, if we suppose him to have been to a greater or less extent an authority for, rather than the author of, the Gospel.

It may, however, well seem strange to us that though the beloved disciple was not the author, or rather all the more

---

[1] E.g. xii. 42.

because he was not the author, his name should not be given, especially if he was one of the original Twelve. To judge of this we must try to place ourselves at the point of view of the evangelist and of the readers for whom the work was intended. It ought not, I think, to be doubted that there were Christian brethren among whom the author of the Fourth Gospel lived, and whose teacher or one of whose teachers he was, and others in neighbouring cities, whom he would think of as probable readers or hearers of the Gospel. For them it would not be necessary to be more precise in referring to his own revered teacher, and the allusive manner of doing so would be impressive and moving. But there are not a few indications that this Gospel was also, and perhaps primarily, intended for Gentiles who were not well versed either in things Christian or things Jewish, and who needed to be convinced of the truth of the Christian faith. Such indications are the explanations of Hebrew words and Jewish customs, the manner in which "the Jews" are referred to as an alien body, and the statement at xx. 31 as to the purpose of the record, "these (signs) are written that ye may believe." Now for this class of readers, also, it would be unimportant that the name even of one of the principal witnesses should be given. The twelve Apostles, though we know so little about most of them, are in our eyes famous men; but they were not so to the Gentile world of the end of the first and first half of the second century. For readers belonging to that world the mention of a name would add little or nothing to such a description as "the disciple whom Jesus loved," or to the strength of the affirmation "he that hath seen hath borne witness." The influence which this consideration might have upon a Christian writer might be illustrated from the works of Justin belonging to a time later than the Fourth Gospel. It should be remembered also that in the Synoptic Gospels the *names* of witnesses are not used as a guarantee of truth. Indeed, in its references to a particular witness, though in a veiled form, the Fourth Gospel exemplifies a transition from the feeling and thought of a somewhat earlier time.

Further, it cannot be assumed that the importance of Apostolic authority was an idea which had been embraced equally at this time in all parts of the Church. It is one which probably appealed strongly to the minds of Roman Christians, and the Ep. of Clement of Rome is evidence that it had done so about the time that the Fourth Gospel was written. But the Twelve themselves had been disciples before they became Apostles, and continued to be so after they had received their commission to be Apostles. It would not be surprising if some of them, and it may be one above all the rest, cherished throughout life the remembrance of that original character, and sought to preserve to the end the attitude of mind which it implied; or that there should have been a circle of inquirers after truth to whom this conception was peculiarly attractive. It is indeed unnecessary to point out how the idea of discipleship is a ruling one in the Fourth Gospel. So much for the contention that if "the beloved disciple" was an Apostle the title "Apostle" must necessarily have been given to him.

My conclusions then from this discussion are (1) that while the framer of the statement at xxi. 24, like those to whom the common tradition of the Church on the subject of the Fourth Gospel is due, was betrayed into exaggeration when he attributed the composition of the Gospel to an immediate disciple of Christ, there was a foundation for this belief in the fact of the dependence of the writer of the Gospel on the testimony of such an immediate disciple; and further, (2) that there are no indications pointing to someone other than John the son of Zebedee having been that disciple such as to countervail the improbability that the very existence of the right person could have been completely ignored in the Synoptic Gospels, and at least almost so by early Christian writers of the second generation, while in Church tradition a wrong one was substituted.

CHAPTER V

THE ENVIRONMENT IN WHICH THE FOURTH GOSPEL WAS PRODUCED AND THE AUTHOR'S OWN ANTECEDENTS

WE need to fix some limits both of place and time for our inquiry into influences the effect of which may be traced in the Gospel.

We shall be allowed to pay so much deference to the tradition of the Church as to assume that the place where the Fourth Gospel first saw the light was Ephesus or its neighbourhood. As regards the possible time of composition we must be ready to note any pertinent facts between A.D. 90 to a little after A.D. 130. Later than this we shall not at the present day be required to look for them. There were new growths of religious thought and feeling and rapid developments at the end of the first and beginning of the second century, and it is not possible in all cases in a period which is in many respects so obscure to determine with certainty the times when all of these began to manifest themselves. But I believe it will be found that there is good reason to assign the appearance of any of the existence of which we have indications in the Fourth Gospel to a time not much, if at all, after the earlier of the limits above mentioned. Other influences with which we shall be concerned were of older standing, and it can only be a question when and how and to what extent the evangelist came under them.

To one topic, certainly not the least important of those properly belonging to the general subject of this chapter—that of the development of genuinely Christian thought and belief in Apostolic and Subapostolic times—I find it impossible to accord separate treatment. This would involve too much repetition and too many cross references, seeing that it necessarily has to be referred to in various connexions in the investigation of the Johannine problem. It came before us when we were considering the relations between the Fourth

Gospel and the First Epistle of St John. It must come before us again when we discuss those of the Fourth Gospel and the Synoptics. In the present chapter also, when examining the effects of influences external to Christianity upon the author of the Fourth Gospel, it must be borne in mind that some of these may have acted upon him not directly, but through Christian thought and teaching which had preceded his own.

Another reason for refraining from any attempt to trace systematically, however concisely, this previous development is that we should thereby be drawn into the discussion of questions connected with St Paul and Pauline literature, in itself a sufficiently large subject. I would only remark here that in spite of the large amount of profound agreement between the author of the Fourth Gospel and St Paul, it is a mistake to regard the later of these two teachers as properly speaking a disciple of the earlier, for he shews complete independence in his mode of statement, in the imagery he employs, and generally in the manner in which he presents different truths. Evidently he had participated in the effects of a movement of thought among Christian believers which may well have been of considerable extent. The teaching of St Paul had given the first powerful impulse to that movement. Any thoughtful Christian some years younger, who was residing one or two decades later in a region where St Paul had taught, would indirectly owe not a little to him. But if he was a truly reflective man his mind would set to work in its own way upon convictions and spiritual experiences, which were not those of St Paul alone, and he would be affected also by associations created for him by his own circumstances.

Different elements in the antecedents of the author of the Fourth Gospel, and his environment when he wrote it, will here be treated under the following heads: (1) Acquaintance with things Jewish in general and with localities in Palestine; (2) Alexandrian Judaism; (3) Gentile Theosophy and Religion; (4) Gnosticism.

The Judaism of the Dispersion

§ 1. ACQUAINTANCE WITH THINGS JEWISH IN GENERAL AND WITH LOCALITIES IN PALESTINE.

There can be no doubt that in the first century of our era there were bodies of Jews living apart from the rest of the inhabitants in the chief cities of the western coast of Asia Minor, as in other cities of the Græco-Roman world. But in many places, and among others those now in question, their numbers, the vigour of their life as a community, and above all their religious spirit and the strength of different parties and tendencies among them, such as might exist within the limits of Judaism, are matters for speculation and can be little if anything more. In some of the cities we have in view the Jewish colony may have existed, as it had in districts further to the East, from a time earlier than that revival of zeal for the Law which was associated with the patriotic movement under the Maccabees. Yet throughout the Dispersion that revival probably exercised some influence through settlers who in the generations following it came from Palestine, and to the impressions received from time to time by those who went up to worship at Jerusalem and returned.

From A.D. 66, or even before this date, and onwards, as the social and economic conditions in Palestine became increasingly miserable, and especially after the siege and capture of Jerusalem by Titus, there was probably a fuller stream of emigrants than before flowing westward, as well, if not in so large a volume, as that flowing east and north.

The effect produced in these ways would in general be greater or less according to distance from Palestine. It would be likely to be felt more, for instance, at Tarsus than at Ephesus. Yet it is reasonable to conjecture that in such a centre as the latter, besides those Jews who had become indifferent to their religion, or had been liberalised by contact with Greek life, there would also be Jews who were well instructed in the Law and strict in their own practice, genuine representatives of orthodox Judaism.

From the time that the traditional view of the authorship of the Fourth Gospel was first challenged it has been a prominent subject of debate whether the work supplies evidence proving the writer to have been a Jew, or a Gentile Christian, who might have acquired such knowledge of things Jewish as he had through study of the Scriptures and through converse with Jews with whom he became acquainted. A further question is whether he was a Jew of Palestinian origin who had come thence to the coast of Asia Minor as others had. These questions have considerable interest and importance in connexion with the genesis of the Gospel and its value as a historical document, even when it is admitted that the author was not the Apostle John. It is true that a Gentile convert might strive to transmit faithfully what had been told him, while a Jew might be chiefly occupied in giving his own exposition of its meaning. Nevertheless the representations of a Jew would in certain ways be more trustworthy. From closer natural sympathy with, and a truer insight into, the habits of thought and conditions of life implied he would be better able to preserve correctly what had been related to him, and it is more likely that when he used his own imagination, as for example in the form given to conversations and discourses, he would convey a right impression. It is also more probable that he would have been in touch with Jewish Christians of the primitive stock and with other Jews from Palestine, from whom he would have received accounts of what was reported there as to the Ministry of Jesus and its ending, which could be compared with, and used to supplement, any special source of knowledge which he possessed in the testimony of a revered teacher.

Further, if the evangelist was not only a Jew, but by origin a Palestinian Jew, he may himself have been brought into contact with the preaching of the Gospel by the immediate disciples of Jesus, and even as a boy himself have seen and heard Him, and thus, as I have suggested, have possessed the qualification for joining in the Apostolic testimony as he claims to do.

The manner in which the evangelist speaks of "the Jews" has been the chief, and is the most tangible, ground on which it has been maintained that he was himself a Gentile. In some cases where it is simply a question of explaining Jewish customs it would be natural enough for any Jew to write as he does. But there seems to me to be force in the objection that

Acquaintance with parties in Palestine 151

at least one who till middle life, if not longer, had been a pillar of the community of Jewish Christians at Jerusalem, and had therefore kept the Law as a religious Jew, and must have been bound to his nation by many ties, could not have expressed himself about the Jews, without explanation or apology, as though they were a people wholly alien to himself, in a way that various passages in the Fourth Gospel would seem to imply. It is easier to suppose that this point of view could have been adopted by a Christian believer who, though a Jew, even a Palestinian Jew, by birth, was younger than the Apostle John, and who had earlier in his life become familiar with the idea of the complete separation of Christians from Jews, after this separation had in many parts been realised. Controversy with rigorous Jews might, also, have accentuated the sense of alienation from them which he independently felt, and he would especially be inclined to dissociate himself from them when he addressed Gentiles, as he does in this Gospel, and, knowing how unfavourably the Gentiles already regarded the Jewish nation, to emphasise its responsibility for the death of Christ.

In this connexion it will be convenient to notice the fact that the author of the Fourth Gospel nowhere mentions the "scribes"—οἱ γραμματεῖς—and that where the other evangelists couple the scribes with the chief priests as contrivers of the death of Christ he names the Pharisees. At first sight this may seem to shew a lack of detailed knowledge of Palestinian conditions, as it has often been said to do. But it should be observed that there was good reason to avoid the use of the word γραμματεῖς in a book largely intended for Gentile readers. Those unacquainted with Jewish life would either fail to derive any impression from it, or would form a wrong one. Luke, indeed, following his documents, has frequently used it, but has also used νομικοί and νομοδιδάσκαλοι, which, though less misleading, would require explanation if the position of the persons in question was to be understood.

And in addition to this difficulty in regard to the term, there was the consideration that a concise representation of the facts, which was broadly true, could best be given by merging the scribes among the Pharisees[1]. The majority of "the

[1] Cp. Mt. xxvii. 62.

scribes" belonged to the Pharisaic party, and eminent scribes were the chief leaders of that party, while at the same time it was from the support of the rank and file of the party, and the influence which as a party it exercised over the people in Palestine, that the leaders derived their own power in dealing with the chief priests. I fail, therefore, to see how the evangelist could better have described the forces whereby the death of Christ was brought about than in the manner he does[1].

I pass to some features, indicative of the author's being by birth and training a Jew, which do not only appear in certain parts of the Gospel, where they might be due to a source that had been employed, but which characterise it as a whole.

We may notice first the style. Though the construction of the sentences is grammatically correct, their simple forms, with few dependent clauses, is Hebraic rather than Greek.

Still more noteworthy is the manner in which a theme is dwelt on through a long passage, by means of restatements of the main proposition, varied in this or that particular, and yet in substance nearly the same, with the object, so to speak, of keeping some great truth for a good while before the mind's eye, and viewing it as a whole and yet from different angles. This method reminds us of many portions of the Old Testament. It is as unlike as possible to the Hellenic "discourse of reason," but it was congenial to the contemplative Semitic spirit which created it[2].

Turning to the subject-matter itself, we note both many express citations from the Old Testament, and also numerous ideas and figures of speech which must in all probability have been suggested by analogues there. In connexion with this fact Holtzmann makes the remark that "the Old Testament rapidly became the Bible of Gentile Christendom." The process, indeed, by which this result was brought about began with the first preaching of the Gospel to the Gentiles. St Paul and others of the earliest preachers of the Gospel appealed to

---

[1] Réville's view that he regards the Pharisees as "a little group of notables in Jerusalem" (*Quatrième Évang.* p. 199) seems to me wholly without warrant. Of course the party acted through its chiefs in its relations with the chief priests in procuring the convoking of the Sanhedrin etc.

Loisy, *Quatr. Év.* p. 515, subscribes to this view of Réville's but gives no better ground for it. [2] Cp. p. 45 above.

Old Testament prophecy in demonstrating to Gentiles that Jesus was the Christ and in setting forth to them the Divine purposes in regard to mankind. They did so, as the Christian apologists of the second century likewise did, in the sure confidence that ancient oracles would be respected and that their fulfilment would make a deep impression. From hearing these appeals Gentiles no less than Jews must soon have become familiar at least with certain proof-texts. Some proselytes to Judaism who afterwards became Christians may also, no doubt, have begun to read the Septuagint before they heard the Christian preachers. But when we have made allowance for the acquaintance with the Old Testament which would have been gained in these ways, it will remain probable that a knowledge of the Old Testament which would enable a writer to introduce allusions to it freshly and naturally even where no point of controversy, or none of the ordinary ones, was involved, was to the end of the first century, and even later, rare among Gentile believers. And this independent knowledge is shewn in the Fourth Gospel[1].

[1] Some of the writer's citations are made also in other New Testament books (i. 23, Mt. iii. 3, Mk i. 3, Lk. iii. 4) and there are also some, which though they do not occur in any other extant early Christian writing were, we may believe, not uncommonly made because of their obviousness, or because they belong to the same contexts as familiar quotations (ii. 17 = Ps. lxix. 9; vi. 45 = Is. liv. 13; xii. 15 = Zech. ix. 9; xiii. 18 = Ps. xli. 9; xv. 25 = Ps. lxix. 4; xix. 24 = Ps. xxii. 18; xix. 36 = Ex. xii. 46; xix. 37 = Zech. xii. 10). The number, however, of these is striking. But, be this as it may, there are others closely connected with the special subjects treated, or type of thought represented, in this Gospel, so that there is no ground for supposing them to have been in common use. Such are the allusion to Jacob's dream in the words "angels of God ascending and descending upon the Son of man" (i. 51 = Gen. xxviii. 12); the bread given from heaven (vi. 31 = Ps. lxxviii. 24); the force of a two-fold testimony (viii. 17 = Deut. xix. 15); the title "gods" bestowed on those "to whom the word of God came" (x. 35 = Ps. lxxxii. 6). Even more striking, perhaps, is the use of images made use of in the Old Testament:—the woman's travail (xvi. 22 = Is. xxvi. 17); the living water (iv. 10 ff. and vii. 37 ff. = Is. xliv. 3 etc.); the shepherd and his flock (x. 1 ff. = Is. xl. 11, Ez. xxxiv and xxxvii. 24); the vine (xv. 1 ff. = Ps. lxxx). Again, the manifestation of the Divine glory (i. 14, ii. 11 etc.) is to be traced to the Old Testament.

A. H. Franke has devoted a treatise to drawing out the correspondence between the Fourth Gospel and the Old Testament: *Das alte Test. bei Johannes*. The above brief statement has been drawn up with the help of this book. He is not by any means always convincing in what he sets himself to prove, and yet on the whole he makes out a strong case for the evangelist's familiarity with the ancient Scriptures.

154 *Acquaintance with ideas of later Judaism*

Familiarity with the ideas known to us in later Judaism is also shewn. The following are instances of this: the belief that the Messiah would appear from some unexpected quarter (vii. 27); the question as to the hereditary punishment for sin (ix. 2); the practice as to circumcision on the eighth day when it conflicted with the Sabbath-law (vii. 22). Christ's appeal to the perpetual activity of the Father, which implies a special interpretation of the statement in Genesis that God rested on the seventh day (v. 17). The date when any of these ideas first appeared in Rabbinic, or other Jewish, literature is not of course the same as that when they first became current. If this could be ascertained it might help us to fix the time of the composition of the Fourth Gospel, and it may be to determine in some measure whether the writer in his accounts of controversies of Jesus with Pharisees and scribes must be supposed to be reproducing controversies held by himself with Jews in the latter part of the first or beginning of the second century, or whether they may not at least be suitable if regarded as representations, which they profess to be, of incidents of Christ's Ministry. It may not be possible for any light to be thrown on these points. But so far as I am aware Rabbinic scholars have not paid any attention to them, though they have borne testimony to the intimate knowledge of thoughts and things Jewish shewn by the evangelist[1].

There are several correct references also to Jewish feasts and other Jewish customs and to the political and social state of Palestine in the earlier half of the first century A.D. Broadly speaking, the picture given of the different classes in the nation, their attitude to Jesus and their parts in the final tragedy, agrees with that in the Synoptic Gospels, and like theirs with historical probability. The differences between them and the Fourth Gospel shew independence on the part of the latter, but not inferior information[2]. The mistake which

---

[1] For illustrations in Rabbinic and other Jewish literature see with regard to the *first* point mentioned above, Drummond, *The Jewish Messiah*, pp. 279 ff.; with regard to the *second*, Wetstein, *in loc.*; the *third*, I. Abrahams, *Studies in Pharisaism and the Gospels*, p. 133; the *fourth*, Franke, *ib.* p. 51 n.

[2] I shall recur to these differences in ch. VI on the *Fourth Gospel and the Synoptics*.

Several Jewish writers, Rabbinic scholars, have of late remarked upon the

the author has frequently been supposed to have made[1] as to the length of tenure of the high priest's office, on the ground of the statement that Caiaphas "was high priest that same year," would imply ignorance so gross as to be inconceivable in view of the amount of knowledge of things Jewish shewn in the book. It would be as impossible for a Gentile who derived that knowledge from the Old Testament, and from intercourse with Jews, as it would be for a Jew. The alternative view that the evangelist meant to imply by the expression he uses that Caiaphas happened to be high priest in that memorable year in which the Saviour of the world was crucified seems to be a reasonable one and sufficiently to explain it. And it may be added that it was rendered the more natural by the frequent changes in the occupant of the office under Herod the Great and the Romans, although it is true that Caiaphas held it considerably longer than most. Instead, therefore, of being a sign of ignorance the phrase used by the evangelist may be a sign of familiarity with the history of the time.

We will now turn to the mentions of localities in Palestine[2].

Even one or two serious errors might be sufficient to render it highly improbable that the author of the Gospel could have been one of the little band of disciples who continually accompanied Jesus as He travelled about Palestine. Such errors

Jewish characteristics in the Fourth Gospel. See I. Abrahams in *Cambridge Biblical Essays*, p. 181, and *Studies in Pharisaism*, p. 12; Güdemann, *Monatschrift für Geschichte u. Wissenschaft d. Judenthums* for 1893, a series of articles on *Das IV Evangelium und der Rabbinismus*; G. Klein, *Der älteste christliche Katechismus und die jüdische Propaganda-literatur*, pp. 49–61. I may mention also Chwolson, *Das letzte Passamahl Christi*, though I cannot regard his solution of the discrepancy between the Fourth Gospel and the Synoptics with respect to the day of the Crucifixion as sound. See below, pp. 250 ff.

Güdemann, *ib.* p. 353, takes, from those whom he believes to be the most expert critics, the middle of the second century as the date to which the composition of the Fourth Gospel is to be assigned. But he does not argue that the Jewish traits were those of that time and not of an earlier time; indeed he would probably deny that there was any substantial difference between the Pharisees of these different times. In the same context he makes the mistake of supposing that the Fourth Gospel was addressed to Jews.

[1] E.g. by Holtzmann, *Einleit.* 3rd ed. p. 459, not to mention older writers.

[2] See on this subject G. A. Smith, *The Historical Geography of the Holy Land*, and *Jerusalem*; Sanday, *Sacred Sites*; Furrer, *Das Geographische in Evang. nach Johannes* in *Zeitschrift d. nt. Wiss.* for 1902, pp. 258 ff.

have been charged against the Fourth Gospel, some of them clearly without ground. Of instances where there may with some reason be thought to be an error into which one of the Twelve would not have fallen, the chief is perhaps that of the distance between Cana of Galilee and Capernaum implied in iv. 46 ff. The best-known Cana is situated a little to the south of Tyre. It would not fit in with the movements generally of Jesus and His disciples, as related in the Fourth Gospel or in the Synoptics, that He should have been there at this time. Moreover, this Cana was not in Galilee, as defined by Josephus[1], though only a few miles outside its borders. The description "Cana of Galilee" would seem, therefore, to be given in order to distinguish the place here intended from the Cana near Tyre, and so far the evangelist appears to shew local knowledge. The Cana here in question has been identified either with Kefr-Kenna about $4\frac{1}{2}$ miles north-west, or with Khurbet-Kana about 9 miles north, of Nazareth. The distance of either of these places from Capernaum might be traversed by a walk of four to five hours. It would be most natural that the father who had come to seek the aid of Jesus for his sick son should start homeward very soon after Jesus had spoken the healing word. If so, and if the time at which this happened, namely "about the seventh hour," is to be understood to have been about 1 p.m. (in accordance with Jewish reckoning), he should have arrived at home by 6 p.m.[2] But the use of ἐχθές is then strange. Even though sunset marked the point from which to reckon a new series of hours, it is perhaps difficult to suppose that the preceding day could be spoken of emphatically as "yesterday" very soon after sunset. Those who had been watching the patient would be feeling rather what a very short time ago it was—one not separated from them by any marked interval—that the fever left him. Dr Westcott held that in the Fourth Gospel the reckoning of time is the same as ours[3]. If so, the father might have reached the neighbourhood of Capernaum soon after midnight, for there would be no reason why he should not walk through the night. In this case, with the

---

[1] *B.J.* 3, 3, 1, cp. Furrer, *ib.* p. 258, n. 1.
[2] E.g. see Clemen, *Entstehung*, pp. 75 and 132.
[3] See detached note in his Com. after ch. xix.

Acquaintance with localities in Palestine 157

hours of darkness and of sleep intervening, it would not be strange that ἐχθές should be used; but the servants would have been less likely to expect the father's return and to have gone to meet him at that hour.

It is also frequently said that want of topographical knowledge is shewn in the statement that Jesus and His disciples left the neighbourhood of the place where John was baptizing with a view to being present at a marriage-festival on "the third day[1]." But surely there is not sufficient reason for assuming error here. We do not know the place from which they are supposed to have started; but we may assume it to have been about 60 miles off. A few young peasants could easily have walked that distance in a couple of days. It would, also, probably not be necessary that they should arrive at the very beginning of the feast, which according to Jewish custom would last several days.

The description of Ænon as "near to Salim" (iii. 23) should also, perhaps, be noticed. There is now a small village called Salim three or four miles to the east of Shechem. It seems once to have been a place of some importance, such as could naturally be referred to in indicating other places in the neighbourhood. No other town of this name is known. There is, also, an 'Ainun seven miles to the north-east by north, and the plentiful springs and waters of the Fârâh valley lie between[2]. The distance from Salim is felt by some to be a serious objection. I doubt this, because, in the first place, the territories belonging to the two places, which may well have bordered upon one another, may naturally be taken into account, especially as it would not be in the village (or town) of Ænon but among the adjacent springs that the multitude would be gathered together. Further, the distance between the two places is not so great that to one who many years before had been for a short time in the neighbourhood they might not in memory have seemed near. A more serious difficulty is the fact that Ænon was in Samaritan territory, and that John the Baptist is not likely to have felt himself called to preach to Samaritans. Nevertheless it is probable enough that the population in the Wâdy-Fârâh was not exclusively or chiefly Samaritan,

[1] Jn ii. 1. [2] See *Memoirs* of Palestine Exploration Fund, II, p. 230.

and the place would be very easily accessible from the Jordan valley[1].

With regard to "Bethany beyond Jordan[2]" the declaration of Origen that he had searched for and could not discover the place, so that he was led to suggest the reading Bethabara, cannot rightly be passed over. At the same time, it should be remembered that—as has often been urged—during the two centuries between the time of the Baptist and of Origen, a period in which Palestine had been the scene of much warfare, the place itself might have disappeared, or the name have been altered[3].

Even should it be felt that in one or more of these instances mistakes have been made which render it difficult to suppose that the evangelist was one of the Twelve, the errors are clearly not such as might not well have been committed by a hearer of one of the Twelve, so that in spite of them the knowledge of localities shewn in the Gospel, if on the whole it appears to be correct, may indicate the derivation of its narratives from an eye-witness. That there are signs of such knowledge in the Gospel should, I think, be acknowledged. The main divisions of Palestine and their relative positions are correctly given—the "Judæan land"—Samaria lying between it and Galilee—and the district "beyond Jordan[4]." The reference to Sychar, nigh unto which was Jacob's well, and the hill on which the fathers of the Samaritan race worshipped, once a favourite ground of objection to the

---

[1] Furrer, who attaches weight to the objections to the commonly received site of Ænon, suggests another one. See *ib.* p. 258.

[2] See Jn i. 28, and cp. iii. 26, x. 40.

[3] Furrer, *ib.* p. 257, suggests a place lying in ruins called Betâne, which is (he holds) the same as the Betonim mentioned at Josh. xiii. 26. The place lay some way from the Jordan, and Origen might have looked only along the river bank. But according to this explanation the Fourth Gospel would have been at variance with Mark and Matt.

Conder (as quoted by Drummond, *ib.* pp. 431 f.) thought the evangelist referred to the well-known district of Batanea, or Bashan, the name of which is still preserved in Ard-el-Bethanîyeh (*Quarterly Statement of the Palestine Exploration Fund*, Oct. 1877, pp. 184 ff.), and he remarks that "if this conjecture be correct, Origen no doubt made his inquiries on a wrong basis." But it would have been natural if a district was intended that the definite article should have been prefixed. Also the reference to so wide an area does not seem probable.

[4] iii. 22 etc., iv. 3, 4, 43, i. 28 etc.

Acquaintance with localities in Palestine 159

authenticity of the Gospel, appears in reality to be a remarkable example of accuracy[1]. Capernaum and Tiberias and "the mountain" are mentioned, by the shore of the Lake of Galilee[2]. The position of the Bethany where Mary and Martha and Lazarus dwelt, and whence Jesus started for His entry into Jerusalem, is defined as "nigh to the city, distant from it by fifteen stadia[3]." A natural site can be pointed out for "the city called Ephraim" in "the country near to the wilderness[4]" to which Jesus withdrew after the raising of Lazarus. In Jerusalem "Solomon's Portico" and "the Treasury" are referred to in connexions suitable to their known positions, as also is the valley of the Kedron[5]. The site of the Pool of Siloam[6] is known; about that of the reservoir near the sheep-gate (v. 2 ff.) there has been difference of opinion, but one that appears to be highly probable has been suggested by Furrer[7]. It may be added that even in cases where we cannot identify a site there is a presumption that the mention of a place-name is due to local knowledge. A writer who was not over-scrupulous about exactitude and who desired to impart vividness to his narrative might not be slow to introduce the names of persons into it, but he would be less inclined to connect events with particular places, because to do this aptly without precise knowledge would be more difficult.

It remains for us to observe, that in one case[8] a name is used, and in another[9] the position of a place is described, in a

[1] See *The Historical Geography of the Holy Land*, by G. A. Smith, pp. 367 ff., and Furrer, *ib.* pp. 258 f.
[2] vi. 1, 15, 17, 23.   [3] xi. 18.   [4] xi. 54.
[5] viii. 20, x. 23, xviii. 1.   [6] ix. 7.   [7] *Ib.* pp. 259 f.
[8] At vi. 1, in the phrase θάλασσα τῆς Γαλιλαίας τῆς Τιβεριάδος, the latter name is in apposition and seems to be added as an explanation. We could imagine that it might be due to a copyist, and that it might first have been placed in the margin. But there is no evidence for this. At xxi. 1, we have simply ἡ θάλασσα τῆς Τιβεριάδος. Writers of the first century A.D. do not use this designation for the lake. Strabo, Pliny and Josephus call it the lake of Gennesar, or Gennesaritis, and the Targums, too, have this form. The name Lake of Tiberias seems to have become more and more the official name from the second century onwards. See Furrer, *ib.* p. 261.
[9] "Bethsaida of Galilee" (xii. 21). The only known Bethsaida was on the left bank of the Jordan, and therefore, according to the boundaries marked out in Josephus, not in Galilee but in Gaulonitis. A little later Julias—as Bethsaida came to be called—was reckoned as belonging to Galilee. See Furrer, *ib.* p. 264.

way which, so far as we know, did not come into fashion till the second century A.D. But naturally the usage in question in these two cases may have begun in some circles earlier than the earliest surviving evidence of it.

The last two references to places which have been mentioned bore on the date of composition of the Gospel. This opportunity may, therefore, be taken of noticing two other points which bear on the date, though they are not topographical. We have in the allusions to the fear that adhesion to Him, or the semblance of it, would lead to expulsion from the synagogues[1], a trait that can hardly have corresponded with the circumstances of Christ's Ministry. It is not likely that a policy of excommunication had been adopted so speedily; but it had no doubt from the latter part of the first century onwards[2]. It has also been supposed by some critics, that in the words at v. 43, "if another shall come in his own name, him ye will receive," there is a reference to Bar Kochba (A.D. 132), who was acknowledged as the Messiah by the famous Rabbi Aqiba. But the description "one that cometh *in his own name*" would not suit a pretended Messiah. On the contrary it fits the Christian conception of Antichrist[3], and this view of the meaning is confirmed by the fact that the expectation of the coming of Antichrist is referred to in 1 John[4].

To conclude this inquiry: That a Christian of the end of the first or beginning of the second century should have visited Palestine in order to familiarise himself with the scenes of the Lord's Ministry lest his account of it might lack local colour is improbable. If his interest in those scenes did lead him to go there it would be because particular places already had associations for him through the traditions he had received.

On the whole the references in the Gospel to localities can best be explained by supposing that the accounts of an eyewitness have been made use of in it. And probably there would even so have been more manifest errors if the writer who embodied the accounts had not himself possessed some local knowledge through having himself for a time resided in Palestine.

---

[1] ix. 22, xii. 42.
[2] E.g. Hilgenfeld, *Einleit.* pp. 738 f., and Schmiedel, *ib.* II. 25 f.
[3] Cp. Loisy, p. 416. [4] ii. 18 and iv. 3; see also 2 Jn 7.

§ 2. ALEXANDRIAN JUDAISM.

The question whether, or how far, the writer of the Fourth Gospel had come under the influence of the Jewish Philosophy of Alexandria is obviously of a very different kind from that of his relations to Judaism in general considered in the last section. On the ground primarily of the place held by the doctrine of the Logos in his Gospel, and also of his employment of allegory, it has been maintained that, before his conversion to the Christian faith, his mind had been steeped in the tenets and modes of thought of this religious philosophy, which is represented to us most fully in the writings of Philo. The Alexandrianism of the Fourth Gospel was a prominent feature of the Tübingen theories, and it is so no less in the treatment of the Johannine problem by some comparatively recent writers[1]. But study of the Gospel has convinced many critics who have not been disposed to take a conservative view of the Johannine problem, that the phenomena of the Gospel cannot be explained to the extent formerly supposed by the one consideration of the author's Alexandrianism. Holtzmann, for instance, while he maintains that the Philonic doctrine of the Logos is a chief moment in the whole Christology of the Gospel, through the thought-sphere of which breathes an Alexandrian atmosphere, at the same time allows that this Johannine sphere of thought has grown together from heterogeneous elements, without attaining to systematic unity. "The discourses of the Johannine Christ," he declares, "recapitulate the whole development of Christology between St Paul, and, say, Justin Martyr[2]."

Others have restricted the Alexandrine influence within still narrower limits. Thus J. Grill and E. F. Scott[3] have con-

[1] I may name the following: A. Thoma, *Genesis des Johannes-Evangeliums*, 1882; Aall, *Geschichte der Logos-Idee in der griechischen Philosophie und in der christlichen Literatur*, vols. I and II, 1897–9; J. Réville, *Le Quatrième Évangile*, 2nd ed. 1902. They admit of course that there are points on which the evangelist does not agree with Philo.

[2] See *Neutest. Theol.* pp. 373 f., 487, and cp. 441, 473. *Hand-Com.* (1908), pp. 5–12.

[3] Grill, *Entstehung d. vierten Evang.* pp. 166 ff.; Scott, *Fourth Gospel*, pp. 154 ff. Cp. also Loisy, *ib.* pp. 54 ff., and Heitmüller, *Com.* in *Die Schriften d. N.T.* ed. by J. Weiss, pp. 716 ff.

ceived of the evangelist as attracted to the Logos-doctrine after he became a Christian, because he perceived that it would aid him in setting forth his Christian belief as to the revelation of God in Christ, while at the same time for this purpose, namely in applying it to the Incarnate Christ, he had to modify it. And it was, they hold, in this modified, adapted form, that it dominated his thought throughout the Gospel. By insisting on this modification of the conception they have sought to combat Harnack's contention that after the Prologue the Logos-doctrine is no longer to be found.

Our inquiry in respect to the doctrine of the Logos in the Fourth Gospel will naturally fall into two parts: first, we will consider the character of the doctrine in the Prologue, and then we will turn to the question whether the doctrine as set forth in the Prologue, or in any shape, was present to the author's mind as the remainder of the Gospel was composed.

1. *The Prologue.* The conception in Jn i, *vv.* 1-18 of the relations of God to the World and to Man as mediated through the Logos corresponds as to its main outlines more nearly with that expounded in the writings of Philo than with any treatment of the subject elsewhere which we possess. There is strong reason, therefore, for holding that acquaintance directly, or indirectly, with the philosophy of Philo, or of that Alexandrian School of which Philo is the chief representative, has had its share in moulding the thought and language of the evangelist. This is allowed on all sides, with very few exceptions[1], and I need not labour the point.

But while there is general resemblance between Philo's Logos-doctrine and that of the evangelist, there are—even apart from the special application of the conception which the latter makes to the Incarnation—important differences between them, and these are of a kind to suggest that the evangelist had not been a regular disciple of the school, and that probably he had not come in contact with, or at least seriously considered, the doctrine till after he had become a Christian.

---

[1] Dr Westcott held that the sources of the Logos-doctrine in the Gospel were Palestinian and Biblical. Recently Prof. Rendel Harris has sought to derive it mainly, or exclusively, from the idea of "Wisdom" in the Old Testament. See note at end of this section, pp. 182 ff.

compared with that of Philo

(α) The Johannine Prologue owes its impressiveness and its enduring value in no small measure to the simplicity of its great outlines. The doctrine as here stated appears unembarrassed with any of those notions taken from Plato on the one hand and from the Stoics on the other with which in Philo's writings it is so closely associated. If the evangelist's mind had ever been impregnated with these notions, and he had perceived the importance of avoiding the introduction of them in the exposition of his Christology, in order not to involve himself in the disputes of the schools, he might by a serious effort have succeeded in this; but that grand simplicity of statement would have been much more easily and naturally attained, if he came to the Logos-philosophy with his Christian beliefs already advanced a considerable way towards maturity, so that his mind would be quick to seize upon just those features in the philosophy which he required for his own purpose, and to appropriate these and no more.

(β) But it will be well to compare the Logos-doctrine of the Johannine Prologue somewhat more closely with Philo's. Réville has protested against the assertion which has been frequently made that the Incarnation of the Logos was an idea wholly inconsistent with the Philonian doctrine because of the contact with matter which it involved. He points out that the contact of the Philonian Logos with matter is continual and also that he acts immanently in human beings[1]. In this contention I believe Réville to be justified. The contact with the flesh implied in the Incarnation does not in itself constitute the fundamental difference between Philo and St John. Nevertheless there is such a difference affecting the whole Prologue, which is closely connected with the climax in the Incarnation. Philo, when he speaks of the Logos in relation to the Absolute Divine Being, or of the mediation broadly considered between God and the Cosmos through the Logos, describes the latter in terms, and attributes to him functions, which at times suggest

---

[1] J. Réville, *ib.* p. 107. On the other hand, Aall, *ib.* p. 119, remarks on σὰρξ ἐγένετο:—"Der kühne Ausdruck geht über dasjenige hinaus was philonisches Denken vorbringen konnte"; and in a note "Das ἐν σαρκὶ ἐλήλυθεν (1 Jn iv. 2, 2 Jn 7) wäre das Höchste wozu derjenige sich erheben könnte, der seiner alexandrinischen Schulung treu bleiben wollte. Die typische philonische Redaktion der betreffenden Vorstellung wäre ἐφάνη ἐν σαρκί."

that he regarded him as a person, though whether he did so or not is doubtful. But in the main the Logos viewed in relation to matter and to individual human beings appears in Philo's teaching to be a diffused spirit, or law, or power, not a personal centre of life and thought. In the Johannine Prologue, on the other hand, the Logos is regarded throughout as a person. He acts upon and in the world from the beginning, but as a person. In each succeeding age He has enlightened men, but as a person dealing with persons. The difference is specially striking in regard to John the Baptist. Instead of John's being said to have possessed a fuller share of the indwelling Logos than men generally, which Philo held to be true of Moses and the prophets, a contrast, which certainly amounts to more than a difference of degree, is drawn between him and Jesus in whom the Logos dwelt.

It might not be impossible that in the thought of one for whom, after he had been an adherent of the school of Philo, the manifestation of the Logos in Jesus Christ had come to be the one all-absorbing object of faith, the whole conception of the Logos and of the mode of His working should have been thus changed, but the difference in question is certainly easier to understand, if he only became acquainted with the Logos-doctrine after he had embraced the Christian faith.

(γ) We have still to notice a difference from Philo in the use made by the evangelist of the ideas of the Life and the Light. Philo does indeed speak of the Logos as the source of light to the human mind, but it is not with him a very prominent notion. And he makes no statement with regard to the Logos as *life* which even remotely resembles that in St John "in him was life[1]." Still less have we in Philo anything to correspond with the words "the life was the light of men," which

---

[1] I cannot pretend to have such a knowledge of Philo's writings as would enable me on my own authority to make this statement. But I can cite J. Réville, *La doctrine du Logos*, p. 67: "Philon ne dit nulle part à ma connaissance que le Logos soit la vie." This is also admitted by J. Grill, *Entstehung*, pp. 207, 218 f. This testimony on the part of these writers is the more significant because it would have suited their theories of the Fourth Gospel if Philo had spoken of the Logos as the source of life.

The history of the ideas of Life and Light in the Fourth Gospel is fully discussed below, pp. 172 ff.

compared with that of Philo

when spiritually applied suggest the profound truth that practical Christian living leads to the enlightenment of the mind[1].

Some affinity with the idea that the Logos is Life might be found in Stoic conceptions. But Stoicism, an atheistic system, in which the Logos is conceived only as a guiding and controlling force, of a subtle and yet materialistic nature, pervading the Cosmos and also belonging to it, could not furnish the foundation for the thought of Philo, whose aim was to provide a philosophic justification for his theistic faith as a pious Jew, and for whom consequently the relation of the Cosmos to God was of as great importance as the relation of the Logos to the Cosmos. He necessarily sought aid in Platonism, an idealistic system; and his refraining from regarding the Logos as the life of men may have been due to a fear that it would involve him in materialistic ideas, and may be an indication that he was not the mere eclectic that he is sometimes held to have been.

Nevertheless it would not be surprising if in those days of eclectic amalgamations someone else less trained in philosophy should have borrowed from Stoicism, or from some other form of contemporary speculation, the conception that the Logos is the Life of the World, and have grafted it upon the Logos-doctrine[2]. The fourth evangelist may have found this step already taken, or he may have taken it himself, in his endeavour to set forth adequately the infinite significance of the Person of Christ. His starting-point in any case was probably the knowledge, founded on experience, that Jesus Christ is the life of souls. He may have been aided also in giving breadth to his thought by the words of the psalmist "in thee is the fulness of life and in thy light shall we see light," which he would readily transfer to the Divine Son. It seems to me most pro-

[1] Cp. viii. 12, also vii. 17.
[2] In Poimandres and other dialogues included in the Corpus Hermeticum references to ζωή and φῶς (often coupled together) are common. The Logos also appears. But there are no statements strictly parallel to those in the Fourth Gospel. The closest are in i. 2, 5, 6. Here Poimandres-Hermes calls himself ὁ τῆς αὐθεντίας νοῦς. A great light is witnessed, that Light is the νοῦς, from the νοῦς, which is the Light, proceeds the shining Logos, Son of God. It will be observed that here the Logos does not proceed immediately from the Absolute. See further the successive emanations, ib. ix. 10.

bable that his idea of Jesus Christ as the Life had attained a large measure of fulness and clearness independently of, and before he combined it with, the Logos-doctrine. And I find confirmation of this view in the opening passage of the First Epistle of St John which, I have argued, was written before the Gospel, and the doctrine of which (as we have seen) is held to be of an earlier type even by many critics who place the time of the composition of the Epistle later[1].

2. From the consideration of the Prologue we proceed now to an examination of the remainder of the Gospel. Is the idea of the Logos to be found there, though the term does not occur? The answer of the great majority of students of the Gospel has been and still is in the affirmative, and this is not surprising. We have all felt the marvellous impressiveness of the great opening doctrinal statement which occupies the first eighteen verses. Through the influence which it exerts upon our minds we are naturally led to suppose that the whole contents of the following work were from the first intended to illustrate and establish the theology of the exordium. This view has accordingly been held by men of the most widely different schools of thought, though they have estimated differently the effect of the connexion. Here I may join together the writers of the classes which I distinguished above. Those of the class mentioned last would not, I think, disagree with what I have written as regards the relations of the evangelist with Alexandrian thought implied in the exposition of the doctrine of the Logos in his Prologue. Indeed they have expressed substantially the same view of the attraction which the doctrine had for him and of the extent to which he adopted it. But they, no less than those who have attributed to the evangelist a thorough-going Alexandrianism, have maintained that, conceiving Jesus Christ to be the Logos Incarnate, he set himself to remould the evangelical history in a way to demonstrate the truth of this conception, imputing it to Jesus Himself in discourses and sayings which are put into His mouth, and

---

[1] For a different view of the history of the connexion between the two conceptions "the Logos" and "the Life," which does not (as it seems to me) agree so well either with the language of 1 Jn i. 1, 2, or the relations generally between the Epistle and the Gospel, see Aall, *ib.* p. 112, note 4.

contriving that it should be suggested also through the accounts of His deeds and by the turn given to the narrative of events.

Further, students of the Gospel who have adhered to the traditional view that it is the work of the Apostle John have explained its differences from the Synoptic Gospels by supposing that the evangelist, though he did not invent, yet purposely selected and arranged, facts in such a manner as to enforce the truths upon which he has dwelt in the Prologue.

Harnack first definitely propounded a different view. He contended that the writer's object in his Prologue was partly to commend his Gospel to educated Gentile and Jewish readers, partly to state the Logos-doctrine in a form less objectionable than that in which it was already held in some Christian circles. When he has effected this purpose, the idea of the Logos is dismissed by him, and he substitutes for it another, which he preferred, namely that of Jesus Christ as the unique Divine Son—μονογενὴς θεός, while, moreover, in the remainder of the Gospel he shews that the retention and employment by the Incarnate Son of His Divine prerogatives in His life on earth were dependent on the Father's will[1].

It is possible to agree with Harnack in his judgment that the idea of the Logos is absent from the body of the Gospel without adopting his theory of the reason for this absence. The suggestion that the evangelist, after he had embraced and so solemnly set forth the doctrine of the Logos, discarded it, does not commend itself as probable. But it is with the question of fact that we are in the first instance concerned. The present writer has become convinced, contrary to what, in common with theologians and critics and readers of the Gospel in general, he had for many years supposed, that as to the fact Harnack is clearly right.

(a) As is well known, the term ὁ λόγος is not after the Prologue used of the Person of Jesus Christ. That the evangelist does not put it into the mouth of Jesus, or of other actors in the Gospel-story, is due, it is said, to a sound historical instinct; for to suppose it to have been used by Him, or by any of His immediate contemporaries in Palestine during His life on earth,

---

[1] See *Zeitschrift für Theologie und Kirche* for 1892; also *Dogmengeschichte*, 4th ed. (1909), p. 109, n. 1.

would plainly have been inappropriate. Some who give this explanation are not generally ready to allow that our evangelist possessed historical instinct to any great extent. But let that pass. The fact is commonly overlooked, though surely it is important, that the term is not employed in remarks by the evangelist himself, where it might have been without impropriety, as in the solemn reflections on the close of Christ's Public Ministry at xii. 36*b*–43, or in the statement of the object with which the Gospel had been written at xx. 30, 31.

Further, as Harnack points out, the phrase ὁ λόγος τοῦ θεοῦ is again and again in the Fourth Gospel applied, in a sense analogous to that in which it is so often elsewhere used, to the teaching of Jesus, or to Divine revelation more generally, and it might have been expected that a writer whose mind was full of the conception of the "Logos-Christ," and whose intention it was to represent Jesus as the Logos speaking and acting, could hardly have refrained from indicating more plainly than he has done, if indeed he has done it at all, that He who spake the "word of God" was Himself the Eternal Word[1]. In one passage (x. 34 ff.) where it would have been specially natural to suggest this thought, the argument takes a different turn: "Is it not written in your law, I said, Ye are gods? If he called them gods unto whom the word of God came, and the scripture cannot be broken, say ye of him whom the Father sanctified and sent into the world, Thou blasphemest; because I said, I am the Son of God?"

(β) Not only is the term "the Logos" as a description of the Person of Christ absent from the Gospel after the Prologue, but there is no hint given in language however veiled of the *cosmical* relations of the Person of the Christ, the place He held in the creation of the World and of Man, and holds in their continual guidance and government and as the source of

---

[1] Holtzmann, *Neutest. Theol.* p. 398, refuses to admit the force of this contention on the ground of the general tendency of the Gospel.

Grill, *ib.* pp. 40 f., when he insists that the knowledge that the term ὁ λόγος might be used in the personal sense would not afford a reason for its not being used in the ordinary sense, appears to miss Harnack's point, which I take to be that it would not have been used so often in the ordinary sense without indications being given of the associations which it had for one to whom its special sense meant so much as is supposed.

with that of the remainder of the Gospel 169

their life. This is a most significant omission. The Logos-doctrine, however simply it may be stated, is essentially a piece of metaphysics; and in metaphysics an attempt is made to ascertain and state permanent laws of being through considering necessities of thought. The idea of the Logos as a means of mediating between the Absolute, Self-existent One and the Created Universe was due to such a necessity of thought, real or supposed. The Supreme acts indeed, but it is timeless action in a transcendent sphere. He creates archetypal ideas; these the Logos has reproduced in the Cosmos after such manner as is possible. This conception lies behind the doctrine of the Prologue. By connecting therewith the fact of the Incarnation the writer is able to bring under one comprehensive view God's revelation of Himself in Nature and in Providence and the consciences of men in all ages, and in the new dispensation of grace. It is the very point of the doctrine of the Logos that it enables us to regard the Divine operations in all these different ways as ultimately one. It is thus that the evangelist in his Prologue teaches us to regard them. If he had intended to set forth the doctrine of the Logos in the body of the Gospel he could not have omitted altogether any suggestion of the thought that He Who had come to reveal the Father in human flesh reveals Him also universally in other spheres of being. Adaptation of the doctrine to the Incarnation of the Christ did not require this. It is indeed not adaptation, but omission of its distinctive element.

(γ) Still less is it conceivable that he should have introduced without explanation sayings which not only belong to a different order of ideas, but are, strictly speaking, incompatible with it. At Jn v. 17 Jesus defends Himself for working a miracle on the Sabbath by referring to the ceaseless working of the Father. The idea suggested is that of parallel working in different spheres; there is no indication of that mode of operation relatively to the Father which is distinctive of the Logos. In the sequel functions of a unique kind are assigned to Him, in the exercise of which He may be truly said to represent God to men, but only two well-defined instances are mentioned. Power has been given to Him to raise from the dead those who have been led to believe on Him through the

Father's drawing, and He has been appointed by the Father to be the Judge in the final judgment.

Again we have sayings at xvi. 28 and xvii. 5 in which the Divine Son speaks of leaving one state of existence and adopting another and then resuming the first. From these it would be not unnatural to infer that He must have been withdrawn for a season from a discharge of the function (inherently belonging to Him if He was the Logos) of mediating between the Absolute and the Cosmos as a whole. But to suppose such a withdrawal would be, according to the thought of the author of the Prologue when he wrote it, impossible without reducing the Cosmos to Chaos.

(δ) We will now go on to scrutinise the relation between the Logos-idea and other lofty conceptions of Christ's Person in the Fourth Gospel. Did they spring from it and were they intended to suggest it? The commonest of them is that of the Divine Son. At i. 18, the last verse of the Prologue, the evangelist introduces this idea through his use of the term μονογενής. And since the term μονογενής was actually applied to the Logos, as we find from Philo's writings, it is possible that to the evangelist's mind it appeared to supply a link between his exposition of the Logos-doctrine and that view which is given us after this point in innumerable passages of the relation of Jesus Christ to God as that of the Son to the Father. If we suppose, however, that this link was designed, it does not follow that the representation of Jesus Christ as the Divine Son was derived from the Logos-doctrine. Philo applies the term μονογενής to the Logos to express the idea of a unique generation, or proceeding forth, from God, and this is the natural meaning for it in a Logos-philosophy. On the contrary in the Fourth Gospel the conception of the relation of the Son to the Father is predominantly an ethical one— that of unity of will and purpose, of filial dependence and loving communion. This is true even though this communion is represented as being so perfect and complete that it implies sameness of nature. The idea is primarily taken, not from a system of philosophy, but from the human relationship of son and father when at its best. That relationship, as it might exist between a human son and the Heavenly Father, was perfectly exhibited in Jesus Christ. At the same time this relationship as seen in Him was felt to have its ground in, and even in its human form to be of a piece with, one that is transcendent, eternal and Divine. But it is remarkable how in the sayings and discourses of the Fourth Gospel indications of an experience of Sonship suited to human conditions are mingled with references to an experience of Sonship surpassing those conditions. Now is there any good reason for supposing that this transcendent aspect of the Sonship was introduced through the effect on the writer's mind of the Logos-doctrine? To translate the Logos-conception—even if it had clearly contained an equivalent element—into this other language, and to do it so thoroughly and extensively, would have required an effort which no one in any age would have been likely to make. Moreover, it supposes that Christian faith, at least in the evangelist's case, first leapt to the conception of the Logos, suited for expressing the relation of the Divine Son to the Cosmos and to Mankind throughout the successive generations of its history, instead of following the far easier and more natural path of first apprehending that the communion which Jesus had on earth with the Father was such as proved Him to be Divine.

Jesus Christ's own consciousness of this eternal life with the Father is perhaps most clearly expressed in sayings referring to His pre-existence. But it is not necessary to suppose belief in the pre-existence of the Christ to be grounded in acceptance of the Logos-doctrine. We meet with it in St Paul's Epistles. Moreover, it was inevitably suggested by the identification of Jesus with the Heavenly Son of man. It is noteworthy that in two of the sayings in the Fourth Gospel on the pre-existence of the Christ the title "the Son of man" is used[1]. In both these sayings we have traces of the process of thought which I have indicated. In the earlier of them the ascent of the Son of man to heaven is made to depend on His having come from heaven[2]. In the latter one, also, the ascent and descent are closely associated. Passages which

[1] iii. 13, vi. 62.
[2] The remark in the text does not rest on a particular interpretation of the passage. But I would observe that it is easier to understand the words if we suppose the sayings attributed to Jesus to end, and the reflections of the evangelist

connect the pre-existence of Jesus with the fact of His being the Son of man plainly belong to a different order of ideas from the Logos-doctrine. There are also two in which Jesus speaks of returning to that sphere which He had left[1]. Though the title "the Son of man" is not here used, they fit in with that conception. I would urge here, as I have done before, that a writer who had been thoroughly grounded in Philo's philosophy and to whom it meant much could hardly have brought himself to introduce such sayings as these two without an explanation. But at least he did not derive them from that doctrine. Other sayings in this Gospel on the pre-existence of the Christ, which are not incompatibly or manifestly unconnected with the Logos-idea like the foregoing, are at the same time not necessarily deductions from it[2].

There is, so far as I can see, no reason to doubt that the original disciples of Christ, if they had not grasped the idea of His pre-existence while they followed Him on earth, did so after His death and resurrection. And St Paul unquestionably held it. In all probability the author of the Fourth Gospel had known this article of faith as one commonly held among Christians, and had accepted it, long before he wrote his Gospel, and the form in which he has presented it there does not appear to have been in any way affected by the Logos-doctrine.

(ε) But because the influence of the doctrine expounded in the Prologue is not to be traced afterwards in certain instances it does not follow that it may not have been even strong in others. And we now come to the teaching about

---

to begin, after *v*. 12. Westcott in his Commentary, as we have already seen above, p. 62 n., supposes such a break to occur after *v*. 15. But after *v*. 12 the first person is no longer used. If in *v*. 13 Jesus is the speaker it is difficult to give a natural meaning to "hath ascended save the Son of man"; for He had not then ascended. The meaning to be then extracted must be the one suggested by the words ὁ ὢν ἐν τῷ οὐρανῷ, which by the majority of textual critics are, however, regarded as a gloss. I.e. He means the Son of man has no need to ascend because He is continually there. But if the words are written from the point of view of the evangelist the meaning is simple and straightforward.

With regard to the gloss ὁ ὢν etc. I would add that there is no other reference after the Prologue to the continuation of the life of the Son of God in heaven during His earthly life.

[1] xvi. 28, xvii. 5.   [2] i. 30 (cp. v. 15), vi. 33, viii. 58.

with that of the remainder of the Gospel 173

Jesus Christ as the Life and the Light in the body of the Gospel, in which the thoughts of the Prologue seem most plainly to recur. I have noticed that Philo does not speak of the Logos as the Life and does not make great use of the figure of the Light, and I have suggested that the prominence given to these ideas in the Prologue itself may have been largely due to the Christian *motif* of its author. But even so the Gospel might have been written from the point of view of the Prologue, and Grill has presented the case for this in the most favourable manner by placing in the forefront of his reply to Harnack the argument that teaching on the Life and the Light is carried over from the Prologue into the remainder of the Gospel.

The teaching on these subjects must be examined with some care. The most considerable passages on Jesus Christ as the Life are the discourse on the parallelism between His working and that of the Father which arose after the cure of the cripple at the pool of Bethesda (v. 17–30, esp. *vv.* 21 ff.); the discourse on the true bread (vi. 24–end); the conversation with Martha before the raising of Lazarus (xi. 21–27). There are besides remarkable sayings on the subject at iii. 15, 16, 36, iv. 14, viii. 12, x. 10, 28, xii. 49, 50, xiv. 6, xvii. 2, 3, xx. 31.

The "life" referred to is everywhere the true, spiritual life, which is not merely the pledge, but the beginning of an eternal life, over which natural death has no power. No suggestion is made that Christ's giving, or being, to men this life is associated in any way with His being also the life of Creation. The only words in which, taken by themselves, this idea could be found are those at vi. 33, where it is said that "the bread of God is that which cometh down out of heaven and giveth life unto the world." But in view of all the other expressions in the context, and of the parallel at *v.* 51, where it is stated that He "will give *his flesh* for the life of the world," it is evident that the meaning is that His life and the means of communicating it, to be perfected through His sacrifice, are *adequate* for the salvation of all men, though this life has to be in every instance personally bestowed and appropriated.

The condition for receiving this gift of life commonly mentioned in the Gospel is faith. But in the sixth chapter it is described as an eating of the flesh of Christ and drinking of His blood (vi. 53–56). This is a plain allusion to His approaching sacrifice and to the Christian Eucharist, and although the bread of life is contrasted with the manna showered upon the Israelites in the wilderness, a comparison which lay ready to hand, and though Philo interprets the manna as allegorically signifying the Logos[1], it is evident that in the discourse in St John we have to do with ideas which are purely Christian.

But there is no indication that the eternal life now communicated, which shall remain untouched by death, is to take the place of the commonly expected resurrection. On the contrary, Jesus declares, emphatically and repeatedly, that He will *at the last day* raise up those who have believed on Him through the Father's drawing[2]. Moreover, with this future raising of the departed who have believed on Him, the summoning by the Son of man of all the dead as well as the living to His judgment-seat is closely linked[3], and is described in language resembling that used in St Matthew and elsewhere about the Judge and the Judgment.

It is, perhaps, conceivable that the evangelist might determine, in writing after the Prologue about the Incarnate Logos, rigorously to exclude from view, alike in words attributed to Christ and in his own remarks, any allusion to a sense in which He was life otherwise than as the salvation of those that believe, and at the same time to mingle with what he said on this subject current eschatological ideas and Apocalyptic language; but it is surely far more probable that the teaching in question has come down to us from a time before the Prologue to the Gospel was written, in a form which does not presuppose the Logos-doctrine.

So as to "the light." In spite of the breadth with which Jesus is declared to be "the light of the world" the manner of His becoming so, which alone appears to be contemplated, is through His incarnate life. It is so at viii. 12. The announcement "I am the light of the world" is immediately followed by the announcement, "he that followeth me shall not walk in the darkness, but shall have the light of life." At iii. 18, 19 it is expressly said, with regard to men's belief or disbelief in

---

[1] See Drummond, *Philo*, index. [2] vi. 39, 40, 44, 54. [3] v. 23 and 27–29.

with that of the remainder of the Gospel 175

the Son of man who has been sent into the world, that "this is the judgment that the light is come into the world and men loved the darkness rather than the light." When His Ministry is drawing to a close Jesus bids His hearers walk in the light while they have it, and a few verses later says, evidently with reference to His presence among them and its consequences, "I am come a light into the world that whosoever believeth on me may not abide in the darkness." At ix. 5 indeed we read ὅταν ἐν τῷ κόσμῳ ὦ φῶς εἰμὶ τοῦ κόσμου, and Westcott presses the ὅταν and translates, "whenever I am in the world I am the light of the world," so that the saying may refer to different comings and modes of coming. Even so the saying would not describe a continuous relation to the world. But in point of fact the usage of New Testament Greek does not appear to justify this rendering. ὅταν with the conjunctive expresses simply a dependent temporal relation. We might translate "being in the world." Even the A.V., "as long as I am in the world," is not far wrong[1].

There is nothing then to shew that the thought of Christ being the Life and Light is in the body of the Gospel inferred from His being the Logos.

(ζ) There are a few more passages to be noticed in connexion with our subject where other points are raised. We will take first those three difficult passages, Jn viii. 24, 28, xiii. 19, where the words ὅτι ἐγώ εἰμι are put into the mouth of Jesus, and it is doubtful what it is intended to predicate. With a view to clearness of thought here it is necessary that we should make up our minds whether the verb "to be" is simply a copula, so that the predicate must be supposed to be supplied from what was in the mind of the hearers, since it cannot in these instances be from the immediate context, or on the other hand—if it contains in itself the predicate, or is at least something more than a copula—what precisely it can be held to predicate. The interpretations of many commentators seem to me unconvincing from their attempting to combine these different views of the grammatical and logical

---

[1] Cp. Blass, *New Test. Gram.*, Eng. trans. p. 218. Mt. ix. 15, ὅταν ἀπαρθῇ ἀπ' αὐτῶν ὁ νυμφίος may be compared where ὅταν cannot possibly mean "whenever," "as often as."

force of the words, without having decided whether, or how far, they can rightly be combined[1].

We shall do well to compare other passages where ἐγώ εἰμι occurs. In the majority of cases there is a predicate plainly to be taken from the context. One, viz. iv. 26, is specially important as furnishing a transition to the instances now before us. The woman of Samaria refers to the expectation of Messiah, and Jesus replies "I am," i.e. He of whom you speak. Even more significant are the words attributed to the Baptist at xiii. 25, where he denies that "I am," and the idea of the person that he is not, is not directly expressed in the preceding context. Jn vii and viii. 12–23 have been mainly occupied with discussions whether He is the Christ and His own declarations about Himself. No single title or description can here be extracted, as that to which Jesus refers when at *v.* 24 He says, "if ye believe not that I am, ye shall die in your sins"; but an intimation of what He claims to be has been given them and He must be understood to say "I am that." This is an explanation in accordance with the general use of the idiom, and if it does not draw out the whole force of the words in this and the other two passages which we are considering, it should go far to do so. It receives strong confirmation from the immediate sequel to *v.* 24. For the Jews demand that He shall put His claim more plainly, while He still refers to what He has been telling them from the beginning. In *v.* 28 He points forward to the day when they will be compelled to acknowledge the truth about Him. Similarly at xiii. 19, Jesus, when He says to His disciples, "From henceforth I tell you before it come to pass, that, when it is come to pass, ye may believe that I am," alludes to that faith in, and conception of, Him, their "lord and master," which they had been led to entertain.

But does the use of the substantive verb in the instances

---

[1] I should make this complaint of Westcott's note, at viii. 24. Again, H. Holtzmann paraphrases ἐγώ εἰμι there "nämlich der ἄνωθεν stammende, die allentscheidende Persönlichkeit." The former of these expressions is taken from the context, the latter must be derived (I presume) from the substantive verb itself, and the question is whether it is legitimate to find it there. See on completing the sense from the context, Loisy, *ib.* p. 561.

with that of the remainder of the Gospel 177

under consideration of itself involve an assertion of Divinity? That has been often held, and the possibility of this has occurred probably to most readers. And the emphatic use of " I am " at viii. 58—" before Abraham was, I am "—may seem to lend colour to this view, though it should be observed that what is there implied is not absolute being but continued existence. Certain passages of the Old Testament are indeed quoted where the Most High speaks :—Deut. xxxii. 39, Isa. xliii. 10, and perhaps also Exod. iii. 14. But, in the first place, these passages are not in point if taken in the original. In the two first there is not even an emphatic use of the substantive verb: it has to be supplied; while the pronoun " he " does occur and is emphatic. It refers to that idea of God which pious Israelites had in their minds. From the famous passage in Exodus on the name Jahweh we learn that " the name did not express any attribute of God, or describe God as to His essence ; but it described Him in this relation to Israel—' I will be with thee[1].' "

It is only from the employment of ἐγώ εἰμι in the Septuagint in these passages that any support can be derived for the notion that this phrase connotes Divine being. And even with this rendering the true meaning is apparent from the context in Deut. xxxii. 39 and Isa. xliii. 10; and the passage in Exodus few venture to quote as applicable.

But in point of fact, to regard the expression as an assertion of absolute, and therefore Divine, being, used of the Most High in the Old Testament, which Jesus transferred to Himself, would prove too much. It would not be in accord with the conception of the Logos; the distinction carefully observed in the Prologue between ὁ θεός and θεός would be ignored.

There will be nothing incompatible, however, with what has been here urged in our recognising that there is a solemn emphasis on the thought of what Jesus is in the instances before us. It is as though He said, " By My nature and place I am indeed what I have told you, and what some among you have surmised. Such are My Person and Work; you are called to believe it, or you will be constrained to acknowledge it; or

[1] See A. B. Davidson, *Old Testament Theology*, p. 71.

if you have done so already you must hold fast by that conviction." He had told them that He was "from above," that He had come to them from the Father, that He was the light of the world; that He would be the source of a new life to those who believed on Him. But He had not said that He was "the Logos," or included in what He said about Himself some of the distinctive elements in that conception.

Let us next note the statement at iii. 35, "The Father loveth the Son, and hath given all things into his hand," and the similar words at xiii. 3. On the former passage Westcott remarks that τὰ πάντα is not to be limited in any way, and I presume would intend the remark to be applied to the later passage also. Undoubtedly one should always endeavour to understand words according to their plain meaning, and the statements now before us do not in themselves suggest a restriction of the "all things" to the work of grace and judgment with a view to which the Son became incarnate. Yet everywhere else in the Gospel, after the Prologue, this alone is spoken of. To this, moreover, reference is made in the immediate context of the former passage, as also in the similar but more precise words at xvii. 2.

The only possible explanation of the features of the Fourth Gospel which we have been observing appears to me to be that in the Prologue and the remainder of the Gospel we have the history of the evangelist's thought in inverse order. In the body of the Gospel we have matter which had accumulated during years of meditation and teaching; it contains statements of Divine truth which he had inherited; it reflects Christological beliefs which he had held, modes of thought to which he had become accustomed, before he grasped the Logos-idea and applied it to the Person of Christ.

There would be nothing strange in his only having become acquainted with that idea, or at least paying heed to it, after he had for some years been a Christian believer and teacher. It would not be necessary, in order that he might have learnt it, that he should have applied himself to the study of Philo's, or any other, writings. In that age when lectures and discussions

with that of the remainder of the Gospel 179

on philosophical subjects in public places were so common, and indeed to a large extent took the place of reading, he might well have heard the Philonic scheme of thought expounded by some "learned Jew of Alexandria," some Apollos who was visiting Ephesus, in some lecture-hall or under some portico. He would then have seized upon its central idea as an aid in defining to his own mind, and in giving satisfactory expression to, a truth which (it may be) he was already feeling after. This kind of use of philosophical terms by theologians and moralists is constantly taking place. It is natural to those earnest men who are spiritual and ethical teachers rather than philosophers.

When, finally, the fourth evangelist composed his Gospel, or put it forth in complete form, prefixing to it his sublime presentation of the conception of the Logos, which he had recently acquired, he did not alter the subject-matter which had gradually taken shape in his mind, or even in part perhaps had been written down, at an earlier stage of his career. And he may well have felt no need for doing so[1]. He would not be acutely, if at all, conscious of differences between his old theological conceptions and that one to which he had now attained. It would be possible for him to contemplate the whole life and teaching which he recorded, and his past reflections upon it, from the point of view of the comprehensive idea which he had reached, and virtually to harmonise more limited or different conceptions with it, just as Christian believers do now in reading the Fourth Gospel. But to suppose this is something quite different from supposing that with the Logos-doctrine already grasped he set about writing the Gospel for the purpose of illustrating it and quite prepared to fashion the matter in such a manner as effectually to do so, and that the result was what we have.

The employment of Allegory in the Fourth Gospel.

The fourth evangelist has also been held to shew his Alexandrine spirit and training in the part which allegory is said

[1] The remarks quoted above, p. 161, from Holtzmann shew that he must have been prepared to admit that there was a good deal of matter in the Gospel which had come down unaltered from an earlier time.

to play in his Gospel[1]. But it may be gravely doubted whether he had allegorical meanings in view to anything like the extent that is supposed, while his motive and purpose in his treatment of the history with which he is dealing, and his attitude towards it, are different from those of the Jewish Alexandrine and other ancient allegorists in regard to the written narratives or the traditions with which they deal.

Let us take first the question of the extent to which the allegorical method has been employed in the Fourth Gospel. The writers whose opinions I am now examining hold that the evangelist had allegorical meanings in view in almost every part of his Gospel, alike in the main features and the events which he records and in details such as names of places, numbers, lengths of periods and seasons. But it is certain that the evangelist rarely gives any indication of these meanings which he intended readers to gather. Can it be believed that he would have refrained from doing so if he had actually had them in mind and attached importance to them? The practice of Philo—whose modes of thought he has been supposed to share, and whose technique even he has been said, though without anything that deserves the name of proof, to follow—is very different. Philo's writings are largely occupied with allegorical interpretations of the Old Testament. He discusses its narratives minutely, leaving nothing to the reader's ingenuity, in order to derive from them support for his theological and philosophical positions. Nor can it be pretended that there was a current language of allegory in which the signification of the traits introduced was clearly fixed, or that names employed bore it on their face. If in two or three instances this may be imagined, it is not broadly true. Moreover, the evangelist was teaching truth new to the world, and it was therefore necessary for him to speak plainly.

Where he desires to enforce a truth by the allegorical application of a fact, he has directly suggested the meaning by the teaching recorded in more or less close connexion with the fact. This is the case with three notable miracles. The feeding

---

[1] E.g. see Thoma, *ib.* pp. 741–755; Réville, *ib.* pp. 80, 81, 300 f.; Loisy, *ib.* pp. 85, 247, n. 4, 259 (e.g. "Quand il parle de la mère de Jésus c'est à Israël qu'il pense, non à Marie").

Use of allegory in the Fourth Gospel 181

of the five thousand[1] affords an opportunity for a discourse on the true bread of life; the opening of the eyes of the man born blind[2] is prepared for and followed by insistence upon the truth that He is the light of the world; Martha is called upon to believe that He is the resurrection and the life[3] when He is about to raise Lazarus, though it is to be observed that the fact seems to be here not that we have in any sense an allegory but an actual instance which demonstrates His power to raise hereafter those who believe on Him.

Besides these we have the following examples:—A saying, in which Jesus may, under the figure of restoring the Jewish temple, have foretold the new order of Divine worship which He would introduce, is interpreted by the evangelist as referring to His own resurrection[4]. The significance which the feet-washing at the Last Supper had (in addition to being an example) is brought out by the saying about spiritual cleansing[5]. The fact that both blood and water flowed from the pierced side of the Crucified Saviour is indeed recorded without any comment on its meaning[6], though with great emphasis on its being a fact. But somewhat at least of its symbolical significance could not but be evident to every Christian. This symbolism of the Fourth Gospel is also characterised by a simplicity and dignity which are often wanting in Philo's allegories. The comparisons employed in the Gospel rest upon real analogies between things in the Natural and Spiritual Orders, like the parables in the Synoptics.

While the evangelist's use of allegory is, so far as he gives any indication himself that he intends it, confined within narrow limits, and his difference from Philo on that score very great, his attitude to the history with which he is concerned is also not the same. It is probably true that Philo accepted, at least in general, the literal accuracy of the Old Testament narratives on which he comments; but it is impossible in reading him not to feel that the allegorical meanings to be found in them are what give them for him their real value and justify the belief that the ancient Scriptures were inspired of God. For the evangelist, on the contrary, the works of Jesus

---

[1] Ch. vi.   [2] viii. 12, and ix. 1 ff., 5 etc.   [3] Ch. xi.   [4] ii. 19–22.
[5] xiii. 4–15.   [6] xix. 34–35.

and all the events of His life were of the utmost importance as facts, quite apart from particular truths which any of them might symbolically teach. In his works Jesus shewed forth His glory; by them He was proved to be the Christ; and alike by what He did and what He suffered He gave life to the world[1]. The evangelist might well, also, be impressed, and there are indications that he was, with the thought that in the Saviour's course on earth everything was Divinely ordered[2], and it may well have been with this feeling in his mind that he recorded details in the evangelic traditions, without pretending that he could explain their significance. This is something quite different from the temper of mind of the allegorist.

It is also to be observed that the fourth evangelist makes many quotations from the Old Testament, but it is in order to shew the fulfilment of prophecy in the history of the Christ, which interests him as it did the author of St Matthew and other New Testament writers. And in his treatment of the Old Testament he does not apply the allegorical method[3]. For examples of this in the New Testament we must go, not to this supposed disciple of Philo, the great allegorist, but to St Paul[4], who derived it in all probability not from Alexandrian but from Rabbinic training.

BP WESTCOTT AND PROF. RENDEL HARRIS ON THE PROLOGUE

Dr Westcott argued that the Johannine Logos-doctrine was framed independently of Alexandrian teaching, at least in the fully developed form in which we see it in Philo. Its principal source he held to be the conception of the *Memra* to be met with in the Jewish Targums,

---

[1] ii. 11, 23, iii. 2, v. 20, 36, x. 25, 32, xii. 37, xiv. 10, xv. 24.
[2] ii. 4, vii. 30, viii. 20.
[3] The *comparison* between the lifting up of the Son of man and the lifting up of the brazen serpent by Moses is plainly not, properly speaking, an allegory (iii. 14, 15), nor is the *allusion* to Jacob's vision (i. 50, 51).
[4] Gal. iv. 21 ff., and 1 Cor. ix. 4.

which are examples of Palestinian teaching. This the evangelist supplemented by the Biblical doctrine of Wisdom[1].

Recently Prof. Rendel Harris has sought to derive the Johannine doctrine of the Logos primarily—indeed it would seem exclusively—from the last-named conception in the Old Testament. He suggests that "the way to the Logos is through Sophia and that the latter is the ancestress to the former," and not only so, but on the ground that "the Logos is quoted as being and doing just what Sophia is said to be and to do in the Book of Proverbs" he propounds the view that "the Logos in the Prologue to John is a substitute for Sophia in a previously existing composition[2]."

It will be convenient to consider first the theory last described. Prof. Rendel Harris would have done well,—even for the sake of his main contention, that in the Johannine Prologue "Wisdom" stood originally where "Word" now does—to distinguish between the conception of Wisdom on the one hand in Proverbs and Ecclesiasticus (where it is virtually the same), and on the other hand in the Wisdom of Solomon, marking the development in the latter, and to allow for the consequences of this development in the Fourth Gospel. In the following brief consideration of the theory we will give it the benefit of this modification[3].

[1] See Westcott, *Gospel according to St John*, Introd. (γ) under the heading *The author a Jew of Palestine*. He treats of the same subject in his early work, *Introduction to the Study of the Gospels*, ch. II, § 4. Dr Westcott did not say whether he would make a distinction between use by the evangelist of the doctrine of Wisdom in *Proverbs* and the Palestinian *Ecclesiasticus* and the Alexandrian *Wisdom of Solomon*.

[2] See *The Origin of the Prologue to St John's Gospel*, 1917, pp. 4–6.

In support of his theory of an evolution of a Logos-Christology from a Sophia-Christology, which had extended even to the substitution of "Logos" for "Sophia" in St John, he appeals to the prominent use by the Fathers from the second century onwards of Prov. viii among their proof-texts on the doctrine of the Person of Christ. See pp. 14 ff. I do not think anyone who considers how freely they were accustomed to quote, and also that no doubt there were not many, if any, passages in the Old Testament which could more directly illustrate or support the Church's Christology, will be much impressed by this argument. On p. 4 he writes, "if the Logos is quoted as being and doing just what Sophia is said to be and to do in the Book of Proverbs, then the equation between Logos and Sophia is justified." Surely because the language about Sophia corresponds to part, it does not follow that it covers the whole, of the conception of the Logos.

It should be needless to observe that although the Divine Wisdom might be regarded as visiting in its plenitude the Christ and might in a sense be identified with Him, there would be obvious objections which must have been felt from the first to using a feminine noun as an actual name for the Son of God.

[3] He makes no distinction between the Alexandrian *Wisdom of Solomon* and the two Palestinian writings, and notices (pp. 10 ff.) the former, composed not earlier than circ. B.C. 30, before the *Wisdom of Sirach*, composed circ. B.C. 200.

That the conception of the Divine Wisdom among the Hebrews, and its personification in the writings which have been mentioned formed part of the preparation for the doctrine of the Person of Christ expounded in the Fourth Gospel is denied by no one. Up to a certain point the Wisdom and the Logos were analogous ideas. And it may well have been also that expressions used of the Divine Wisdom in those writings were present to the evangelist's mind, and were employed by him, with regard to the Logos. The parallelism of his language does not indicate more than this. The real question is whether the various elements in the thought of the evangelist are to be found in the doctrine of Wisdom of the Sapiential books to the same extent as elsewhere[1].

In the Book of Proverbs and in Ecclesiasticus Wisdom is set forth as characteristic of all God's works and displayed in them, and therefore as prior to them. As personified she may be thought of as sharing His counsels; but it is He Who effects things. The notion of an *efficient* cause, of an instrument, or agent, is not connected with Wisdom, or at most only in a single expression in each of these books, in which expressions also the notion of skilful design is more prominent than that of force. On the other hand, in the Wisdom of Solomon she is said to be the "worker of all things" (ἡ πάντων τεχνῖτις), and is described in terms, some of which remind us of the subtle, all-pervading, all-penetrating *anima mundi* of the Stoics.

But even in the use of the word τεχνῖτις the intention may chiefly be to emphasise the skilfulness of the work, while in the passage as a whole it is the marvellousness of the universe as an object of knowledge with which the writer appears to be mainly occupied. Anyway he does not in the book as a whole consistently attribute force (as distinguished from designing and direction) to Wisdom, and even in this book as in the Canonical Old Testament, Divine power and operation are associated with His Word. We have two remarkable instances where signal Divine interpositions are to be described. "It was neither herb, nor mollifying plaister that restored them to health, but thy word, O Lord, which healeth all things[2]." And again, "Thine Almighty word leaped down from heaven out of thy royal throne, as a fierce man of war into the midst of a land of destruction[3]." In another passage also where both "word" and "wisdom" occur the more comprehensive creative action is associated with the former[4]:

---

[1] The chief passages to be examined are Prov. viii. 22–31; Ecclesiasticus i. 1–10, and xxiv; and Wisdom of Solomon vii. 22–28.
[2] xvi. 12.   [3] xviii. 15; see also context.
[4] ix. 1: Θεὲ πατέρων καὶ Κύριε τοῦ ἐλέους σου ὁ ποιήσας τὰ πάντα ἐν λόγῳ σου, καὶ τῇ σοφίᾳ σου κατεσκεύασας ἄνθρωπον.

"O God of my fathers, and Lord of mercy, who hast made all things with thy word, and ordained man through thy wisdom." It is moreover to be noted that the instrumental preposition ἐν is used before "thy word," whereas τῇ σοφίᾳ has no preposition and should probably be regarded as the dative of the manner rather than of the instrument.

It is further to be observed—and this is still more important—that while any true wisdom which men possess flows from the Divine Wisdom, and God's prophets derive thence their inspiration, the process of communication is here regarded as an inward one, or on its inner side. But God has also, according to the Old Testament, revealed His Mind and Will as it were objectively, and these objective revelations were made through His Word. As, therefore, the ideas of the exercise of Divine power in creation and in the sustenance of all things, and above all of an objective revelation of God, are so prominent in the Prologue to the Fourth Gospel, it seems to me altogether a mistake on the part of Prof. Rendel Harris that, when tracing the history of its thought, he should exclude almost entirely from view the teaching of the Old Testament and the Apocrypha about the Word of God, and confine his attention to that about the Divine Wisdom which certainly in regard to these points is decidedly less suggestive.

Dr Westcott has greatly the advantage in that he seeks to take account of the influence of both Biblical conceptions. But his theory does not supply the means of explaining their fusion, or of accounting in any other way for the difference between the idea of the Word not merely in the Old Testament itself but in the Targums, and in the Prologue to the Fourth Gospel. In the Targums the Memra is a personality, perhaps most resembling the Angel of the Lord. But his appearances are occasional on his being sent when a special Divine interposition is required. On the contrary in the Prologue we have the comprehensive statement of great truths about permanent Divine relations and operations, or such as connect together successive stages in a course of action which in principle is one throughout. And among these permanent relations there is included one internal to the Godhead for which the Targums afford no suggestion, though a resemblance to it may be found in some of the speculation in regard to Wisdom in the Sapiential books. The use of the Greek term λόγος which signifies both speech and reason, and had been employed also by Heraclitus and subsequently by the Stoics to denote a law and subtle force pervading the universe, afforded a means of combining different views. But it could hardly have done so for anyone who did not add to his knowledge of the Old Testament and Palestinian teaching upon it some slight acquaintance at least with Greek philosophy, or who had not at all events gone through a somewhat arduous process of reflection with a view to forming a comprehensive idea out of different applications of the term. Now since in the writings of Philo, composed 60 or more years before the Fourth Gospel, we find a doctrine of the Logos, which in certain of its broad features (to say at present no more) resembles that of the Prologue; since in Philo the Logos appears under a two-fold aspect, the one interior to the life of God, the other as conditioning God's relation to the universe; since there too it is through the Logos that God created and that He sustains and guides all things, and even the title Son of God is there given Him; since through the Logos He reveals Himself to man, and only in the Logos that He can be known, it is surely unreasonable to suppose that the thought of the Prologue is wholly independent of that of the Alexandrian School, of the doctrines of which the writings of Philo are the representatives to us[1].

[1] Philo distinguishes between the Logos in relation to the Cosmos, and as indwelling in God. This indwelling does not for Philo imply personal communion, but neither does the indwelling of Wisdom in God according to the Sapiential books do this. In Christian theology the terms ἐνδιάθετος and προφορικός have been used to distinguish between the Logos within the Godhead and as manifested in creation etc. It is to be observed that though Philo uses them to distinguish between reason in man and the spoken word, he does not use them to mark the analogous distinction in regard to God. The reason may be that in the use with respect to man he was following the Stoics, or (as Drummond suggests) that he felt it to be inappropriate to apply an adjective to God's expressed thought "which at once recalled a mouth and a tongue." On the whole subject see Drummond, *Philo*, II, pp. 171 ff.

Westcott, *ib.* writes, "When Philo speaks of 'the divine Logos' his thought is predominantly of the Divine Reason and not of the Divine Word. The conception of a Divine Word, that is of a Divine Will sensibly manifested in personal action, is not naturally derived from that of a Divine Reason." This is misleading. The *efficiency* of the Divine Logos in Creation, in Providence, and in the Revelation of God's character and Will is a fundamental principle of the Philonian doctrine. In connexion with the study of Philo, Zeller, *Phil. d. Griechen*, III. 2, II. 1, Soulier, *La Doctrine du Logos chez Philon d'Alexandrie*, and Drummond, *Philo Judaeus*, may be specially recommended.

The mystery-religions 187

§ 3. GENTILE RELIGIOUS THOUGHT AND FEELING[1].

Religious thought and feeling in the Græco-Roman world at the beginning and for the first centuries of our era, as every one knows who is even slightly acquainted with the period, contained many diverse elements strangely intermingled, and of which the precise nature and mutual relations are in some instances hard to determine. In order not unnecessarily to confuse the issues with which we are concerned in this volume, in themselves sufficiently complicated, it will be advisable to confine our attention as closely as possible to those features in connexion with which it is more or less probable or at least conceivable that Christian, and more particularly Johannine, thought may have been affected through actions and reactions from and upon surrounding conditions, or where at least instructive analogies may be observed. In regard to these also it must be our endeavour to indicate broadly the character of the phenomena, while avoiding as far as possible the mention of such details as are not important for our purpose.

One—perhaps the most outstanding—phenomenon which claims our attention is the spread of mystery-religions in the Græco-Roman world from a little before the Christian era, and for some three centuries after it. These mystery-religions have been the subject of a great deal of investigation and discussion in recent years. Some fresh evidence in regard to them has been brought to light through archæological discoveries, and there has been not a little speculation as to the causes and extent of the influence which they exerted. Even upon the thought of the Apostle Paul and the author of the Fourth Gospel it is supposed to have been important. There has been too much readiness in some quarters to put to their account tendencies of thought and of religious feeling which did not originate with them. It is easy to speak largely and loosely of "the mysteries-language," "the mysteries-literature" and "the mysteries-conceptions," wherever a mystical element is dis-

[1] *Die hellenistisch-römische Kultur in ihren Beziehungen zu Judentum und Christentum*, by P. Wendland, 1907, is the best comprehensive treatment of this subject.

cerned. But if care is not taken these are apt to be question-begging and misleading expressions.

In the age and the regions of the world we are considering there were various movements which were in some respects similar and congenial to one another, but which were in reality independent growths. They must be duly correlated, not confounded, if we would really understand the thought and feeling of the age; and this is in a peculiar manner necessary if we would do justice to the relations between them and the Pauline and Johannine literature.

But, first, let us consider the mystery-religions[1]. Through the intercourse of different races from the time of the conquests of Alexander onwards, religions of this kind emanating from Egypt and from the East took hold increasingly in the Greek Dispersion and among Romans, in spite of the opposition which as foreign cults they at first encountered. Their adoption amid populations which were not Greek, but had at least been familiarised to a certain extent with Hellenic culture, may perhaps seem stranger to us than it should, from our being chiefly acquainted with ancient Greece as represented in its literature and its philosophy when freest and greatest.

That there was nothing fundamentally uncongenial to the Greek temper, or new to Greek habits of mind, in the mystery form of religion will be apparent if we recall how great was the fame of the Eleusinian mysteries throughout the classical period, and how Greeks from far and near gathered together for them at the seasons when they were chiefly celebrated. Essentially these mysteries did not differ from other mysteries[2],

[1] On the subject of the mystery-religions let me name especially the following books: G. Anrich, *Das antike Mysterienwesen in seinem Einfluss auf das Christentum*, 1894; F. Cumont, *Les Religions Orientales dans le Paganisme Romain*, 1909; R. Reitzenstein, *Die hellenistischen Mysterien-Religionen*, 1910; Dieterich, *Eine Mithras-Liturgie*; A. Meyer, *Inwiefern sind die neutest. Vorstellungen von ausserbibl. Religionen beeinflusst*, 1910; P. Gardner, *The Religious Experience of St Paul*, esp. ch. IV, 1911; C. Clemen, *Einfluss der Mysterien-Religionen* in *Versuche und Vorarbeiten*, vol. XIII, 1913; H. A. A. Kennedy, *St Paul and the Mystery-Religions*, 1913; A. Loisy, *Les Mystères Païens et le Mystère Chrétien*, 1919.

For those readers who desire a single book on the subject, or one with which to begin their study of it, the first in the above list, though the earliest, is specially and strongly to be recommended.

[2] Reitzenstein, *Die hellenist. Myst.-Rel.* pp. 7, 9, sharply distinguishes between what he calls the "personal mysteries," and the "national or community mysteries,"

The mystery-religions

and it may be asked why, when in various parts of the world a demand for mysteries arose, men who had participated in ordinary Greek civilisation did not turn to those which Greeks had already learned to value, rather than to those of Isis and Osiris (or Sarapis) introduced from Egypt, or of Cybele from Asia Minor and Mithras from Syria or Persia. Possibly in the case of the former the local associations with a famous sanctuary were such as not to allow of their transplantation, while this was not the case in regard to the latter, the diffusion of which also happened to be favoured by special circumstances. One recommendation which the Egyptian rites had is obvious. They came from a land whose institutions were of great antiquity and whose priesthood laid claim to the possession of a lore handed down to them from a very distant past. Wisdom, more particularly knowledge of the origin and end of things, the secrets of the universe and of man's destiny, was generally held to have been to a peculiar degree the privilege of early ages. A similar advantage may have been supposed to belong in greater or less degree to other religions coming from the distant mysterious East.

Some adaptation also no doubt took place of the cults to fresh worshippers through the removal or modification of

as though there was a difference in kind. He is surely mistaken in this. Undoubtedly, when religious rites which had been wholly foreign, and were still regarded as such by most of the population, began to make their way in any region, individuals adopted them at first from strong personal conviction or hope, and the whole celebration of the connected worship, even those parts of it which were not necessarily secret, had to be confined within a small circle of worshippers who had banded themselves together. But there must have been a time when mysteries such as the Eleusinian, which became a great national institution, had passed through the stage of gradually winning acceptance. Moreover, while large numbers participated in certain public parts of the ritual, initiation continued always perforce to be an intensely personal affair, undergone probably in every generation only by the few. This is implied in the contrast which Plutarch draws (*De Consol.* 10 *init.*) between what he and his wife knew, as having been initiated, and common opinion. He does not say that the mysteries in which they had been initiated were the Eleusinian, but this is certainly most probable, true Greek as he was, and living as they did at Chæronea.

It may further be observed that the Mysteries of Isis in the centre from which they spread to the Græco-Roman world, the Ptolemaic kingdom, were most certainly an established state-religion, and there is also some reason to think that the most distinctive features of a mystery-religion were introduced into it there from Eleusis, not from Egypt. (See next note.)

features which might seem barbarous, and the assimilation of different mythologies to a greater or less extent[1].

But however recourse to these rites was facilitated for many whose ideas and habits of life were different from those of the races amid which they originated, and however it was encouraged, through the power which the ritual that was employed had to impress many natures, through the appeal it made to the imagination and the emotions, there is good reason to think that their success was due mainly to the idea itself and the aim which lay at the heart of them all. They were designed to give, and apparently often were able to give, to the initiated an assurance of safety in passing through death, and of happiness in another life.

Great obscurity surrounds the manner in which this assurance was conveyed by means of the experiences through which the initiated were taken. It probably differed somewhat in the case of different rites, but in all it was a secret which was jealously, and it would seem effectually, guarded. Precisely for this reason, when for no other, the presumption is in regard to any of the rites included in the mystery-cults which are actually described or to which there are express allusions, such as drinking of the "cyceon" in the Eleusinian mysteries, or even the "taurobolium" in the worship of Mithras, that its significance lay in its being, not itself the effectual thing, but an appointed step in the approach to participation in some final ceremony, or to the moment for hearing some authoritative utterance, which would be the consummation of the whole series of rites.

Nevertheless the chief purpose of all the mystery-cults without distinction may be gathered from those parts of them which were comparatively public, and about which we have information. In all of them purificatory rites figured largely, and it would seem that their intention was not only, and probably not so much, to fit the worshipper for the worship then

---

[1] In one important instance Eleusis itself seems to have exercised a direct influence in such adaptation. Early in the third century B.C. Timotheus, one of the Eumolpidæ, hailing thence, is said to have taken part along with Manetho, the learned Egyptian priest who wrote in Greek about the rites and creed of Egypt, in shaping the institutions of the famous Serapeum which Ptolemy Soter founded at Alexandria as part of his plan for uniting different classes of his subjects.

to be engaged in, as to remove stains which the soul had contracted through life in the flesh, and so to deliver it from liability to punishment and to render it capable of a better life in another world. The importance attached to the mysteries under this aspect is clearly indicated in a passage of Plutarch[1].

To the deities of the mystery-religions rule over the underworld in some way belonged, and in the legends connected with them the idea was involved of a struggle between life and death and the victory of life. The story was recalled of some super-human being who had undergone sufferings, and even met apparently with extinction, but who emerged triumphantly. The hope was here held out to the true devotee that he similarly would find deliverance from all his woes, and in the process undergone by himself a sure ground for this hope was given him, through the close knitting somehow of the bonds between himself and the god. He believed that there and then he was brought into a mystic fellowship with the divine being, and that he was delivered from the power of malign spirits. This would be of value even for the present life; but most valuable of all would be the pledge of safety thus afforded when the soul at death passed finally to another world.

The spread of the mystery-religions in this age is evidence that a sense of the reality of the world of spirits and anxiety about the life to come were widely experienced then. The calamities of the time have often been assigned as the reason for this. But for the generality of men, especially of the heathen population, the conditions of life were surely not peculiarly unfavourable in the first few centuries of the Roman Empire. The causes of movements of thought and feeling at a particular epoch are often hard to trace satisfactorily. In regard to that one which we are now considering it may not be possible to say more than that the great problems of the meaning of life and death, of the reality of a spiritual world, and of human destiny, are always there, and that it is natural that recurrently the minds of men—or of a larger number of them than usual, for that is all that actually happens—should turn to them, owing to satiety for the time being with other interests, if for no other reason. It is the fact that there was this widespread concern

---

[1] See *De Consol.*, passage referred to above, p. 189 n.

about another world at the commencement of our era which is of importance to us, however it is to be explained. To it the mystery-religions owed the fascination which they had for many minds, while at the same time undoubtedly they fostered it. They presupposed the ideas and fancies which had long been in men's minds as to punishments that might await men in that world and its possibilities of bliss; but they made them more vivid. They roused into activity both the fears and the hopes that might be entertained in regard to it, and offered a way of being delivered from the fears.

They also appeared to satisfy an aspiration for knowledge, namely that kind of knowledge so much coveted in that age which is not to be acquired through the perceptions of sense, or discourse of reasoning, but must come through Divine revelation. And yet it does not seem that the mysteries had anything of value to communicate, any doctrines to teach which were properly speaking their own. With the exception of that sense of the reality of something spiritual which they contrived to impart, men found there the ideas which they brought with them. In devotees whose conceptions of the world of spirits and the future state were of a low or commonplace type they served little if at all to raise them, but on the contrary led them to put confidence in rites as having a magical power to secure their future well-being. Hence Plutarch[1] who always treats the mysteries, as he does the Pagan religions in general, with respect, and who (as we have had occasion to remark) had himself been initiated, nevertheless thinks it necessary to utter a warning that they are liable to be misinterpreted, and if so to do serious harm. In order that we may learn the right lessons from them we must, he says, "take with us the teaching of philosophy as our mystagogue[2]."

This interesting remark of Plutarch's shews us that the philosophy, or quasi-philosophical thought, of the time had indeed its points of contact with the mystery-religions, but that it did not derive its ideas, or necessarily take its tone, from them. Bearing this in mind, we will now proceed to notice some of its characteristics.

[1] J. Oakesmith's *Religion of Plutarch* is a careful study.
[2] λόγον ἐκ τῆς φιλοσοφίας ἀναλαβόντες μυσταγωγόν, de Iside, 378 A, B.

On the one hand there was undoubtedly a growing disposition to adopt a monotheistic creed. In Greek philosophy the conviction had always made itself felt that the world was essentially one. In the generations near to and preceding the Christian era the pantheism of the Stoic philosophy in its own way encouraged the belief in the world's unity. Moreover, its adherents, especially it is believed under the influence of Poseidonius (circ. B.C. 135–50), in spite of the materialism which the school had formerly shewn, endeavoured to conceive an Invisible Universe which no less than the Visible formed a single, harmonious Order. Other thoughtful men, who were unable to rid themselves of the belief in a Divine Nature which was above and not a part of the world, fell back on Platonism and especially on those elements in it in which a religious and monotheistic attitude was most apparent. It may well be, also, that the teaching of Judaism, the representatives of which were so widely dispersed in the Græco-Roman world, had no inconsiderable effect in promoting monotheistic views. Large numbers of Gentiles actually we know became more or less closely attached to Judaism, and it is certainly possible that this Jewish faith in their midst may in a more secret and subtle manner have influenced other minds.

But the bent towards Monotheism was encountered by a strong attachment in many minds to inherited and established religious beliefs and practices. Many men, also, doubtless who did not value these highly themselves pretended to accept them out of deference to their wives for the sake of domestic peace, or because of the public opinion in their favour, and because they regarded them as a means of controlling the masses. The polytheism which threatened to become more irrational than ever through the combination of cults from different parts of the world was rendered a little more palatable to educated men by explanations to the effect that the gods worshipped in different countries were in reality the same gods known under different names. The endeavour was also made to discover valuable truths enigmatically taught in the various legends of the gods. But it was also recognised more or less clearly that something further was required. Polytheism had to be somehow reconciled with the principle of *monarchia* in the universe.

The gods whether they were regarded as having been always spirits, or according to the theory of Euhemerus, which exercised wide influence, as having been all or some of them deified men, were conceived of as all subordinate to one supreme Divine Being, or Principle. Thus by the great religious problem to which I have referred, which forced itself upon Gentile minds when polytheism began to be in danger of collapse through internal causes of decay, before the assault upon it by Christianity was made in full strength, attention was turned upon the spirit-world. The gods were already held to be of divers degrees of rank and power and as fulfilling various functions therein; imagination further filled it with a multitude of nameless spirits, some of them malicious, but many of them good, who were charged with messages to men, or entrusted with the continual shepherding in this present life of individual men.

The movement of thought of which I have been speaking arose among those who had received in the main a strictly Hellenic training. The writings of Plutarch classed as *Moralia* illustrate it well. I pass now to that pre-Christian Gnosticism, as we may term it, in which Oriental influences were far stronger. Out of it by a syncretistic process the Gnostic systems chiefly known to us through the Christian fathers grew. The non-Christian elements in these systems, those of a theoretic kind no less than distinctive usages, could in any case be most naturally supposed to have existed independently before their amalgamation with Christianity, and their history can to some extent be traced.

The Gnostic doctrines concerning the constitution of the universe as a series of concentric spheres under the government of their respective "archons," as also of the means by which the soul is to ascend till it attains to absorption in the Deity, had evidently required considerable intellectual effort to think them out; and certainly it was not merely by participation in rites such as those of the mystery-religions that they had been apprehended. The foundations of these doctrines, if not their more elaborated forms, are probably to be traced to the astrology taught by the learned priests of Babylon, and to ideas embodied in the religions of Persia and of ancient Egypt. The civilisations of these countries were what Cumont has well

Pre-Christian Gnosticism

described as "sacerdotal civilisations." But it does not follow that the religions they favoured were exclusively, or predominantly, of the mystery-type. And there is certainly no good reason to think that the learning of their priests, and the religious philosophy taught by them, were connected with any such feature. At the same time in the notion of *gnosis* which we find generally in Gnosticism, and which has suggested a class-name for its various systems and schools, the idea of *revelation* is included which is more plainly expressed in μυστήριον. And in part this idea in the Gnostic systems may be due to its origin in authoritative teaching by priests in close association with religious beliefs; though in part at least it is probably also due to the circumstance that, though they received contributions in course of time from Greek as well as Oriental sources, they sprang up among a people whose habits of thought were Oriental rather than Greek, intuitive rather than logical.

Some of the points on which I have touched are well illustrated in writings included in the *Corpus Hermeticum*. In the precise form in which we have it this collection belongs to the fourth century but there must be a ground-work which is considerably earlier, for there are references to it in Clement of Alexandria and Tertullian[1]. Gnostic doctrines are taught in these dialogues, but in a comparatively simple form. It is a curious point that they are put into the mouth of Hermes who imparts them to Thoth, a figure of Egyptian mythology, and to Asclepius, neither of whom apparently, when the instruction is given, has yet been deified, but who represent disciples of Gnosticism who are instructed in the process of being re-born and attaining to a perfect state. No expectation is shewn that

[1] Reitzenstein, the most recent writer upon the subject, maintains (*Poimandres*, pp. 11 ff.) that this ground-work belonged to the first century. His main reason is that he holds that the figure of the Shepherd in the Christian writing of the *Shepherd of Hermas*, belonging to the earlier part of the second century, was borrowed from that of *Poimandres* in which Hermes appears in treatise No. 1 of the *Corpus*. This is possible, but he does not seem to me fully to prove his point. See *Poimandres*, by R. Reitzenstein, 1904. This work includes an edition of cc. 1–13 (numbered by Reitzenstein 14) of the *Corpus*. There is a more comprehensive edition by G. Parthey, 1854.

any knowledge of divine things is to be derived from any mystery-religion. It is when pondering the subject of real things (τὰ ὄντα), and much perplexed thereby, that Thoth falls into a trance and receives instruction from Hermes[1]. Nowhere is there any indication that with a view to being granted knowledge a ceremonial initiation must be undergone. In preparation for having the hymn of new birth communicated to him, he is to stand under the open sky, looking towards the south, about the time of sunset, in complete silence[2]. The sacrifices that he is bidden to offer, and that he does offer, are λογικαὶ θυσίαι[3].

The value of the *Corpus Hermeticum* seems to me to consist largely in the fact that here we have a Gnostic strain which does not appear to be connected with any mystery-religion, for such use as is made of Egyptian and Greek mythology does not involve this. There is no justification for describing, with Reitzenstein, the teaching given as "the spiritualisation of the mystery-religions[4]," as though these had furnished the basis for it. Nor, on the other hand, is it associated with any Christian doctrines; nor does the teaching given appear to be offered out of hostility to Christianity, as a substitute for it, the spirit which animated some neo-Platonic writings.

The sketch of Gentile religious thought and feeling which I am here attempting, brief as it is, would be incomplete without an allusion to the magicians—miracle-workers and prophets —who in divers places arose and travelled about, and who claimed divine sonship, or to have Hermes, or some other god, dwelling in them, and who no doubt in some cases more or less sincerely believed it, and whose prayers that such an indwelling might be realised have been preserved to us on papyri which have come to light[5]. In this connexion, too, I may recall

---

[1] *Herm.* I. I.

[2] *Ib.* XIII. 1, 3, 4. Cp. I. 19–31. Plainly here it is not through the rites of any mystery-religion that salvation is attained.

[3] *Ib.* I. 31, XIII. 18, 19, 21.

[4] *Hell. Myst. Rel.* p. 25. This writer and some other recent writers seem to have had their balance of judgment quite upset in regard to the mystery-religions by their interest in them.

[5] For instances see Reitzenstein, *Poimandres*, pp. 17 ff., and the references there.

The Mysteries and Christianity

the well-known fact that divine honours were paid to Roman emperors both after death and while living, especially in the Eastern part of their dominions.

Into close contact with these beliefs and modes of thought the Apostle Paul and the author of the Fourth Gospel were brought as Christian teachers;—how were they affected by them? Owing to the abhorrence which from their Jewish training they naturally would, and plainly did, feel for idolatry, they would be repelled by the mystery-religions. There is no sign that they in any way distinguished these from any other heathen rites, or paid any special heed to them. It is, therefore, most unlikely that they could have consciously and of set purpose imitated them. Unconscious imitation would be possible, but is not to be hastily assumed. They do not, like Christian writers at the end of the second century and afterwards, contrast Christian with Pagan mysteries, in which case we might suspect a desire to shew that Christianity supplied what those whom they addressed craved for, which might have led to the introduction of, or at least to increased emphasis upon, features in Christian faith and worship akin to those of the Gentile mysteries. Further such terms as we find them using, which had any connexion with the mysteries—μυστήριον itself, and words signifying new-birth—had come to be more widely used, and from this wider usage they, like γνῶσις, would more probably be taken[1].

Again, where ideas and forms, which might conceivably have been derived from the Gentile mysteries or other Pagan observances, might also have had a Jewish origin, the latter is clearly the more probable. It is more natural to find a prece-

---

[1] μυστήριον had before St Paul's time been used by Jewish Alexandrian writers of a Divine knowledge to be communicated to the rightly disposed without participation in any mystic rites, e.g. Wisdom ii. 22, vi. 22, Ecclus. iii. 18, Philo, *de Cherub.* ch. xiv. Philo in the passage quoted implies a contrast with the heathen mysteries, but in part no doubt the use he made may have been suggested by a use disconnected from the mysteries which had already grown up.

For "new birth" see above, p. 70, the references to the *Corpus Hermeticum*; also Apuleius, *Metamorph.* XI, chs. 16, 21 and 27 ("reformatio"), and comp. note at end of this section. Cp. also "transfigurari," for a moral change in Seneca, *Ep.* 6, 53, 8, and 94, 48 (quoted by Wendland, *ib.* p. 46).

dent for the institution of Christian baptism in the Jewish baptisms of proselytes and in "John's baptism," and in point of fact the analogy in these cases is closer than in the use of ceremonial washings in any mystery-rites known to us; while the sacrifices under the Jewish law could teach anything that was to be learned from heathen sacrifices.

Nevertheless the strongly mystical element in Pauline and Johannine teaching—not merely in that connected with Baptism and the Eucharist, but as regards the whole life of the Christian—is a feature demanding comparison with a temper of mind which, as we have seen, was a characteristic of Gentile religion in that age, manifested in the vogue of the mystery-religions and in divers other ways as well. Unless I am much mistaken it should in its Christian manifestation—except in so far as it sprang out of distinctly Christian principles and beliefs—be regarded as belonging to the spirit and modes of thought of the age rather than as copied from any single contemporary phenomenon. Some students are far too apt to assume derivation on one side or the other when in any age they meet with parallel instances of thought and expression and practice. It is in point of fact to be expected that human minds working under similar conditions, subject more or less to the same general influences, should independently frame similar conceptions and express themselves similarly in word and act. In the case now in question some Pauline and Johannine language concerning the indwelling of one person in another, which may seem strange to us, is most probably to be explained, not by the idea having been transferred from the mystery-religions or magical formulæ, but by the want of definiteness in the conception of personality then prevailing.

Again, we have the titles "son of God" and "saviour" used in heathendom of some who in outward appearance were men, and in Christianity of One Who in outward appearance was a man. But we ought not to stop at a comparison as to the use of names. There was an underlying belief in heathendom, which was fundamentally a right belief, in the possibility of communion between God and man, and in the direct interposition of divine beings in the affairs of men through their actual presence in men. In Judaism such a belief in the pre-

The Mysteries and Christianity

sence of God in man was precluded by its far loftier conception of God, till at length even in Jewish hearts and minds it arose and was allowed free play, when One came Who could be regarded as in a true and unique sense the Son of the Most High in that He participated in His nature and was perfectly one with Him in character and will[1].

It will be suitable to compare Pauline and Johannine teaching with Gentile religion on one other point, the belief in a future life. It is only as regards the expected lot of the individual after death that there can be any comparison, and this in Christian teaching was subordinate to the expectation of the Return of Christ and triumph of the Kingdom of God. Herein we see the relation of Christian to Jewish teaching, in which latter also the happiness of Israel in a regenerated earth is the great object of hope. And in St Paul's eschatology, more particularly, what is most remarkable is the transfiguration of that hope into the conception of the coming final victory of Divine Goodness, which he sets forth in the Epistle to the Romans (chs. viii and xi).

It should be remembered that in Judaism also, in the interval between Old Testament times and the Christian era, there had been great development in ideas about the condition of souls after death before the day of resurrection, or without mention of it. Of this both Jewish Apocalypses and the Book of Wisdom afford evidence, and in these writings the reference is plainer and more direct than in the mystery-religions to the future punishment of wickedness and reward of virtue, and the righting of inequalities and injustices, apart from which there is nothing specially noble in the doctrine of a future life.

At the same time the widespread concern in the Gentile world about the future life, and occupation of men's minds with the spirit-world, may have helped to stimulate thought about the condition of the individual soul after death among

---

[1] The manner in which Gentile conceptions of divinity were affected by Polytheism is not sufficiently recognised by G. P. Wetter (*Der Sohn Gottes*, 1916). In heathenism we have this and that person claiming to be or described as "a son of a god," but no one who is ὁ υἱὸς τοῦ θεοῦ, the (unique) Son of the (One true) God, Mt. xxvi. 63; Mk xiv. 61. Dölger, *Icthys,* p. 395 f., rightly observes: "Das Wort θεός hatte in der Sprache des zweiten Jahrhunderts nicht den engen Sinn den wir Christen vom heute dem Worte geben."

Christians. Moreover, we may gather that for St Paul and the author of the Fourth Gospel the ground of hope for the individual Christian believer lay in the experience which he had of communion with Jesus in this life. It was inconceivable that one capable of this communion should perish. Even now he derived from Jesus a life which was essentially, one might almost say perceptibly, eternal, as being free from elements of decay. This was in some degree analogous to the ground of hope of continued existence offered in the mysteries, but distinguished therefrom by the intensely ethical character of Christian faith, and consequently of the communion with the Divine which it seeks. And clearly it was Christian experience itself which did teach the hope, and could have taught it even if there had been no mystery-religions.

ADDITIONAL REMARKS ON THE QUESTION OF THE INFLUENCE OF THE MYSTERY-RELIGIONS ON CHRISTIAN RITES, IDEAS AND LANGUAGE

As regards communion with the Deity through sacrifice, St Paul (1 Cor. x. 18-21) appeals first to the Jewish example: "Behold Israel after the flesh; have not they which eat the sacrifices communion with the altar?" In the sequel the Apostle also treats the partaking of the feast in the idol's temple (not specifically a rite of a "mystery-religion") as an act of communion.

On Prof. P. Gardner's theory of the origin of the Christian Eucharist let me quote Anrich's comment, *ib.* p. 111, "Als *Curiosum* erwähnt sei die Ableitung des Abendmahls aus den Eleusinien bei Percy Gardner, *The Origin of the Lord's Supper*, 1893. 'Der Centralpunkt der Eleusinienfeier appears to have been a sacred repast of which the initiated partook and by means of which they had communion with the gods,' p. 18 (davon ist nichts bekannt). 'Der Bericht des Paulus über die Einsetzung des Abendmahls, auf den alle übrigen Berichte zurückgingen, entstamme einer Vision desselben in Korinth ($\pi\alpha\rho\acute{\epsilon}\lambda\alpha\beta o\nu$ $\mathring{\alpha}\pi\grave{o}$ $\tau o\hat{u}$ $K\nu\rho\acute{\iota}o\nu$), zu der die in der Nähe gefeierten Eleusinien den Stoff geliefert.'"

The drinking of the Cyceon has been called a sacramental act, "doch mit zweifelhaftem Rechte," observes Anrich (*ib.* p. 29), "da uns leider ihre Bedeutung vollkommen unklar ist." As regards the source of ideas, we have the sprinkling with the blood of sacrifices

The Mysteries and Christianity

in the Mosaic ritual. This may be compared with the Taurobolium. As a matter of fact the latter does not appear to have been practised in the Græco-Roman world before the middle of the second century (cp. Cumont, *ib.* pp. 100 f., and Anrich, *ib.* p. 43), so that it is not likely to have been known to Christians of the Apostolic Age. But even if it had been, the figure of the sprinkling of the Blood of Christ would have been far more probably derived from the Old Testament, from which the author of the Epistle to the Hebrews actually takes it (chs. ix, x).

The idea that the god was eaten in the sacrificial meal does not appear before the second half of the second century A.D.

Baptism. In the account of preparation for initiation in Apuleius, *Metamorph.* xi, ch. 23 ff., a bath and sprinkling by the priest come first, but these are not in themselves the admission to a new spiritual position that even the Jewish baptisms mentioned above are. The completion of Baptism required according to Christian teaching was the laying on of hands which betokened the bestowal of the Holy Spirit, and which was suggested by its being a common sign of blessing among the Jews. It was not practised, so far as I am aware, as a mystery-rite. The bath and sprinkling are followed (not preceded) by a ten days' fast, and it is only after this that the priest takes Apuleius by the hand to lead him into the "penetralia." There is nothing in Apuleius' account to justify the statement of Reitzenstein [*Archiv für Religionswissenschaft*, p. 406] that after the bath "als Wiedergeborener wird dann der Täufling der Göttin vorgestellt." The idea of new birth is not connected by Apuleius with the bath, nor indeed with the process of initiation at any point, but with that moral transformation, figured by him as his restoration from the form of an ass to that of a man, as a sequel to which he became an aspirant for initiation into the mysteries. If the idea of new birth was associated with the mysteries themselves it was probably regarded as the result of the whole process of initiation.

§ 4. GNOSTICISM (COMMONLY SO CALLED).

In the last section some ideas came before us which I described as Gnostic, though they were not associated in any way with Christian teaching. But from the closing years of the first century to the latter part of the second, the integrity of the Christian Faith was, as is well known, menaced by attempts partly to combine such ideas with Christian doctrines, partly to conceal conceptions essentially incompatible with Christian Faith under Christian expressions. To these hybrid doctrines and systems the name of Gnosticism has commonly been given.

When we were engaged in examining the relations between the Fourth Gospel and the First Epistle of St John we met with evidence in both writings of the existence of such Gnostic errors at the time they were written[1]. We have now by considering this evidence in connexion with the history of Gnosticism to determine, if we can, the type of Gnosticism which the author of these writings knew. Was it Christian Gnosticism in an early stage, while it was still unsystematic, and the character of which was largely Oriental, or was it one of those elaborate systems, of which that of Basileides was the earliest, in the shaping of which ideas derived from Greek philosophy had a distinct share? The latter has been maintained by numerous critics from Baur onwards. In the former case the Fourth Gospel and the Johannine Epistles might have been written a little before or a little after the end of the first century; in the latter they could not be assigned to a much earlier time than circ. A.D. 130[2].

We shall see, I believe, that the indications which are to be found in the Johannine writings are not only all compatible with the form of Gnosticism aimed at being an early one, but that on the whole they suggest this.

As we have observed, it is not clear from the language used whether the Christological error pointed at was pure Docetism or "Cerinthianism." But even if we knew this it could make little or no difference as to fixing the date of the documents; for both these theories, it would appear, from such evidence as

---

[1] See above, pp. 93 ff.

[2] This approximately is the time to which, on account of their relations to Gnosticism, Pfleiderer assigns St John's Gospel and Epistles. "The Johannine theology," he writes, "is to be understood in the light of its connexion with and opposition to the Gnosticism of the Hadrianic period," *ib.* p. 167. So also Schmiedel, "Der Gnostizismus, mit dem der vierte Evangelist ganz vertraut ist, ja, den er nachdrücklich bekämpft, erst um das Jahr 100 in die christlichen Gemeinden eingedrungen ist....Joh. hat es aber schon mit einer fortgeschrittenern Gestalt des Gnostizismus zu tun. Nur die seit etwa 140 aufgekommenen Formen scheint er noch nicht zu kennen," *Evang. Briefe d. Joh.* II, p. 19.

we possess, had been put forth not later than the first years of the second century[1].

It is also noteworthy that this false teaching was communicated, or confirmed, by pretended utterances of the Spirit[2]. So far as we know such voices of the Spirit ceased soon after the Apostolic Age, only to be revived in Montanism, when the burthen of the utterances was of an entirely different character. For the nearest parallel to the present instance we have to go back to the assurance given by St Paul to the Corinthians that "no man speaking in the Spirit of God saith, Jesus is anathema; and no man can say, Jesus is Lord, but in the Holy Spirit" (1 Cor. xii. 3). He explains that it is necessary for him to instruct them as to this, because as Gentiles they had not been accustomed to spiritual gifts in their religion. The impostors here were probably Jews. The employment of such appeals to special inspiration in propagating doctrine would be far less natural among the representatives of Greek Gnosticism

---

[1] The tradition of the second century made Cerinthus a contemporary of the Apostle John. See Iren. *Adv. Hær.* III. iii. 4. Cp. Eus. *H.E.* III. 28. Cerinthus and his doctrine fell into the shade after the rise of the great Gnostic teachers of the second quarter of the second century. He is only briefly noticed by the writers on heresies, or passed over in silence, as by Clement of Alexandria. Pfleiderer perversely writes again and again, Basileides and Cerinthus. This is an inversion of the natural order and seems to suggest also that their teaching was the same. Their lives may have overlapped, but there is every reason to suppose that Cerinthus "flourished" before Basileides. Pfleiderer grossly and inexcusably misrepresents the views of Lightfoot as to the relations to one another in order of time of the Cerinthian and other forms of Docetism. Pfleiderer writes (*Primitive Christianity*, Eng. Trans. IV, pp. 156 f.): "As Lightfoot well remarks, the distinction is not to be overlooked that the Ignatian false teachers taught the pronounced Docetism which entirely denied that Christ had come in the flesh and declared His manhood to be a mere appearance, whereas the Ep. of John has only one passing allusion to this (iv. 2), and generally combats the milder Cerinthian Docetism or Dualism....But that is not, as seems generally to be thought, an earlier, but as Lightfoot has remarked with unquestionable justice, a later form of Gnostic Docetism which became less pronounced as time went on." Lightfoot expresses himself quite clearly in a manner which implies a view the opposite of that which Pfleiderer attributed to him. (*Apost. Frs.* Pt II, vol. I, pp. 379 f., 2nd ed.) He describes the Cerinthian form and that referred to in the Ignatian Epistles as "the two earlier forms," i.e. earlier than the Valentinian and than that ascribed by Irenæus to Basileides. He does not even imply that the one attacked in the Ignatian letters was the earlier of the two which preceded the Valentinian and Basileidian. On the contrary he mentions the Cerinthian first and says of the other "this type also appears on the confines of the Apostolic age."

[2] 1 Jn iv. 1, 2.

in A.D. 130 than among men of Jewish extraction, and partly Jewish training, twenty or thirty years earlier.

While the teachers who had separated from the Church, referred to by the writer of the First Epistle of St John, held erroneous views in regard to the Person of Christ (the subject on which, as was natural, differences first arose), they do not seem to have taught what he regarded as erroneous with respect to God as the Father and Creator. From the passage in which the author of the Epistle urges that no one can "have" the Father who does not truly receive and believe in the Son (ii. 22, 23), it may be inferred that the persons whom he has in mind desired to be orthodox as to the Father. He could not have written thus of Basileides and other later Gnostics, nor even it would seem of Cerinthus, if the account given by Irenæus (*Adv. Hær.* I. 26, 1) is correct[1]. Some critics have indeed discovered an allusion to the theory of the existence of two opposite principles in the words "God is light, and in him is no darkness at all" (1 Jn i. 5). However this may be, the emphasis there is laid wholly on the thought that he who would have fellowship with God must not live in the darkness of sin and lovelessness.

The proposition about God just quoted, like "God is love" (1 Jn iv. 8), and in the Fourth Gospel "God is Spirit" (iv. 24), shews that already in Christian circles men were occupied with the subject of the nature of God; but we have no indication that as yet Christian believers were likely to come in contact with speculations on this subject which were plainly at variance with Jewish as well as Christian faith.

We pass to another point. From the fact that the writer of the Epistle insists on the impossibility of there being any true knowledge of God which is dissociated from holiness of life and love of the brethren, some critics infer that he is thinking of those disciples of Gnosticism who maintained that the Gnostic is not subject to law, and who are charged by Church-writers with licentiousness of life[2]. But this reference in the words of the First Epistle of St John would not fit with what we know of the chief Gnostic Schools even of the second

---

[1] Cp. Wurm, *Bibl. Stud.* VIII, for 1903, pp. 3 f.
[2] Cp. Cone, *The Gospel and its earliest interpretations*, pp. 321 f.

the Gospel and First Epistle of John 205

quarter of the second century. According to the most trustworthy information which we possess such a charge could not be brought against the founders of these schools, but only against certain of their followers in the latter half of the century[1], which would now be generally admitted to be too late a date for the Johannine writings.

There is, however, good reason to think that the point of the rebuke of the writer of our Epistle has here sometimes been misapprehended. For it is evident that antinomianism could not have been combated by urging that ἡ ἁμαρτία ἐστιν ἡ ἀνομία. That saying implies that ἀνομία is recognised as a very grave thing, but suggests that there were those who excused themselves for committing acts which by an enlightened conscience were held to be sins on the ground that they were not breaches of "the law." They were in truth, he implies, breaches of the law as interpreted by the Gospel. The writer does not anywhere in the Epistle denounce gross sensual sins. He holds up before his readers a positive standard of conduct which is the highest conceivable, the purity and righteousness of Jesus Christ. The fault on which he dwells most is want of love to the brethren. We can well imagine that those who valued themselves on their "knowledge" may often have shewn contempt and want of consideration for simple Christians who may sometimes no doubt have been very ignorant. St Paul had to rebuke this spirit and the acts proceeding from it, among Corinthian Christians, at a considerably earlier time. Moreover, in separating themselves from the Church the false teachers had committed a very definite and grievous offence against love. Whether the writer has them in mind when he speaks of the duty of giving bread to the needy I do not feel sure. He may simply have been led on to this point as one

[1] With regard to the Basileidians Clem. Alex. (*Strom*. III. i. 3) expressly says that the licence, which the later ones claimed as the right of "the perfect," was not encouraged by οἱ προπάτορες τῶν δογμάτων. So also he attributes similar teaching to the successors of Carpocrates and Prodicus, not to these men themselves (*ib*. III. ii and IV. 30). Cp. also Irenæus, in speaking of Gnostics of his own time, "Ptolemæus and his party, the flowering of the School of Valentinus" (*Adv. Hær*. I. vi. 2, and Præf.). No weight can of course be attached to the statement of Hippolytus as to the immoral doctrine of Simon Magus (*Ref. Omn. Hær*. VI. 19), or the obiter dictum of Epiphanius in regard to Carpocrates (*Adv. Hær*. XXXVIII. 1).

connected with the subject of the practical observance of the law of love. It is, however, quite possible that such men might have been hard to the poor[1]. Just as there would seem to be a word pointed at them where it is said that "sin is lawlessness," so there may be when it is said (v. 17) that πᾶσα ἀδικία ἁμαρτία ἐστίν—"all unrighteousness"—one might almost venture to translate "every form of unfairness"—"is sin."

It clearly appears, also, that the flattery of the world had been a snare to them (iv. 5). It had induced in them a worldly temper, the love of preeminence among men, of pomp and show, and it may be also of money.

Unhappily there is no reason to think that, in order to find traits such as these in men professing in some sense to be Christians, it would be necessary to come down several decades in the second century.

Once more, it has been frequently said that the distinction drawn between "children of God" and "children of the devil" at 1 Jn iii. 10, and other similar language both in the Epistle and the Gospel[2], shews that the Gnostic idea of an absolute difference of nature between different men had been adopted.

If the force of those expressions in the Johannine writings is to be rightly estimated, they must be compared with similar ones in writings which have never been supposed to be infected with Gnosticism. In the interpretation of the parable of the tares we read, "the tares are the sons of the evil one" (Mt. xiii. 38); again, the scribes and Pharisees are said to make a proselyte "two-fold more a son of hell than themselves" (Mt. xxiii. 15); Paul, also, addresses Elymas the sorcerer as "son of the devil" (Acts xiii. 10). It will be generally admitted that the intention of these expressions in Matthew and Acts was to convey the idea that the men in question reflected the character of the devil as completely as if they had been his actual children[3]. The possibility would not be excluded that they

---

[1] Remarkable confirmation for this view may be found in a passage in which Ignatius speaks of the indifference of the heretical thinkers to the needs of the destitute. *Ad Smyrn.* VI. 2. Ignatius does not accuse them of sensuality.

[2] See above, p. 95 n.

[3] Other expressions which illustrate this use of the idea of parentage are γεννήματα ἐχιδνῶν (Mt. iii. 7, Lk. iii. 7), and υἱοὶ ἀπειθείας (Eph. ii. 2, v. 6).

had through their own fault surrendered themselves to become what they had shewn themselves to be. The case may be the same with the corresponding expressions in the Johannine writings. So also those who were "of the world," or "of the things below," had suffered themselves to become impregnated with the spirit of the world.

Again, the idea conveyed in the title "the prince of this world" is the same as in the figure of "the strong man armed who keepeth his goods," or in the offer of Satan in the temptation in the wilderness to give to Jesus all the kingdoms of the world and the glory of them.

Whether the creed of the author of the First Epistle of St John and of the Fourth Gospel was Dualism, or not, depends on whether he held that the power of the devil had, or had not, been allowed to arise, and might, or might not, at any moment be terminated, by the Will of God. On a review of the teaching of these writings there can, as it seems to me, be no doubt that the former is the true alternative[1].

But be this as it may, I would observe that the Dualism—if Dualism it is—of the Johannine writings is a moral and spiritual one. There is no contrast suggested between spirit and finer and grosser forms of matter, nor between the absolute and the finite. It has an affinity with the Dualism of the East, by which Jewish thought before the Christian Era, and through Judaism Christianity from the time of its rise, had been affected, not with the doctrine of the Greek Gnostics, such as Basileides and Valentinus, who were not properly speaking "dualists," but whose aim was to reconcile, if they could, the Monism of Greek philosophy with those aspects of human nature and of the world to which the dualistic thought of the East had drawn attention[2].

---

[1] It may also be pointed out that at Jn viii. 44 it seems to be implied that the devil was not originally what he afterwards became. "He *stood not* in the truth."

[2] It may be right to notice an argument of Holtzmann's, *Z. f. Prot. Theol.* VIII, p. 336. He observes that "the Gnostics" (in 1 Jn) "now stand outside (ii. 19) and form their own conventicles, which at all events could first happen in the course of the second century." But surely, that the heretical teachers should draw off, and arrange for meetings of their own partisans, as soon as they had any, in some private house or elsewhere, is no more strange than the action of

Seeing then that the traits which are distinctive of the fully developed Gnostic systems of the second century are absent from the Gnostic thought of the existence of which the Johannine Epistles and Gospel give evidence, these writings ought to be referred to an earlier period and may reasonably be placed at the end of the first or beginning of the second century, by which time Gnosticism in its incipient stage was already affecting Christian teaching[1].

St Paul described at Acts xviii. 7, xix. 9, and is indeed what would naturally happen in similar circumstances among any set of people in any generation.

[1] In confirmation of this conclusion I may cite the strong and clearly given judgments of Loisy quoted above, p. 13; and of v. Soden: " Die Irrlehre (in 1 Jn) trägt nirgends Züge die ins zweite Jahrhundert wiesen," *Urchrist. Litt.-gesch.* p. 195.

CHAPTER VI

THE FOURTH GOSPEL AND THE SYNOPTICS

THUS far in the present volume, and in the two preceding, I have been examining the evidence, external and internal, as to the dates of our Gospels, the conditions under which they were produced, and the influences affecting the writers, because right conclusions on these points may help us to form a true estimate of their value severally as historical documents. But in the subject of the present chapter we are at once brought face to face with important aspects of the history itself. The difference between the Synoptic representation of the Person and the Ministry of Jesus and that in the Fourth Gospel is such that we are compelled to ask whether we can use them both. To many critics it has seemed to be a case of *entweder-oder*. *Either one or the other*—they contend—must be adopted as our guide, while we decline to follow the other; and they give their preference to the Synoptics. Although they do not by any means regard them as fully trustworthy, they hold them to be so by comparison with the fourth evangelist. It is held that a presumption in favour of the Synoptic accounts is raised by their greater naturalness and lifelikeness, and the absence of the appearance of any such special doctrinal purpose as there is in the case of the Fourth Gospel, by which their character as narrators might be impaired. And it is held also that the result of a detailed comparison is to demonstrate their superiority to such an extent and in so many instances that, even where the best case can be made out for the Fourth Gospel, it is most probable that the others are in the right.

In regard to the view which I have just described—the *entweder-oder* one—Dr Moffatt in his *Introduction to the Literature of the New Testament*[1] has indeed declared that "the day is now over, or almost over" for it. I should be glad to think it completely antiquated, and I believe it may become so.

[1] P. 540.

Liberal critics as well as conservative ones have had to abandon many positions in the course of time, and they should realise that they may have to abandon more. But for the present that *entweder-oder* view must still, it seems to me, be reckoned with by anyone who desires to make sure of his own position in regard to the Fourth Gospel.

I would ask that the present attempt, to see whether information supplied by the various documents ought not to be in some measure combined, should not be regarded with suspicion because of the unsatisfactory methods of the Harmonists in former generations. No instructed student would employ those methods now. Where there are clear contradictions it must be recognised that one or other statement is erroneous. In all the writers concerned there may in many cases be imperfect accuracy. In reports handed down for a considerable period orally before being committed to writing this would be inevitable apart from a Divine interposition, which there is no good ground for assuming. On the contrary, it is evident that the evangelists, as also the other Scriptural writers, however truly they may have been in certain respects inspired, were in others left to the use of their ordinary human faculties and consequently liable to error. It will not, therefore, be legitimate to adopt the Harmonistic device of assuming that narratives which resemble one another in two or more Gospels do not refer to the same occasion, because of differences by which they are marked, where we should make no such assumption in a similar instance in comparing other ancient documents. For reasoning of this kind it may certainly be said "the day is now over." But again with regard to the explanation offered for some discrepancies by writers who did not adhere to the doctrine of Scriptural infallibility, but who were concerned to defend the Johannine authorship[1], that owing to advanced age the Apostle's memory was at fault, I would observe that I shall not be tempted to have recourse to this expedient because, as I have said, it seems to me most probable that the author of the Gospel according to St John was at most a disciple of the Apostle, not the Apostle himself. And as we shall not apologise for the author, when he does not

---

[1] E.g. B. Weiss.

appear to be in the right, on the ground that he was old, so also we shall not maintain that he necessarily possessed a more intimate knowledge of all the facts than the other evangelists. But on the other hand there are strong objections against supposing, as many modern critics are ready to do, that while the resemblances were derived by him from what he read in the other Gospels, the differences are due to his having been guided in the use of their narratives simply by the desire to illustrate his own leading ideas and to work out the plan of his Gospel in the manner that seemed to him most effective, or that he found most convenient. At whatever precise epoch he wrote, and however different his idea of the duties of a historian were from ours, it would have been strange that he should have been so indifferent to historical truth, and to the Synoptic Gospels as authorities, if they were his only ones. I am well aware that his conception of truth was not primarily that of truth to external fact. But it seems to me that a sense of the importance of the latter must have been included in his larger notion of truth in such a manner as would have prevented him from wholly disregarding external evidence as to facts, especially as unquestionably he believed God's supreme revelation to have been made through the facts of a human life.

We should probably indeed be compelled to make that hypothesis of mere invention on the part of the author, if the composition had to be placed as it was by Baur and his earlier followers at, or later than, the middle of the second century, and we might likewise be so if we were driven to adopt the latest date now suggested, namely, circ. A.D. 130. But we have seen that there is no good reason for placing it later than quite the beginning of the second century, and that it may have been written some years earlier than this. Living at this time the author might well have been a man who had derived information at first hand from one of the Twelve; and apart from this traditions might then still have been current in the Church, which were independent of those in the Synoptic Gospels.

Moreover, consideration for the views of other Christians would provide a check on his following his own fancies. If he was, as is most probable, the writer of the First Ep. of St John, he was a pastor no less than a theologian and thinker—a man who was living in the most intimate communion with, and felt the most anxious solicitude for, the general body of Christians in the district where he lived. If the same man was not the evangelist, the latter was at least one of the same spirit. He would not be the man lightly to run counter to what the Christian flock had been commonly taught.

I do not mean that the evangelist's own ideas as to what was fitting may not have helped to shape his conception of events, but that there were limits to the extent to which he could feel himself to be independent of external proof. Still less need it be supposed that what he had read of certain occurrences may not have affected his narration of others, without his having in reality confused them. Such influences may have combined with what he independently knew in determining the form of his own accounts. But along with this the probability of the presence of historical elements in this Gospel, even when it diverges from the other Gospels, must be allowed. Tradition itself, which might weave the narrative of the same event, or set of events, into a different connexion, may have been responsible for the divergence, and the truer form of the tradition may lie behind the Fourth Gospel. Moreover, although, as I have already said, we must be cautious about reckoning similar events as different because of discrepancies between various documents, yet when the marks of identity are not clear, we may fairly bear in mind that history does sometimes repeat itself.

Most interesting and important will be the consideration of those cases in which there is a correspondence between the Synoptics and the Fourth Gospel of a subtle kind, namely, a real likeness but one shewing itself in different situations and largely in a different manner, or again in broad features of the Lord's Ministry and its reception; or where thoughts much dwelt on in Christ's teaching in the Fourth Gospel appear, even if only partially, in certain sayings rare of their kind in the Synoptics. In such cases it may justly be said that there is mutual confirmation.

In order that we may rightly compare the Synoptics and the Fourth Gospel we must bear in mind the history of the composition of, and mental tendencies displayed in, the former as well as the latter. They, too, as historical witnesses have their drawbacks—drawbacks which are commonly far too much ignored when it is a question of comparing them with the Fourth Gospel. Misrepresentations can arise through lack of insight and reflection on the part of narrators and expositors as well as through prolonged meditation. Few, if any, students of the Gospels, familiar with critical methods, would (I believe) at the present day maintain—and it is not here pretended that it would be possible to do so satisfactorily—that the Fourth Gospel has in reproducing the teaching of Jesus preserved it in all respects in its original form, or according to the true proportion of different parts. But this cannot be said of the Synoptics either, and it is therefore a question deserving of earnest and repeated examination whether they and the Fourth Gospel may not act as correctives to one another. It has often been in the past, and is sometimes still, too little acknowledged, that although the course of the narrative in the former may appear to be more continuous, yet the slightness of the records embodied therein, and the elementary character of the information required by those to whom the Gospel-message was first delivered, taken with the plan of the Fourth Gospel as a mere selection of typical scenes and discourses, lessen the force of objections founded on omissions, or differences of arrangement; while on the other hand, the significance of comparatively slight notices is thereby increased. It should be remembered, also, that the value of particular contributions from one side or the other cannot be a question of mere quantitative measurement. This in itself is a reason for giving full consideration to any addition to our knowledge which may be furnished by the Fourth Gospel. One fact may obviously chance to be of far greater importance than many others; still more may the evidence for one trait, in framing our conception of a character. Moreover, much in the records of the past besides the literal reproduction of a great man's sayings, or exact account of his actions, may be of the highest significance for our knowledge of him. The impression that we perceive was made by an original personality may be the most momentous of all historical facts about him, even when the evidence of that impression is to be seen chiefly in the stimulus given to other minds, which have proceeded to work to a greater or less degree after their own manner. But assuredly we should generally be able from the impression made to infer not only that the personal influence which made it was a powerful one, but also something as to the character and methods of thought and action of him who produced it.

In the following comparison of the Fourth Gospel and the Synoptics we shall be compelled to go over much ground that has been well-trodden and is more or less familiar to all students of the Gospels. But this cannot be avoided in an attempt to deal comprehensively with the Gospels as historical documents, such as that made in the present work. Before we consider the treatment of the history by them respectively, and the questions of historical and psychological verisimilitude involved therein, it will be well, I think, to examine the evidence for the use of the first three Gospels by the Fourth, mainly as arising from similarities of expression, apart from the treatment of the history by them respectively.

The Use of the Synoptic Gospels by the Fourth Evangelist.

In proof of use the amount of agreement in subject-matter and of phrasing cannot of course be produced which was forthcoming when the use of the Marcan document by our first and third evangelists was in question; and it is not required because it evidently suited the plan and disposition of the fourth evangelist to be more independent in the treatment of his subject; and further because his Gospel was later, and as years passed, it would necessarily have been more difficult to preserve close agreement through oral tradition, so that for a smaller amount of agreement than before one must have recourse to the explanation of a documentary connexion.

It will be most satisfactory, I think, to consider *first* the parallelisms where they are found in incidents and episodes which clearly appear to be the same. Under this head, if there are several points of agreement between the Fourth Gospel and the three others the fact will be stated in general terms, and the reader will be left to refer to them if he desires to do

acquaintance with the Synoptic Gospels 215

so. Whether these common agreements should be accounted for by the fourth evangelist's use of one of the three in particular will be considered at the end of our review of all the facts. Agreements specially with one or with two of the Gospels will be expressly mentioned. *Secondly*, the instances will be taken in which words might have been suggested to the fourth evangelist in the description of a different event, or his imagination stimulated to introduce a trait, or to mould a fresh narrative, by what he had read in one of the others. Here a distinction will be made between what appear to be the more and the less probable cases. *Lastly*, we will notice sayings occurring in the Fourth Gospel and in one or more of the Synoptics, but differently placed.

I. Agreements with portions of narrative.

1. *Testimony of John Baptist: sign at Baptism of Jesus.* Jn i. 19–28, 33–34; Mt. iii. 11, 16; Mk i. 7, 8, 10; Lk. iii. 16, 22. Besides agreeing in various points with the three Synoptics, Jn agrees with Mk and Lk. against Mt. in having the figure of loosing the shoe-latchet instead of carrying the shoes; and with Mk against both Mt. and Lk. in not adding καὶ πυρί to πνεύματι ἁγίῳ.

2. *Allusion to John the Baptist's imprisonment.* Jn iii. 24, it had not taken place and Jesus was still in Judæa. In Mt. iv. 12, Mk i. 14, John's imprisonment is used to mark the time when Jesus began His Ministry in Galilee. In Lk. iii. 20, it is recorded without being connected with the Ministry of Jesus.

3. *Andrew Simon's brother; and the name Cephas, i.e. Peter, given to Simon.* Jn i. 40–42, vi. 8; Mt. iv. 18, x. 2; Mk i. 16; Lk. vi. 14; Mt. xvi. 18; Mk iii. 16; Lk. vi. 14.

4. *Feeding the five thousand.* Jn vi. 1–15; Mt. xiv. 13–21; Mk vi. 31–44; Lk. ix. 10*b*–17. Besides agreements with the three Synoptics, Jn has, like Mt. and Lk., that the multitude ἠκολούθει αὐτῷ. The same phrase is, however, also used in Mk in preceding chap. (v. 24). A more noticeable point is that according to Mk the disciples asked whether they should buy 200 denarii worth of bread, which is not in Mt. or Lk., and that Jn puts into the mouth of Philip the observation that 200 denarii worth of bread would not be sufficient. In Jn, Mk and

Mt. but not in Lk., the grass for the multitude to sit on is mentioned.

5. *The crossing of the lake which followed upon the feeding of five thousand.* Jn vi. 15-21; Mt. xiv. 22-28, 32, 33; Mk vi. 45-52; Jn, like Mk, refers to the disciples rowing (ἐλαύνειν); he has σταδίους like Mt. but adds an approximate number in place of Mt.'s "many." There is no reference in Jn to the incident with regard to Peter told in Mt.

6. *The demand for a sign like "the bread from heaven" which Moses gave.* Jn vi. 30-32. Cp. the demand for "a sign from heaven," Mt. xvi. 1-4; Mk viii. 11, 12; Lk. xi. 16.

7. *"The twelve."* Jn vi. 67, 70, 71, xx. 24; Mt. x, xx. 17, xxvi. 14; Mk iii. 14, 16 etc.; Lk. vi. 13 etc.

8. *The anointing at Bethany.* Jn xii. 1-11. There are agreements with both Mt. xxvi. 6-13, and Mk xiv. 3-9. Jn has with Mk alone νάρδου πιστικῆς, and likewise with Mk alone gives 300 denarii as the price at which it might have been sold, though the latter prefixes ἐπάνω. Again Jn has ἄφες αὐτήν like Mk's ἄφετε αὐτήν, whereas in Mt. a different phrase is employed. On the other hand, there is a slight similarity between Jn and Mt. in that in Mt. "the disciples" murmur, and in Jn "one of the disciples," namely Judas, whereas in Mk it is "certain persons."

9. *The foreknowledge and prediction of the betrayal.* Special emphasis is laid in the Fourth Gospel on the act of the traitor. For his Satanic inspiration, Jn xiii. 2 and 27 are to be compared with Lk. xxii. 3.

10. *Jesus withdraws after the Last Supper beyond the brook Kedron.* Jn xviii. 1: in the Synoptics the place is described as the Mt of Olives; Mt. xxvi. 30; Mk xiv. 26; Lk. xxii. 39.

11. *The arrest.* Jn xviii. 3-10; Mt. xxvi. 47-52; Mk xiv. 43-49; Lk. xxii. 47-51. Besides agreements with all three Synoptics, we have βάλε τὴν μάχαιραν εἰς τὴν θήκην with, in Mt., ἀπόστρεψον τὴν μάχαιράν σου εἰς τὸν τόπον αὐτῆς, and the *right* ear as in Lk.

12. *Peter obtains admission into the high priest's house, and his denials of Jesus.* Jn xviii. 15-18, 25-27; Mt. xxvi. 58, 69-75; Mk xiv. 54, 66-72; Lk. xxii. 54-62. Besides agreements with all three Synoptics, Jn like Mt. and Mk separates

acquaintance with the Synoptic Gospels

the mention of the entry of Peter from the denials, whereas Lk. tells the whole story of Peter in the high priest's house continuously. Jn and Mk speak of Peter "warming himself"; Lk. is more periphrastic.

13. *The trial in the high priest's house.* Annas, according to Jn, after interviewing Jesus sends Him to Caiaphas, xviii. 23. In Mt. and Mk there is a trial in the night; in Lk. in the morning.

14. *The trial before Pilate.* Jn xviii. 28–xix. 16; Mt. xxvii. 11–31; Mk xv. 1–20; Lk. xxiii. 1–25. There are agreements with the three Synoptics in common, and some with Mt. and Mk but not with Lk. Cp. the form of the question about releasing Jesus in Jn *v.* 39 with Mk *v.* 9. It should be noticed that there is no trace in Jn of the additions which in Mt. and Lk. are made here to Mk.

15. *The Crucifixion.* Jn xix. 17–30; Mt. xxvii. 33–50; Mk xv. 22–37; Lk. xxiii. 33–49. There are agreements with the three Synoptics in common, but the name of place, Golgotha, given as in Mt. and Mk is not given in Lk. The sour wine also is offered as in Mt. and Mk just before the end; in Lk. it is offered earlier by the soldiers in sport.

16. *The body of Jesus is obtained from Pilate by Joseph of Arimathæa and the Burial.* So also in the three Synoptics; but in Jn Nicodemus is joined with Joseph in the Burial. Jn xix. 38–42; Mt. xxvii. 57–61; Mk xv. 42–47; Lk. xxiii. 50–56.

II. Possible reminiscences of other (distinct) narratives.

(*a*) *The more probable instances.*

1. Jn vi. 3 introduces the account of the Feeding of five thousand, as Mt. xv. 29 does that of the four thousand, by stating that Jesus "went up into the mountain and sat there."

2. *Miracles on the Sabbath are an offence in Jerusalem as well as in Galilee.* Jn v. 9, 10, 16, vii. 22, 23, ix. 14; Mt. xii. 10; Mk iii. 1, 2; Lk. vi. 7.

3. *The impotent man at the pool of Bethesda, like the paralytic at Capernaum, is bidden to take up his bed and walk.* Jn v. 8; Mt. ix. 6; Mk ii. 11, 12; Lk. v. 24. The same word for bed κράβαττον is used in Jn as in Mk; in Mt. there is κλίνην and in Lk. κλινίδιον.

4. *Jesus heals a blind man in Jerusalem by anointing his eyes with clay moistened with His spittle.* Jn ix. 6, 7. In Mk vii. 32–34 He anoints the ears of a deaf man, and in Mk viii. 22–26 the eyes of a blind man, with His spittle.

5. *An anticipation and an echo of the Agony in Gethsemane.* Jn xii. 27 and xviii. 11; Mt. xxvi. 38, 39; Mk xiv. 34–36; Lk. xxii. 42. Compare especially with Mk where there is parallelism with the expression at the former passage in Jn.

6. *A voice from heaven.* Jn xii. 28 may be compared with the voice at the Baptism and Transfiguration.

7. *The meal at Bethany and the two sisters, Martha and Mary, of whom Martha served,* may be compared with the meal in "a certain village," Lk. x. 38 ff., where there were the same two sisters and the same one served. Some touches might conceivably have been suggested to the fourth evangelist by Lk. vii. 36 ff.

(*b*) *Instances suggested on much slighter grounds.*

1. At Jn ii. 4 Jesus declines to act on a hint from His mother, while at Mt. xii. 46 ff. = Mk iii. 31 ff. = Lk. viii. 19 ff. He refuses to be interrupted by His mother and brethren in His teaching. But the occasions are not similar and the spirit and the purpose of the intervention are not the same.

2. Some critics have held that the narrative of the raising of Lazarus was suggested to the fourth evangelist by the parable of Dives and Lazarus in Lk. xvi. 19 ff. The associations of ideas that are traced are far too subtle to be probable, and the whole theory is connected with a distorted conception of the evangelist's allegorising tendency.

III. Sayings differently placed.

1. "*A prophet hath no honour etc.*" Jn iv. 44; Mt. xiii. 57; Mk vi. 4; Lk. iv. 24. This saying is introduced at different points and perhaps with different intention, but is employed as in the Synoptics to describe a feature of the Ministry of Jesus. It is nearer in form to Mt. and Mk than to Lk.

2. *Quotation from Is. xii. 35 on spiritual blindness;* placed, Jn xii. 39, 40, in the final condemnation of the Jews by the

evangelist. In the Synoptics it is placed in connexion with the teaching by parables: Mt. xiii. 13; Mk iv. 12; Lk. viii. 10. It is found again Acts xxviii. 26, and was doubtless a quotation often made by early Christians.

3. "*He that loveth his life etc.*"; placed Jn xii. 25 in the last days at Jerusalem after the saying about "the corn of wheat"; in the Synoptic Outline after the prediction by Jesus of His crucifixion: Mt. xvi. 25; Mk viii. 35; Lk. ix. 24. There is also a similar saying in the charge to the disciples, Mt. x. 39 (Lk. xvii. 33). The phrasing in Jn is not so close to the latter as to the former, and here it is somewhat nearer to Mk and Lk. than to Mt.

4. "*He that receiveth whomsoever I send etc.*"; placed Jn xiii. 20 at Last Supper. At Mt. x. 40 in charge to disciples, and at Lk. x. 16 though not so close. Used also in Synoptic Outline in connexion with the dispute among the disciples about precedence, and the example of receiving a child: Mt. xviii. 5; Mk ix. 37; Lk. ix. 48.

5. "*The servant is not greater than his lord etc.*" Jn xiii. 16, after the feet-washing and referred to again xv. 20. Cp. Lk. vi. 40.

We may now summarise as follows:—in the 16 sections in which we have noted above definite parallelisms of narration between the Fourth and other Gospels, the parallelism is not merely generally but fully covered by Mk, except in 5 and 11, in each of which there is one parallelism specially with Mt., and in the second of these one slighter one with Lk. There are also very noticeable points and expressions common only to Jn and Mk in 1, 4, 5, 8, 12, 14. There is no trace even of the whole incidents which we find added by Mt. and Lk. to Mk in Marcan contexts. As to suggestions which might have been taken by Jn from distinct though similar accounts in one of the other Gospels, we have one from Mt. in (*a*) 1; but the source of those noted in (*a*) 3, 4, 5, must be looked for in Mk; while it is also not necessary to go beyond Mk for those in (*a*) 2 and 6. Those in (*a*) 7 if derived are from Lk. Further it is specially noteworthy that all the *sayings* of Jesus which in form closely resemble any in the Synoptic Gospels are contained in Mk. The absence of any Logian matter closely corresponding with Mt. and Lk., as well as other matter of the same kind contained in one or other of these two Gospels, is singular. Reference may here be made to the healing of the king's officer's son in Jn iv. 46–54, which bears much resemblance to that of the centurion's servant in Mt. viii. 5 ff. and Lk. vii. 2 ff., not improbably derived by them from the Logian document[1]. The differences in the Fourth Gospel are such that the evangelist can hardly have taken it from either of them. A different rendering orally made may have been the channel through which he came to know it.

From these facts we must draw our conclusions as to the fourth evangelist's acquaintance with the other Gospels, and they may give rise also to some interesting speculation on the early circulation of the several Gospels. The parallels with St Mark certainly seem to afford evidence of an amount and kind sufficient to prove that the fourth evangelist knew that Gospel fairly well. That he knew either of the others seems more than doubtful, and strange as this may seem at first sight, it is hardly to be considered so when allowance is made for the conditions which then hindered the rapid multiplication and distribution of copies of books. It should also be remembered that the interval between the composition of the Fourth Gospel and the two later Synoptics need not have been of more than one or two decades, if so much, and that these two Gospels were probably produced in other parts of the Christian Church.

From the limited question whether or to what extent the fourth evangelist was acquainted with and has used the Synoptics we will now pass to such a comparison of their representations of the Gospel-history, including the teaching reported, as must involve an endeavour to determine how the case for historical probability stands between them, or to what degree they may fairly be taken to supplement one another.

We have to compare some Johannine and Synoptic accounts which differ materially, though the events intended are plainly the same. But to a large extent the events which the fourth evangelist has chosen to relate are not the same, and are placed

---

[1] See vol. II, p. 85.

The work of John the Baptist

by him through indications of time, of which he gives more and clearer ones than the Synoptics, in periods which are left unoccupied, or nearly so, in their narratives. Discrepancies of the same kind cannot occur here; but the question has to be faced whether, in spite of the silence of the Synoptics, these portions of the Johannine narrative have a historical basis.

Lastly, there is the strange fact of the attribution to Jesus in the Fourth Gospel and the Synoptics of teaching in the main so different. We have to ask whether room is left in the Fourth Gospel for teaching similar to the Synoptics; and more important still whether there are not indications in the Synoptics of conceptions in the mind of Jesus which might furnish at least the great themes enlarged upon by the evangelist in the discourses of the Fourth Gospel.

The work of John the Baptist in its relation to the Ministry of Jesus Christ. Mt. iii. 1-17, iv. 12, xi. 1 ff.; Mk i. 1-11, 14; Lk. iii. 1-22, vii. 18 ff.; Jn i. 6, 15, 19-36, iii. 22-36.

The fourth evangelist, no less than the Synoptics, introduces the Gospel-history by treating of this subject. With a view to a fair comparison between the accounts it is important in the first place to note that the Synoptic one virtually ends with the Baptism of Jesus, while the whole of the Baptist's testimony related by the fourth evangelist is represented as subsequent to it. Further the latter says nothing of the widely extended work of the Baptist in preaching repentance among all classes as a preparation for the Coming of the Kingdom of God. He is concerned only with the Baptist's testimony to Jesus as the Christ, the Son of God, the Lamb of God.

In the accounts of the Synoptics it is a point of great interest to notice that according to both St Mark and St Matthew the vision of the descent of the Spirit in the form of a dove was seen by Jesus; while according to St Mark and St Luke the words from heaven were also addressed personally to Him. This address in the second person, in place of the announcement in the third person, which we find in the parallel in St Matthew (and at Mk ix. 7 and parallels), may have been due to the language of the second psalm. But at least the description of the vision in the basal account in St Mark implies that it was primarily intended for the assurance of Jesus Himself on entering upon His arduous career, and we may therefore be justified in supposing this of the voice also. It would certainly seem, also, from this form in which the facts are told, especially as to the vision, that Jesus must Himself have spoken of the signs granted Him, just as we must suppose confidences of His to have been the source of what is related of His temptation in the wilderness.

Yet it might well be that John the Baptist also might have been allowed to have through spiritual sympathy a perception of the signs, or of the one which according to the Fourth Gospel was granted him.

And, further, in whatever way the signs came to be known, there is no probability that any of the Synoptic evangelists, or the preachers of that oral Gospel which formed the foundation of the written ones, were interested in the point which deeply interests our generation, namely, the light that may be thrown upon the human nature of Jesus by any indication that the signs were needed by Himself. They desired only to make it known that Jesus had been declared from heaven to be the Christ. Thus the simple narration of what happened at the Baptism would quite naturally supersede any mention of the Baptist's own subsequent testimony. The tendency in the early days, as later among the hearers and readers of the story, would be to suppose, in spite of those traits in certain of the Synoptics which we have been noticing, that the signs were witnessed by many, and they would not be likely to reflect that this would have been inconsistent with the history of the manner in which belief in Jesus actually grew. On the other hand, that a revelation should have been made from the early time of the Baptism to one preeminent man of God, which is what we gather from the Fourth Gospel, is not incompatible with the subsequent course of events as related in the Gospels.

Presented in the manner that it is in the Synoptic Gospels, the Baptism of Jesus forms a dramatic close of the Ministry of John, as well as the beginning of that of Jesus. It is the latter also in the Fourth Gospel, but the work of John does not there terminate abruptly. It overlaps that of his greater successor (iii. 22–3). Surely this is not what a writer who was mainly desirous of magnifying Jesus would have invented, even in

The formation of a band of disciples

order to have an opportunity of introducing such an utterance as "he must increase but I must decrease." He would have been more likely to represent the Baptist as giving up his independent work to become a follower of Jesus. And yet one can well understand that, as we find described in the Fourth Gospel, the Baptist, even though he realised that Jesus was far greater than himself, should still go on with his own preaching, leaving Jesus to come forward when and as He saw best. There was still work preparatory for the Coming of the Kingdom which the Baptist might do according to his own methods.

It remains to notice the Message of the Baptist to Jesus from prison, taken, it may be, by our first evangelist and by Luke from the Logian document (Mt. xi. 1–6; Lk. vii. 18–23)[1]. Undoubtedly the Baptist appears in a very different light here from that in which he does in the Fourth Gospel. But we must consider the passage carefully in order to guard ourselves against unjustifiable inferences. From the introductory words in both Gospels it might seem that the thought that Jesus might be the Christ had recently occurred to John in consequence of the reports made to him about the Ministry of Jesus. But another view is suggested by the reply of Jesus. It ends: "Blessed is he whosoever is not offended in me." It may be inferred that the Baptist having at one time believed was now experiencing doubt and perplexity, because of the line of conduct followed by Jesus. One whose disposition to inquire was only just being aroused could not be "offended." The use of this word implies that a conviction once strong had become weaker, as would be possible under the stress of disappointment and depression, in spite of those strange intimations which he thought he had received.

The gathering of a little group of disciples around Jesus. Jn i. 35–51, ii. 2, 11, 12, 17, 22, iii. 22, iv. 8, 27, 31, 33; Mk i. 16–20; Mt. iv. 18–22; Lk. v. 1–11; Mk ii. 14, 18; Mt. ix. 9, 14; Lk. v. 27 f., 33; Mt. x. 1–4; Mk. iii. 13–19; Lk. vi. 12–16.

Before the commencement of the Public Ministry of Jesus, according to the Fourth Gospel, a few men attached themselves to Him as disciples from among those who had already been disciples of John the Baptist, or who had at least come, it would

[1] See vol. II, pp. 85 ff.

seem, to the place where they were, to listen to the Baptist's preaching. They of their own part now come to Jesus. Of one only it is said that Jesus seeks him out and bids him follow Him, and in this case His own departure for Galilee is given as a reason for His so doing. In no instance does it appear that the step then taken of attending upon His teaching involved giving up permanently forthwith the occupation by which they earned their livelihood. Jesus is, however, in this Gospel seen from this early time moving about accompanied by a little body of disciples. It is not implied that this body was in the earliest period of the Ministry of Jesus a constant one. Doubtless from time to time there were accessions, and the presence even of the whole number of original members may have been affected by circumstances. The appointment of twelve is at no point described; but allusion is made, when the Galilean Ministry was drawing to a close[1], to its having taken place, and among them were those whom we hear of as attaching themselves to Jesus at the beginning, or at least several of them. It might be imagined, perhaps, that all these had remained in attendance upon Him from the first without a break. But this is not necessary.

In the Synoptic Gospels the course of things appears differently, but there are points in the accounts there given which we should have been glad to have had explained. When Simon and three others, and soon afterwards Levi, were summoned by Jesus to leave the work by which they earned their livelihood and did so immediately, they had had, so far as appears, no preparation for taking this decisive step, and He had had no opportunities of knowing their characters and spirit. This hardly seems natural. Again somewhat later He withdrew, we are told, into the mountain and called to Him whom He would, and they came to Him, and He appointed twelve, whose names are given, that "they might be with him, and that he might send them forth to preach and to have power to cast out devils." Among them were five who had already been called to abandon all in order that they might ever after be His companions, and four of whom had been told that henceforth they should be "fishers of men." How then is that second call to be adjusted to that

[1] vi. 67, 70, 71.

The formation of a band of disciples

former one? No doubt the fact of finding themselves members of a definite body of Twelve to which they had been thus solemnly appointed would increase their sense of responsibility. But the Synoptics say nothing to make clear the meaning of this new stage in their vocation relatively to what had gone before.

In regard to the history of his own discipleship the reminiscences of Simon Peter, on which there is reason to think Mark largely relied, would be specially vivid; and the narrative of the call on the shore of the Lake of Galilee must therefore be allowed to relate to a decisive turning-point in the lives of the disciples there mentioned. Previous contact with Jesus is not, however, precluded by anything there stated; but plainly there could not have been before that day a continuous and pledged attendance upon Him.

On the other hand that, as the fourth evangelist represents, the earliest followers of Jesus should be drawn from among those whose hearts were full of the expectation of the Coming of the Kingdom of God and of the Christ, men who had already been attracted to the Baptist and deeply stirred by his preaching, is entirely what one would expect. The manner, too, in which, according to this evangelist, they attached themselves to Him in the first instance without being required at once to make a decision which would have life-long consequences, is natural.

I have endeavoured to bring out clearly the differences between the two accounts, and at the same time not to treat these differences as involving actual incompatibility, where that could only arise from assuming something to have been meant which has not been stated. I have also indicated the reasons for giving weight to each account; in the former it is more particularly that due to Mark as the hearer of Peter, in the latter the inherent probability of certain features of the narrative.

It seems to me that this is a case in which there is good reason to hold that, although either owing to imperfect information, or the lack of a conception of what was required for a satisfactory narrative, the impression given by the narrators severally is defective, there are elements of truth in each account which we may rightly seek to combine.

Early belief that Jesus is the Christ. Jn i. 41, 45–51, iv. 25, 28–30, 39–42.

It is a feature of the Fourth Gospel that not only is Jesus pointed out by the Baptist as the Christ; but that immediately after this the two who heard the Baptist and some others declare this to be their own belief, and that He either virtually or expressly accepts their professions of faith in Him.

The Synoptic Gospels are silent as to any such professions of disciples in the early days of their discipleship; but this is not to be taken as implying that this faith was lacking. In the view of the evangelists their act itself in attaching themselves to Him no doubt proved that they held this faith; and it is in point of fact easier to understand that men might embrace it, and surrender themselves to it with generous enthusiasm, at the opening of His Ministry under the influence of the strong hope of the speedy appearance of the redeemer of Israel which they cherished, than that they should arrive at it, which some appear to think they did, as a slowly-formed conviction after difficulties had been caused to their minds by His delay in working the deliverance of Israel, and by the warnings He gave to them as to what He their Master and they themselves would have to endure. This is not to say that their belief in the Messiahship of Jesus was of the same quality at the beginning as afterwards. It needed to be strengthened and deepened through fuller personal knowledge of Him, while being at the same time tested through having to face doubts in their own minds, and the doubts and hostility of other men. The significance of the incident at Cæsarea Philippi[1] is that it had come triumphantly out of this testing. They were able to retain their faith in Jesus in days of widespread perplexity about Him. Their conception of what His Messiahship meant, however, still stood in great need of being spiritualised and exalted. A history of the belief of the disciples of this kind, starting from an early beginning, is required by the evidence generally which the Gospel-story supplies, and is rendered natural by the prevailing Messianic expectation.

The view has, indeed, also been held that a considerable period of time, occupying the earlier part of the Ministry of

---

[1] Mk viii. 27 ff.; Mt. xvi. 13 ff.; Lk. ix. 18 ff.

Early belief that Jesus is the Christ

Jesus, must be allowed for His Messianic claims to take shape in His own mind. This raises the whole question of the consciousness of Jesus as to His own Person and Mission. The evidence of the Synoptic Gospels and the Fourth Gospel in regard to it will be compared in a later part of this chapter. All that I can at this point say is that the accounts in the Synoptic Gospels of the Baptism and the Temptation imply that before His Public Ministry began the assurance had been Divinely communicated to Him that He was endued with an authority and entrusted with a mission which involved the conception of Messiahship.

There does not then seem to be anything essentially inconsistent between what we are told in the Synoptics and in the Fourth Gospel as to the faith of the disciples, or the attitude of Jesus towards it. But in regard to the full historicity at any rate of another narrative occurring early in the Fourth Gospel, in which the truth of His Messiahship is set forth, there are difficulties which are suggested by considerations of general probability, and by a comparison of the view given in the Synoptics of the course of action adopted by Jesus. It is related that Jesus, on returning from Judæa through Samaria, revealed Himself as the Christ to a woman by Jacob's well, and that her fellow-townsfolk, after hearing her report, and listening to His teaching for two days, declared their conviction that He was "the Christ, the Saviour of the world." There are no instances of a conception of the work of Jesus so large as this even among the disciples in the days of His Ministry on earth. Furthermore Jesus elsewhere waits for men to confess Him to be the Christ; He does not take the first step in declaring Himself to be so, as in the case of the Samaritan woman. And before the people, before any persons, indeed, save the innermost circle of His disciples, He shews the greatest reserve with regard to this claim. There was not indeed among the Samaritan population, cut off as it was from the life of the Jewish people, the same danger that mischief would arise from false expectations as there was in other districts where He preached. And yet here, too, He might well fear to encourage them, seeing that from the shortness of the time that He would be there, He could not guard them from error and guide their faith and hope into right channels.

15—2

Visits of Jesus with His disciples to Jerusalem prior to that at which He was arrested and put to death.

The fourth evangelist not only gives us a view different from that which the Synoptics do of the manner in which the discipleship of some of the chief disciples of Jesus began. He also proceeds from the formation of that first little band of adherents as the point of departure to relate the history of the course taken by Jesus during a period about which the Synoptics are silent, and which, whatever the original intention may have been, turned out, according to the Johannine account itself, to be of a certain "preliminary" character. He first paid a visit to Galilee. This was natural. For as we learn from the Fourth Gospel, Jesus Himself also was, at least through the residence of His family before His birth and His own residence from early childhood, a Galilean, and He had family friends at Cana; and three at least of the disciples who met with Jesus in the neighbourhood where John was preaching and baptizing were Galileans. But He did not in the brief length of time which He spent in Galilee on this occasion begin public work. He wrought indeed one miracle, but its object appears to have been the confirmation of the faith of those who had already become disciples, not a wider appeal. From Cana He and His disciples went to Capernaum, and after a few days, of which nothing is recorded, started for Jerusalem in order to be present at the Passover, which was close at hand.

As every one knows, visits of Jesus to Jerusalem before that at which He was crucified, together with one to its near neighbourhood[1], the remarkable miracles performed and the teaching given there, recorded in the Fourth Gospel and peculiar to it, form one of the chief differences between it and the others.

There are considerations in regard both to the historical character of these visits and to their significance in connexion with the Person and Work of Christ which apply to them collectively, and these may be examined before we touch upon any one of the visits apart from the rest, except to observe how they are distributed in the record relatively to the Ministry as a whole.

---

[1] To Bethany for the raising of Lazarus, xi. 1, 18, 54.

Visits of Jesus to Jerusalem

The first preceded the opening of the Galilean Ministry described in the Synoptic Gospels. This is clearly indicated by a comparison of one of the rare marks of time occurring in those Gospels, with one in the Fourth Gospel—the imprisonment of John the Baptist[1]. Further, with at most one exception, the others are all subsequent to the close of that Ministry. For there is no suggestion that after the occasion described in Jn vii. 10, when Jesus left Galilee and appeared in the temple in the midst of the Feast of Tabernacles, He again returned to Galilee.

I have said that, with at most one exception, the Galilean Ministry remains unbroken, according to the Fourth Gospel, by any visit to Jerusalem. That exception occurs in ch. v in the form in which the work has come down to us. But it is not altogether improbable that there may have been a dislocation at this point, and that the matter connected here with some unnamed Jewish feast is really the beginning of the account of the visit for the Feast of Tabernacles, the remainder of which is given in ch. vii[2]. If so, the fourth evangelist brought in the whole of his additional matter relating to a ministry in Jerusalem and Judæa partly before and partly after the limits of the Galilean Ministry, as they are marked out in the Synoptic Gospels. The fact, if such it is, of this arrangement would affect somewhat the significance of the absence of corresponding accounts from the Synoptic Gospels. If, after a brief ministry in Jerusalem and Judæa, Jesus desisted, and then began a ministry in Galilee which lasted for a year or more, and which He carried out to its completion without interruption, while after this Jerusalem became the chief centre where His work finally culminated, it seems more intelligible that the early preachers in those brief oral accounts of the Saviour's Life and Work which they gave, and which formed the basis of the earliest written Gospel, should have concentrated attention on two divisions of their subject, (1) the Galilean Ministry, which opened so impressively with the proclamation "the Kingdom of God is at hand," and in the sequel shewed the labour of Jesus for men in all its charm; and (2) the Last Days at Jerusalem, which likewise opened most impressively with the

[1] Cp. Jn iii. 24, with Mk i. 14, Mt. iv. 12.   [2] See above, pp. 67 ff.

Triumphal Entry into the city, in the sequel to which that other aspect was presented which it was necessary for all to know of—the rejection of Jesus by men and the suffering He endured on their behalf.

On the other hand, it is true, some account of the earlier time spent in Jerusalem might have been suggested by a due perception of its significance as regards the probation of the Jewish people and Christ's own conception of His Mission. This perception we may with good reason say the fourth evangelist had. But it came through deeper spiritual insight and longer meditation, and the lack of it can be understood.

Independently, however, it may be said, of the interest that should have been felt in any work done in the Holy City, one might have expected those visits to Jerusalem to have been noticed, even where instruction in the facts of the Gospel was of a simple kind, for the sake of deeds of Jesus which, if the Johannine narrative is trustworthy, took place at them. Here, however, the objection founded on the silence of the Synoptic Gospels lies not against the credibility of the visits, but against that of the particular incidents which, if true, one would have expected to find mentioned, and which would have led to the notice of the visits. We are now considering the historicity of the visits, and we should be bound here to take account of an objection as to the incidents, only if it were more likely that a miracle judged to be legendary would come to be connected with an occasion that was itself legendary than with a historical one; but there seems to be no good reason to think this.

As a matter of fact, while the absence of all particulars from the Synoptic Gospels has created doubt as to any ministry of Jesus in Jerusalem before those last days when He came there to die, they supply evidence of not a little weight, partly in sayings which they put into the mouth of Jesus, partly in indications in their narratives, that there must at some time have been such a ministry.

Our attention may first be given to the words in the apostrophe to Jerusalem, contained in St Matthew and St Luke: "How often would I have gathered thy children together." In St Matthew (xxiii. 37–39) this apostrophe forms

Visits of Jesus to Jerusalem

the conclusion of the denunciation of the scribes and Pharisees, which is the last public utterance of Jesus. But even if it is rightly placed here, ποσακις, "how often," could not naturally be used only of the teaching given during the few preceding days. In St Luke it is placed earlier (xiii. 34, 35) among those discourses and sayings which he has introduced into the Marcan Outline between the departure from Galilee and the final going up from Peræa, or somewhere in the Judæan borderland, to Jerusalem. In St Matthew the apostrophe is preceded by the saying (vv. 34–36) "Behold, I send unto you prophets, and wise men and scribes etc.," which is found in St Luke, in partly different phraseology, at a still earlier point in his "great insertion" (xi. 49–51), where it is quoted as from "the Wisdom of God." Now it is contended by those critics who deny that Jesus exercised any ministry in Jerusalem before that of which we have an account in the Synoptic Gospels, that the two sayings given separately in St Luke form properly one saying as in St Matthew, and that the whole was taken from a document which professed to give utterances of "the Wisdom of God," and which was not an authentic source for the Words of Christ.

But this argument is not based on any observations that I am aware of as to the general procedure of the two evangelists. On the contrary our studies of the Logian element in the first and third Gospels[1] have led to the conclusion that our first evangelist is disposed to combine together sayings that seemed germane to one another, while the third is disposed to keep apart sayings that came to him separately. The apostrophe to Jerusalem made a very effective ending to the discourse denouncing the scribes and Pharisees; so the former might very naturally place it there even if it did not stand there in his source, while the latter who gives, somewhat briefly, the same discourse down to the saying "Lo, I send unto you etc." could have had no sufficient motive that one can imagine for removing what, on the hypothesis we are considering, was the conclusion of the saying in the original context in which he found it.

Whatever then may be the case with regard to the earlier

[1] See vol. II, pp. 74 f.

part (*vv.* 34-36) of the passage in St Matthew, with which Lk. xi. 49-51 corresponds, the position of the words "O Jerusalem...how often would I have gathered thy children together" in the third Gospel confirms their right to be regarded as Words of Jesus.

But this saying does not stand alone. There is another not less significant put by Luke into the mouth of Jesus when He paused in His Triumphal Entry into Jerusalem "and beheld the city and wept over it," and exclaimed, "Thou knewest not the day of thy visitation." It is inconceivable that Jesus should not have regarded His own coming, His own preaching and working amongst them, as not included in their "day of visitation," their day of opportunity (as we should more commonly say), and should regard that day as already over though He had never exercised any ministry there. He would indeed still continue to do so; but He could speak as He does only if He knew the uselessness of it so far at least as the population as a whole, the city and its chief representatives, were concerned, because He had already discovered the hardness of their hearts.

There is another saying, occurring in St Mark (xiv. 49) and in the parallel contexts in the two other Synoptics, which, though it does not point so clearly to previous visits, is deserving of consideration in the present connexion. On being arrested Jesus said, "I was daily with you in the temple teaching and you took me not." In the Marcan narrative the public teaching of Jesus in Jerusalem appears to be comprised within two days. Evidently the expression "daily" would be unsuitable if that was the whole length of time in view, which is moreover, even with twelve hours or so at the beginning and at the end added, too short for all that the evangelist represents as happening in it, namely, for the decision to be reached that Jesus must be put to death and the plan for seizing Him to be matured and carried into execution. This incongruity, both as regards the saying of Jesus at His arrest and the time allowed for the development of plans for His destruction, may be removed if we suppose that Jesus had been longer in Jerusalem before He was seized than appears in Mark's narrative[1]. And in point

---

[1] Wellhausen, *Ev. Marci*, p. 94, who points out the objection to so much being crowded into so short a time as it is by Mark, adopts this explanation. He

First visit to Jerusalem

of fact Luke implies this. Still it may be asked whether, as the fundamental Synoptic narrative, that in St Mark, is not self-consistent, the wiser course is not to turn to another tradition according to which teaching given by Jesus on earlier occasions may be referred to, when also seeds of hostility had been sown, which had had time to bear fruit.

The supposition therefore that Jesus exercised a ministry in Jerusalem before that visit at which He was put to death is required by allusions contained in the Synoptic Gospels themselves, and also in order to understand the final crisis as they describe it.

Over and above this, as I would insist, that supposition is in itself a highly probable one. Even as a pious Jew there was reason for Jesus to visit Jerusalem at the times of the great feasts, and when there He could not, after He had received His call to His prophetic office, hold His peace.

We have come to the conclusion that the public appearance of Jesus in Jerusalem on the occasion described in the Synoptic Gospels was not the earliest. But so far we have decided nothing as to the number of His visits, or the probability that they were made at the points relatively to the Galilean Ministry at which in the Fourth Gospel they are placed.

The First Visit to Jerusalem recorded in the Fourth Gospel.

Here then first we have to notice the interesting fact that this Gospel represents the young prophet as going up very soon after He has received His call to the Holy City, and there beginning His work. It was psychologically and in the circumstances natural that He should do so. There seemed to be a fitness in the place owing to all its associations, and it promised opportunities of a unique kind, especially at times of great festivals, of reaching earnest-minded Jews from all parts of the world, which could not but be attractive to any man, especially any young man, with a prophet's rôle to fulfil. There might be force in the suggestion that He could not have exercised influence and authority in Jerusalem before He had

declares that the supposition of former visits will not serve because He could not then have appeared as "the great prophet from Galilee." But even if this was necessary, it could not at least apply to the time spent at Jerusalem, according to the Fourth Gospel, at the Feasts of Tabernacles and Dedication. For this was after He had not only reached, but passed, the zenith of His influence in Galilee.

acquired fame by His success in Galilee (see above, p. 232, n. 1), if the people to be addressed had only been Jerusalemites. But this view will be seen to be baseless, if the variety of elements to be found in the crowd assembled at such a time be remembered. It was also not surprising that ere long experience shewed that the conditions were not in reality favourable, at all events for a prolonged stay. The evangelist appears to be anxious that it should not be supposed that Jesus failed there to make an impression by His works and words, yet he implies that there was something untrustworthy in the attitude to Him of the many who were impressed. Later in the Fourth Gospel, Jews at Jerusalem who believed are spoken of; and yet when Jesus implied that they were not truly free they turned against Him[1]. It is stated also that there were members of the ruling class who believed and yet were afraid to confess their belief openly for fear of the Pharisees[2]. It might well be so. In Jerusalem were to be found in the largest number those who would be most withheld by old ties and by fear of worldly loss from becoming wholeheartedly and openly His disciples, though they might be secretly convinced of the truth of His teaching, or at one time have hoped that He would prove to be the Christ.

So far then the points in the account of this visit that we have considered are credible enough. It remains for us to ask whether a cleansing of the temple is rightly connected with it. There does not seem to me to be anything in itself unlikely in Jesus having performed this act so early. It has often been argued that He would thereby have publicly made known His claims before it accorded with His purpose and plan so to do. But the claim which He long kept veiled was that of being the Messiah; in the cleansing of the temple a claim to be the Messiah was not necessarily implied. What He did was only what any prophet might have felt moved to do. It has also been said that after such a challenge to their own authority the priests could not have desisted from crushing Him. But there may have been too much sympathy with the action of Jesus among the people and among many also of the party of Pharisees, who were in general hostile to the Sadducean chief priests, readily to allow of this, and the authorities might thus

[1] viii. 31 ff.   [2] xii. 42 ff.

Journey through Samaria

have had good reason for pretending to acquiesce in it at the time.

But though all this may be true we must further inquire whether it is likely that such an act can have been performed twice; and if probably only once whether most reliance is to be placed on the Fourth Gospel or the Synoptics.

Undoubtedly incidents which in character are virtually identical do recur in the same lives; and it is not difficult to imagine that the same abuse after being suppressed might have crept in again; and if it was observed by Jesus to have been flourishing once more He could hardly have refrained from treating it as before. Still when in different ancient documents we find two accounts in many respects so similar referring to different times, it is on the whole most probable that we have to do with different traditions about the same event. It seems to me impossible to choose between them in the present instance with any confidence. Inherent probability appears to be on the side of the Fourth Gospel. It was, as I have said, natural that the young prophet should visit Jerusalem early in His career, and that if He found a gross abuse flourishing in the temple there He should attack it, while it is unlikely that an abuse had then not appeared which was rampant two years later. On the other hand Mark is entitled to preference as a historical witness. He was more simply a reporter, and he wrote down earlier what he had learned.

Journey through Samaria. Jn iii. 22–iv. 42.

After remaining for a time in the neighbourhood where John, who had not yet been cast into prison, was baptizing, Jesus returned into Galilee through the district of Samaria to the east of Shechem (Neapolis), and a few miles further to the east of the city of Samaria (Sebaste), avoiding these important places, and passing through the comparatively insignificant township of Sychar, and thence taking the most direct road into Galilee. The terms of these topographical allusions afford no just ground for suspecting the truth of the narrative, and the evangelist's knowledge of the geography of Palestine[1], as was freely alleged in the earlier periods of the controversy

---

[1] See above, pp. 158 f.

about the Fourth Gospel. But, as we have had occasion to notice already in the present chapter, there are features in the account of what occurred in this Samaritan township, which must be reckoned improbable[1].

The Galilean Ministry. Jn iv. 43–54, vi. 1–vii. 9.

In passing to the Ministry in Galilee the fourth evangelist observes that the Galileans received Him having seen all the things that He did at Jerusalem at the feast. So according to him, too, as well as according to the view, to which I have referred, of some modern writers, there was a connexion, though of an opposite kind, between the effects produced by the ministry in each region, and it is one which (as it seems to me) is in itself more probable. If so, the experience of Jesus in this was that of many others who have sought to do the Will of God; namely that when some work upon which they have entered hopefully, and which they have striven to carry out faithfully, appears to have failed and has had to be abandoned, it has presently been found to have prepared the way for successful work somewhere else, or in some other form[2].

From the Galilean Ministry the fourth evangelist selects a few episodes. He relates the Healing of the son of the king's officer, the Feeding of the five thousand on the eastern shore of the lake, which was followed by the Recrossing of the

---

[1] See p. 227.

[2] I have avoided committing myself in what I have written above to any interpretation of the very difficult verse, Jn iv. 44: αὐτὸς γὰρ Ἰησοῦς ἐμαρτύρησεν ὅτι προφήτης ἐν τῇ ἰδίᾳ πατρίδι τιμὴν οὐκ ἔχει. The evangelist's intention in these words must be either to justify Jesus for leaving Judæa or for not going to Nazareth. The difficulty in the actual context is to apply πατρίδα to either. πατρίς may be used in the larger sense of one's country as at Heb. xi. 14, or in the narrower sense of the town, or other local division, where one has been born, or where one's family is settled. It is used of Nazareth in this sense at Mk vi. 4 and parallels. But at Jn iv. 44 Jesus was on His way into Galilee, within which Nazareth was. On the other hand if the word is applied to Jerusalem, or Judæa, it must be in a broader sense, for He had not been near Bethlehem, and his connexion with Bethlehem could not determine that with Jerusalem and Judæa. But it may be doubted whether Jerusalem could be called His πατρίς in contrast with Galilee, which was Jews' country, a part of the ancient inheritance of Israel. One is tempted, therefore, to think that there must be some words missing here or some slight transposition. If πατρίς could be contrasted with Cana of Galilee, mentioned in v. 46, the application to Nazareth would be clear. I do not therefore think that the fourth evangelist can here, with the use made of the saying by St Mark known to him, have wished to put forward a different view of the πατρίς of Jesus.

The Galilean Ministry

lake, when Jesus rejoined His disciples by walking over the water.

I have suggested that the fourth evangelist derived the narrative of the Healing of the son of the king's officer ultimately from the same Aramaic source as that from which the Healing of the centurion's servant came in St Matthew and St Luke, but through a different channel[1]. Possibly in that source it was the first miracle told. As it did not occur in the Marcan document different views might be held of its proper position relatively to the Marcan sequence. In St Matthew and St Luke it is placed early, though not first. The author of the Fourth Gospel may have had two reasons for selecting this miracle for narration. As being a cure wrought upon a patient at a considerable distance, it might be reckoned as one of the more remarkable miracles; while it also afforded an example of the blessedness of a strong faith such as was demanded from those for whom the fourth evangelist wrote, when the visible presence of the Lord had been withdrawn from the earth.

The two Galilean miracles in the Fourth Gospel which are taken from St Mark—the Feeding of the five thousand, and the Walking on the water—are the mightiest works of Jesus related in any of the Gospels. They are those in which it is most difficult to imagine a mode of operation even remotely analogous to anything that we know, since even in the raising of the dead there might be supposed to be an extension of what happens in cases of suspended animation. It is worth while to note this because we are thereby reminded that difficulties as to the historical character of the Fourth Gospel owing to the inclusion in it of accounts of miracles are not essentially, if at all, greater than even in the case of St Mark.

I have spoken of the narratives of these two miracles as taken from St Mark. In them, as we have seen above, some of the similarities in points of detail and forms of expression occur which afford the strongest evidence of the fourth evangelist's acquaintance with St Mark[2]. We also noticed in the sequel to the account of this miracle in the Fourth Gospel

---

[1] See above, p. 220.
[2] *Ib.* pp. 215 f., 219.

another coincidence—the demand for a sign from heaven—which points to the use of St Mark[1]. But there are also some other resemblances between the Fourth Gospel, in that portion of it which relates to the Galilean Ministry, and the Synoptic Gospels, which are not so close as those before mentioned, and which it seemed to me best to disregard when the question to be determined was simply whether the fourth evangelist was acquainted with the Synoptic Gospels or any of them. These additional resemblances to which I now refer are to be found for the most part in the general representation of the course of events rather than in details. They are accompanied by differences which shew that if such similarity as there is arose from the fourth evangelist having read St Mark, he set himself after this reading to form his own idea and to give his own account of what happened; while the relation of his own narrative to the Marcan might also be explained by a measure, greater or less, of independent knowledge. In the comparison between the Gospels which we are now making this broader relation between the narratives must be considered.

When after the crossing of the lake the multitude that had been present at the great miracle of feeding had (according to the fourth evangelist) followed Jesus and again gathered about Him on the western shore, Jesus rebuked them because the effect of the miracle had been to make them look to Him to satisfy their temporal needs. It is interesting to compare the lesson here taught with that taught from the two miracles of feeding at a later point in the Marcan Outline (followed in St Matthew, but not by Luke in this part of his Gospel). There the Twelve misunderstand a saying about the leaven of the Pharisees, supposing it somehow to contain an allusion to their not having taken sufficient bread with them in the boat; and Jesus rebukes their spiritual dulness by reminding them of those miracles, which should have proved to them that He was well able to provide for their bodily wants. The indication given in the Fourth Gospel of the purpose of the miracle is thoroughly in character with the leading ideas of that Gospel, but should not be dismissed as unhistorical for that reason alone. That the effect of His miracles should not have been

[1] *Ib.* p. 216.

The Galilean Ministry

what Jesus desired, and that He should have been troubled by the misuse of them, is not in itself improbable. Moreover the saying employed, " Labour not for the meat which perisheth etc.," whether originally spoken with the reference here given to it or not, is not dissimilar in its main purport from such as are to be found in the Synoptics, and especially from some of those derived presumably from the Logian document.

The demand for a sign from heaven follows immediately in the Fourth Gospel, and Jesus replies that the bread from heaven is the sign and that He Himself is that bread, and this theme is then dwelt upon at length. Whether Jesus did teach this about Himself we shall consider presently, when comparing generally the teaching given in the Fourth Gospel and in the other three. We are examining now only the historical framework, the evangelist's setting here for the teaching. To accepting this as true to fact in this place there is the serious objection that Jesus could hardly have addressed to the audience described, composed as it was largely of the common folk of Galilee, and including along with them hostile " Jews," as well as disciples, this advanced teaching, which even to the disciples present was new, as appears from the evangelist's own account.

Again it is to be observed that at the conclusion of the teaching it is said that these things were spoken in the synagogue in Capernaum (*v.* 59). Since from the beginning of the teaching (*v.* 26 onwards) there is no mention of His having entered the synagogue, the natural inference would be that the whole of it, or at all events all after some point very near the beginning, is to be included in what was spoken there. And yet there is a certain artificiality in those disputings, placed near the middle and again before the last portion (at *vv.* 41 and 52), which afford fresh starting-points for the fuller development of the main theme. And the probability is that the evangelist would not care to be exact about the precise occasion on which each thing was spoken; what he was anxious to secure would be an orderly unfolding of the claims of Jesus.

We may then reasonably conjecture that he was led to place the whole of this discourse-matter where he does, just after the miracle of feeding, from his having been accustomed to use that miracle in his instruction of Christian assemblies as a text for setting forth Jesus as the living bread.

If I mistake not, the evangelist gets back on to firmer ground and shews knowledge, or a right view, of the history when he places at this point in his narrative a great crisis in the Galilean Ministry. The time is the last five months between the Feast of Passover (vi. 4) and the Feast of Tabernacles (vii. 2). There is an extensive defection of those who had till then reckoned themselves adherents. But the faith and devotion of the Twelve shine forth brightly by contrast in a confession of faith made in their name by Simon Peter in response to an inquiry of Jesus. So also in the Marcan record in the conversation at Cæsarea Philippi the firm faith of the twelve is shewn in a confession made on their behalf by Simon Peter. The occasion of this profession of faith on the part of the Twelve appears to be somewhat earlier in the Fourth Gospel. No interval is allowed for the consequences of the misgivings that arose out of the teaching at Capernaum to become manifest. In the Marcan record there have been some journeyings between the crossing to Capernaum and the profession of faith reported[1]. But a crisis in thought and feeling such as that which forms in both accounts the background to the profession of faith of the Twelve belongs to a period of weeks or months at least, not to any particular moment within such a period.

There is a difference in the contrasts depicted in the Synoptics and the Fourth Gospel. In the former it is between the faith of the Twelve and the speculative and non-committal temper, and the virtual denial that Jesus could at all events be the Messiah, which had taken possession of the minds of men generally in place of the widespread enthusiasm and spirit of expectancy shewn at an earlier time. In the latter the contrast is with the falling-away of many who had accounted themselves "disciples." In the Synoptic Gospels, too, the existence of

---

[1] The interval will appear to have been less considerable than in our St Mark, if the view advocated, vol. II, pp. 152 ff., is accepted that our St Mark is a second edition in which some matter has been introduced in this portion of the Gospel from a tradition parallel to that in the original Gospel, actually referring to the same events as have already been narrated.

The Galilean Ministry

"disciples" other than the twelve has been indicated[1]. But from the moment of the selection of the Twelve there is little or nothing to remind us of them[1]. They disappear from view. We have only on the one side the Twelve, on the other the crowds. But that there should also have been not a few who, throughout the portion of the earthly Ministry of Jesus when His influence was greatest, were deeply impressed by His teaching and Personality, and who regarded themselves as, or wished to be, His followers, but who nevertheless fell away under the stress of the perplexity caused them by elements in His teaching which they could not appropriate, or by the hostility of the ruling class, is entirely probable. There ought to be no doubt that the fourth evangelist in representing this to have been the case in Galilee, as he does also in Jerusalem, has preserved an important feature of the Ministry of Jesus; and there is also a touch of truth in his having given the fear of men as a cause of disloyalty only in connexion with a class of disciples in Jerusalem.

We have still to notice a difference in the Synoptic and Johannine form of the profession of faith of the Twelve. In the one it is, "Thou art the Christ"; in the other, "Thou hast the words of eternal life; thou art the Holy One of God." The recognition that He has the words of eternal life is in character with the leading ideas of the Fourth Gospel, but it should not be forthwith regarded as wholly unhistorical on that account. The Messiahship of Jesus has been fulfilled in the manner indicated by these words, in the generations and ages subsequent to His work on earth. Is it to be thought that He had no notion Himself that thus it would be; and if He had, may we not suppose that some of those who were most intimate with Him had some inkling of this, even while they retained their inherited ideas?

Lastly, we must compare the reply of Jesus to the profession of faith of the Twelve in the Marcan record and in the Fourth Gospel. In the former while plainly accepting that which they believed concerning Him as true, He bids them keep it to themselves, and then begins to instruct them, as to

[1] Mk iii. 7, 13, 14. Instances are also given later of men who professed a desire to follow Him, but whom He frightened away. Mt. viii. 19-22; Lk. ix. 57-62.

the sufferings that await Him, His rejection by the rulers and leaders of the people, crucifixion and resurrection. In the Fourth Gospel also it is evident that He accepts their faith in Him, and here too He points to the coming catastrophe, though only by a veiled allusion to the betrayal. The terms of the prediction in the Synoptic Gospels may very likely have been rendered as precise and full as they are through the after-knowledge of the writers, or of the reporters on whom they relied. But the warning in the Fourth Gospel, though not marked by the same precision, is, it should be freely allowed, even less likely to be historically accurate, since it is inconceivable that Jesus would have instilled mutual suspicion into His little band of constant companions a whole year before the end.

The interval between the final departure of Jesus from Galilee and His coming to Jerusalem for the Passover at which He suffered. Mk x. 1–52; Mt. xix. 1–xx. 34; Lk. ix. 51–xix. 28; Jn vii. 10–13, v. 1–47[1], vii. 14–xi. 57.

Mark, followed in St Matthew, represents Jesus as removing to "the borders of Judæa and beyond Jordan," and states that multitudes flocked to Him again there, and that "as he was wont he again taught them." He tells at least two incidents as happening in this district, in connexion with which valuable pieces of teaching are given. The period of time within which these two incidents happened, and to which the preceding general notice referred, may well have been one of several weeks or even of some months. Mark's account of the Ministry throughout consists mainly of a series of incidents related in some detail with sayings thereto appertaining, which severally can have occupied only portions of days and between many of which there must have been considerable intervals of time, while we are told only very briefly, or often not at all, how the intervals were filled[2]. I have said that at least two incidents belong to this time; the words which introduce a third, "when he was going forth into the way," probably mark the beginning of His final journey to Jerusalem, the continuance of which is indicated at

---

[1] I have included this passage in accordance with the supposition defended above, pp. 67 ff. and 229, that there has been a dislocation in this part of the Gospel.

[2] E.g. i. 39, vi. 56.

The last months of Christ's Ministry 243

v. 32. On the other hand in St Matthew a new departure, that for Jerusalem, is clearly marked in the parallel to this latter place (xx. 17), and this is the more noticeable because our first evangelist frequently connects narratives closely in time where in St Mark there is simply juxtaposition[1].

By Luke the period is differently treated. He represents the journey as a continuous one from Galilee to Jerusalem but evidently as a slow one, on which Jesus passed through cities and villages, teaching as He went (xiii. 22). Luke introduces in connexion with it much of the matter that he derived from the Logian source. At the beginning of it Jesus passes near a Samaritan village (ix. 51 ff.) but later in it also He is "between Samaria and Galilee" (xvii. 11), while early in it He enters a village where dwelt two sisters named Martha and Mary. He makes no mention of Peræa, but rejoins Mark's outline just before the point at which, according to the latter, the start from Peræa was made. Probably Luke the Gentile had only vague ideas about the topography in these eastern parts of Palestine. But plainly he believed that there was a considerable interval between the time when Jesus left Galilee and His coming to Jerusalem for the last Passover, and that it was spent in the region to the south of Galilee and east of Jerusalem.

In the Fourth Gospel we are not told the route which Jesus took for Jerusalem when He left Galilee. But if He went by way of the eastern side of Jordan He cannot have paused on His journey, since the Feast of Tabernacles was already nigh at hand at the time of His departure from Galilee, and His kinsfolk had already started in order to be present at the Feast, and He Himself arrived before the middle of it. It is more probable that He chose the more direct road. It is also natural to suppose that when at x. 40 the evangelist states that after the Feast of Dedication, three months later than the Feast of Tabernacles, Jesus "went away again beyond Jordan" the reference in "again" is to the occasion of His being there before His Ministry in Galilee began, described in this Gospel, not to some intervening one unmentioned in it. And there

---
[1] See above, II, p. 37.

is the more reason to think so in that he recalls the fact that this was the neighbourhood where John baptized.

There is no clear break between the teaching of Jesus and His disputations with opponents at and after the Feast of Tabernacles and at the time of the Feast of Dedication. It seems that we are intended to understand that Jesus spent the whole of this time in Jerusalem, or that if He withdrew at all, it was only to some place in the immediate neighbourhood. On the whole then the time to which the fourth evangelist refers at x. 40 may be held to be in his view the same as that referred to at Mk x. 1. If we suppose the fourth evangelist to have been of opinion that Jesus must have visited Jerusalem in the latter part of His Ministry but before the last Passover, though he did not know when such a visit took place, he could not have introduced it more skilfully into the Marcan outline than he has done. It seems to me more probable that he was guided by actual knowledge. The news of the illness of Lazarus apparently found Jesus in Peræa[1]; but after going up to Bethany to raise him, He did not return to Peræa, but went to Ephraim in the north-east of Judæa "near the desert[2]." There seems to be no imaginable reason for the evangelist's mentioning this place, except a definite reminiscence, if not on his own part, then on that of his informant, or preserved in tradition. Through Ephraim, if it has been rightly identified, there was a road which passed by way of Jericho to Jerusalem. According to the Fourth Gospel the miracle of the raising of Lazarus had an important part in bringing about, or in hastening, the final catastrophe. It produced a profound impression on many who witnessed it, who were thereby led to believe in Jesus. But others who were present reported to the Pharisees what had happened, and thereupon the chief priests and along with them the Pharisees, that is, no doubt the responsible heads of the latter party, came to a more definite determination than before that Jesus must be destroyed[3]. Before this, though we are told that "the Jews" sought to kill Him, the only measure adopted by the authorities appears to be that they endeavoured, though in vain, to get Him arrested. So far they may have put off any decision upon the difficult question what the next step should

---
[1] Jn xi. 6.   [2] *Ib. v.* 54.   [3] *Ib. vv.* 45 ff.

The supper at Bethany

be, till they had Him in their power. Now, however, they resolve that He must be put to death.

From the approach to Jerusalem to the day before the Crucifixion. Mk xi. 1–xiv. 11; Mt. xxi. 1–xxvi. 16; Lk. xix. 29–xxii. 6; Jn xii. 1–50.

From the point we have now reached onwards, the fourth evangelist is not merely treating of the same, or approximately the same, period as the other evangelists but of the same few days. His narrative of one incident which then occurred is, as we have seen above[1], one of those which most forcibly suggest that he must have been acquainted with and have used St Mark. The independence which he shews here, as in other parts of his Gospel, is nevertheless remarkable. He shews it in narrating incidents which he has in common with the others, as well as in introducing to so large an extent matter that is wholly peculiar. Jesus came to Bethany, he tells us, six days before the Passover, and the house He stayed in was the home of Lazarus and his two sisters Martha and Mary; there it was that He was entertained at supper, and Martha served. The woman who anointed Jesus was Mary. She poured the ointment not on His head but His feet. The remark about waste he assigns to Judas. It was on the next day that Jesus had His popular triumph on entering Jerusalem. The fame of the raising of Lazarus had no small part in bringing it about.

All these points may have been due to the fourth evangelist's own imagination and reasoning. He may have calculated that six days was the number which must probably have been required according to Mark's narrative; and the various events may have seemed to him to follow one another most naturally if this supper preceded the Entry into Jerusalem. Again in view of what he had already told of a certain family which had a home at Bethany, he could hardly suppose, or let it be supposed, that Jesus would stay at any other house but theirs. He may have represented Mary as anointing the feet not the head because he felt certain that she would choose to do that which betokened the most profound reverence. In making Judas the critic of the action he may have simply been actuated by the same feeling with regard to the traitor as appears in other

[1] See p. 216.

passages of his Gospel. And the introduction of the effect produced by the miracle that had been wrought on Lazarus fits with other indications of his view of the course of events which ended in the death of Jesus.

At the same time we should judge from the injunction at Mk xiv. 9 that the story of this anointing was one which was often told, and from some of those other ways of telling it which the fourth evangelist may with good reason have held to be as trustworthy as Mark's, he may have derived some of those traits which we know only through him. It may also be observed that the connexion of sentences in Mark does not make it perfectly clear that the supper, as well as consultations of the rulers how Jesus might be taken by craft, and the betrayal of Judas, is to be understood to have taken place "two days before the Passover." The statement about the supper may be parenthetical. The significance of its position here arises from the preparation made for the death of Jesus by the service of love while others were compassing it. The evangelist himself may have chosen to mention it here on that account; or it may have been attracted into this place in the common tradition through that association of ideas. The Johannine day for the occurrence may, therefore, have as much title to be regarded as correct as four days later. For another feature in the Fourth Gospel, the family of the entertainers of Jesus, a certain measure of indirect confirmation may be obtained from St Luke in the well-known narrative concerning two early believers, sisters, who lived in some village between Galilee and Jerusalem, whose names were Martha and Mary, and their characters not dissimilar to those of the two sisters at Bethany noticed in the Fourth Gospel. That the remembrance of two such women should have lasted on in the Church in Palestine for a generation or more after their own deaths, even without the aid of any documentary record, would be natural enough.

The form and contents of the account in the Fourth Gospel of the conclusion of the Public Ministry of Jesus in the days which followed His Triumphal Entry are wholly different from those in the other Gospels, while they are thoroughly appropriate. The incident of Greek proselytes being desirous

of speaking with Him, and the forecast thus called forth of the
far-reaching effects that His death would have, an exhortation
to the people to walk in the light for the brief time that it
remained with them, a statement just afterwards that Jesus,
this Divine Light, was hidden, a solemn reflection by the evangelist on the blindness of the Jewish people, and a final cry of
Jesus respecting His Mission from the Father, through rejecting
which any man cannot but bring condemnation on himself,
take the place of the conflicts with and denunciations of scribes
and elders, Pharisees and Sadducees, and the prophecy spoken
to the Twelve of the coming destruction of the temple and
punishment of the Jewish nation and return of the Son of man,
together with exhortations as to faithfulness in the discharge of
the trust committed to them, and warnings to be watchful, which
occupy the corresponding portion of the Synoptic Gospels.

*The Last Supper of Jesus with His disciples, and His
Arrest, Trial, Crucifixion and Burial.* Mk xiv. 12–xv. 47;
Mt. xxvi. 17–xxvii. 61; Lk. xxii. 7–xxiii. 56; Jn xiii. 1–xix. 42.

We have first to consider the days of the month on which
the twenty-four hours in question fell, with all that this implies
as to the character of the Last Supper. According to the
statements of the Synoptics, understood in their natural sense,
the supper was the Paschal meal of the year, partaken of at
the time appointed by the Law, that is in the early hours of
the 15th of Nisan by Jewish reckoning, or the evening of the
14th by that to which we are accustomed. On the other hand,
in the Fourth Gospel it is nowhere implied that the Last
Supper was the Paschal meal, and it is moreover expressly
said that on the following morning the Jews who led Jesus
to Pilate would not enter the prætorium lest they should be
defiled and so be prevented from eating the Passover (Jn
xviii. 28), thus making it impossible to regard the preceding
evening (or night) as the time for it[1]. This appears to be a clear
contradiction, and attempts to shew that the contradiction is
only apparent have been and will continue to be, so far as I can
judge, unsuccessful. Let me notice a couple of those likely to
be the best known to English readers, and one other for a

[1] Cp. also Jn xiii. 29, which shews that the 15th of Nisan kept as a Sabbath
could not have begun, and παρασκευὴ τοῦ πάσχα at xix. 14.

different reason, namely that it is not only (I believe) the most recent, but that it has been put forward and discussed in writings not easily accessible to students who have not a large library at hand, but who may have seen references to it, and feel curiosity about it. Dr Westcott, in his *Introduction to the Study of the Gospels*[1], maintains that the clearest statement of what was the actual fact in regard to the days of the Last Supper and following events is to be found in the Fourth Gospel. But he argues that the Synoptics *mean* the same. The question about preparing the Passover, which, according to Matthew, Mark and Luke, was asked by the disciples on "the first day of unleavened bread"—with the addition in Mark and Luke that it was the day on which the Passover was sacrificed—was, Dr Westcott suggests, " asked immediately upon the sunset of the 13th"; and "the preparation which the disciples may have destined for the next day was made the preparation for an immediate meal which became the Paschal meal of that year, when the events of the following morning rendered the regular Passover impossible." But it must be observed that properly speaking the " first day of unleavened bread" followed the day on which the Passover was killed; and although it seems to me not improbable, as I have allowed below, that where two modes of reckoning days, the Jewish and the Roman, were in use, some lack of precision might not be uncommon in referring to the hours which would be differently assigned according to the two modes, this would be unlikely in cases where there could be no such confusion. Hence in regard to the afternoon of the 14th of Nisan when according to Jewish reckoning a new day was about to begin, without any change of day for a few more hours in the Roman reckoning, the expression "first day of unleavened bread" might be loosely used, and all the more so because the removal of leaven had already begun. But there would be no disposition to use the incorrect expression as to the time nearly twenty-four hours earlier. There is even a more serious objection to Dr Westcott's further supposition that a meal—the "preparation" for which could not have included, if made only immediately after

---

[1] See note at end of ch. VI, *On the Day of the Crucifixion*; the position adopted remained unaltered in the last edition of the work.

The Last Supper

sunset on the 13th, the obtaining of a Paschal lamb, duly slain in the temple—could have been regarded by the disciples and without explanation described as "the Passover."

Dr Edersheim[1], on the other hand, held that, as may be naturally gathered from the Synoptic account, Jesus ate the regular Passover at the legal time, and sets himself to reconcile the Johannine narrative with this view, (*a*) by interpreting the words "that they might eat the passover" in Jn xviii. 28, as equivalent to "that they might offer the Chagigah," the offering to be made on the first festive day. He contends that the defilement incurred by entering the prætorium would not have continued beyond sundown and would therefore not have interfered with participation in the Paschal meal, and also that the term "pesach" was applied not only to the Paschal lamb, but to all the Passover sacrifices, especially to the Chagigah. But he fails to establish satisfactorily his point as to the length of time that the defilement would last; and while one can understand that a reference to the Chagigah might be included in a general reference to the Passover feast, it would require far clearer evidence than any which is forthcoming to shew that it could be spoken of thus specifically as "the Passover," and stress be laid on *eating* it rather than offering it, even if eating followed, when the most significant part of the feast— the eating of the Paschal lamb—was already over; (*b*) Dr Edersheim renders $\pi\alpha\rho\alpha\sigma\kappa\epsilon\nu\grave{\eta}$ $\tau o\hat{u}$ $\pi\acute{a}\sigma\chi a$ (Jn xix. 14), "Friday in Passover week." But although $\pi\alpha\rho\alpha\sigma\kappa\epsilon\nu\acute{\eta}$ could designate Friday in an ordinary week, as being the day of preparation for the weekly Sabbath, it is quite another matter to suppose that $\pi\alpha\rho\alpha\sigma\kappa\epsilon\nu\grave{\eta}$ $\tau o\hat{u}$ $\pi\acute{a}\sigma\chi a$ can mean "Friday *in* Paschal week," especially when, according to the view we are considering, it was in point of fact the first day of unleavened bread.

But even if these interpretations were allowed to pass there would still be other difficulties to be overcome, and in particular the notion of some who were present that when Judas left the room the object could be that he should make purchases for the feast (xiii. 29), which would no longer have been possible.

The third treatment of the question of the day of the

[1] Vol. II, pp. 566–8, and cp. pp. 479–482, 7th ed.

Last Supper and of the character of the meal, which I will examine, is that by Chwolson[1]. In the first place he insists that the statement that the disciples inquired on the first day of unleavened bread where they were to prepare is plainly incorrect, since the first day of unleavened bread was the 15th of Nisan, following the day of preparation on which the lambs were slain. To explain how this erroneous statement found its way into all three Synoptic Gospels Chwolson has the following theory. On the authority of certain of the fathers he assumes that our Greek Gospel according to St Matthew is a translation from a Hebrew one, and that the translator at Mt. xxvi. 17 overlooked four Hebrew letters which happened to be repeated in immediate proximity, with the result that he has given us what we have in place of "the first day of unleavened bread drew near, and there drew near the disciples to Jesus and said" etc.[2] Then in course of time the text of St Mark and St Luke in the corresponding passages, which had originally conveyed a right meaning, were, in imitation of this wrong rendering in St Matthew, altered into their present form, by some Gentile Christian, ignorant of Jewish customs.

The extreme precariousness of a theory which requires us to find corruption of the original text in all three Synoptic Gospels, without any documentary evidence that indicates it, will be generally recognised. It must also be pointed out that in the account given of the manner in which the whole mistake arose one of the surest conclusions of Synoptic study is completely ignored and contravened, namely, that our first Gospel is not a translation from a Hebrew Gospel but is based on Mark.

These hypotheses, however, about the text of the three Synoptics serve only to remove from each what appears to Chwolson to be a manifest blot. There remains the apparent inconsistency that while the Last Supper is represented in the three Synoptics, and according to Chwolson also in St John, as the Paschal meal, it may be inferred from the last-named,

---

[1] *Das letzte Passamahl Christi und der Tag seines Todes* 1908.

[2] *Ib.* p. 11, "Der ursprüngliche Text des Matth. xxvi. 17 hat, wie wir glauben, also gelautet: ... יומא קדמיא דפטיריא קרב וקרבו תלמידוהי לות ישוע ואמרו Die Buchstabengruppe kof, resch, bet und waw, die wir absichtlich überstrichen haben, folgt hier wie man sieht zweimal hintereinander."

The Last Supper

and also probably from the three former, that the day following was a working day. To explain this he adopts measures that are even bolder. He propounds the view that—although unquestionably from the beginning of the second century A.D. onwards and (so far as we know) only as the continuation of an established practice, when the 14th of Nisan fell on a Sabbath, the requirements of preparation for the Passover were held to supersede the duty of Sabbath-rest—yet there had in fact been a change in the preceding century. The rule at the earlier time had, he asserts, been that in the case supposed the slaying of the Paschal lambs, and the rest of the preparation of them, should take place on the 13th or even, in order to make sure that there should be no invasion of the Sabbath-rest, on the 12th. He proceeds next to assume that the day after the Crucifixion, which was the Sabbath in that week, was in that year the 14th of Nisan, and that the Paschal lambs had been slain in the temple on the 12th, so that one would be obtainable by Jesus and His disciples on the Thursday. But we are not yet at the end of Chwolson's hypotheses. He supposes that there were two views among the Jews as to the proper time for eating the lambs, when for the reason given they were slain before the 14th. Some held that the meat should be put aside for consumption at the beginning of the 15th, as the Law appointed. To this party those belonged who, according to the Fourth Gospel, had not on the morning of the Crucifixion yet partaken of the Passover. Others, among whom were Jesus and His disciples, attached more weight to another injunction of the Law, viz., that the lamb was to be eaten in the night following the afternoon when it had been slain.

Chwolson cites a story from the Talmud[1] about Hillel's treatment of the question of the conflicting claims of the Sabbath and due preparation for the Passover, and infers from the question having been put to him as to which were the strongest, that a different practice from that which Hillel justified and which alone we know of must at some time have existed. But the purpose of the story may quite as well be, or indeed seems far rather to be, not to determine the choice that should be made between competing practices, but to meet the scruples

[1] *Ib.* pp. 20 ff.

that might be felt in following the customary practice, by shewing how an exception to one precept of the Law, rendered necessary for the sake of the observance of another precept, can be itself traced back to general rules or principles, and so differentiated from exceptions which men may be inclined to make for their own convenience and in a spirit of self-will. Another object is to display Hillel's greatness as a scribe of the Law. At the one point at which he fails—namely, in being unable to recall some traditional precept to meet the difficulty that, inasmuch as it is the Sabbath, the people have come not wearing knives for slaughtering the lambs—the sequel certainly does not allow us to suppose that there was any actual uncertainty as to what should be done when the 14th was a Sabbath. Hillel says: "Leave it to the people, they will find the right way out"; and presently it is observed that they have attached the knives to the horns of the beasts or stuck them in the wool of the lambs, so that these and not the men are carrying them.

As to a diversity of view about the time for eating the Passover if the lambs had been slain before the 14th, Chwolson admits that no trace of it remains, except where he thinks that he finds it in the Gospels. And it is surely incredible that in spite of the absolutely clear instructions given in the Law the Paschal meal should ever have been separated from the Feast of unleavened bread.

It seems almost superfluous to add any other criticism of Chwolson's theory; yet I will point out that he finds it necessary, in order to explain the notices in the Gospels, to put back the preparation *two* days, namely to the 12th. If it was put back at all, surely it would not be by more than twenty-four hours. The danger of an invasion of the Sabbath-rest, which he alleges as a reason for interposing a longer interval, would not be greater than in other years when the Preparation was followed by "the first day of unleavened bread" which ranked as a Sabbath.

As I do not know of any other devices than those which I have mentioned for reconciling the Fourth Gospel and the Synoptics on the subject of the day of the Paschal meal, I feel constrained to hold that there is error on the one side or

The Last Supper

the other; it remains to determine, so far as we can, on which in this particular instance it lies.

It cannot be denied, I think, that there are strange features in the Synoptic accounts, although it may be doubtful whether attention would have been drawn to them to the same extent, if there had been no Fourth Gospel, or if it were allowed on all hands that the testimony of that Gospel must necessarily give way to that of the earlier Gospels. Accordingly it may be convenient, and conducive to a fair judgment, if we consider what may be said to remove or diminish difficulties in the Synoptic narratives. I have already above had occasion to suggest an explanation of the loose use of the expression "the first day of unleavened bread." The more serious difficulties all consist in the mention of things done on what appears according to them to have been properly the first day of unleavened bread, which ought not to have been done on that day since it ranked as a Sabbath. It must be allowed that if the occurrences related were not merely unsuitable to the day on which they are said to have taken place, but impossible upon it, the evangelists could not have recorded them as happening then. What was possible in the circumstances must have been known to Mark, a Jew, and to one so versed in things Jewish and in Jewish ideas as our first evangelist, and even to Luke, who, though probably a Gentile, had lived much with Jews. We must beware, therefore, of exaggerating the seriousness of the infringements of the feast-day rest recorded. Men of the class employed by the Saducean chief priests to arrest Jesus would no doubt not be over-scrupulous about bearing arms on a day forbidden by Tradition. Again, the chief reason for holding a trial on a Sabbath, or day similarly regarded, seems to have been that it might issue in a condemnation to death, and that it was customary to carry the sentence immediately into execution. In the present case, however, the plan was that the Romans should be persuaded to put Jesus to death. The members of the Sanhedrin seem to have failed in accomplishing speedily enough what they originally purposed doing[1]; but they counted that when Jesus had been handed over to the Roman power they would be

[1] Mk xiv. 1, 2; Mt. xxvi. 3–5.

comparatively safe from the danger of a popular commotion even "during the feast."

The touch that Simon of Cyrene was ἐρχόμενος ἀπὸ τοῦ ἀγροῦ (Mk xv. 21), though it naturally suggests that he might be coming from work on his field or farm, is susceptible of a different meaning.

Again speedy burial may have been regarded as a work of necessity, and the purchase of a shroud by Joseph of Arimathæa, and the first steps towards embalming the body taken by the women, may have been held to be for that reason permissible. When also a virtual Sabbath was to be followed by the Sabbath of the week there would be special grounds for acting promptly. These considerations suffice, I think, to shew how the Synoptics could give the account they do, and that it might be true. Nevertheless the fact remains that the Johannine account is more clearly self-consistent, and so far is the more probable.

But there is one further question of probability to be considered. Is it more likely that if the Crucifixion actually happened on the 15th of Nisan the fourth evangelist should have represented it as having happened on the 14th; or that if the Last Supper was not the true Paschal supper eaten at the proper legal time, the Synoptics should have represented it as being so? It has often been said that the fourth evangelist was influenced by the desire of setting forth the contrast between the lambs which were being offered in the temple on the 14th and the Lamb of God Who was at the same hour being offered upon the Cross. That the times of these offerings should have been the same is indeed an impressive thought. But it seems to me that if this thought had been present to the mind of the evangelist, and his conception of the order of events was moulded thereby, he would have drawn attention in some way to the coincidence, for fear that his readers should fail to notice it; and this he has not done. And on the other hand, the consideration has been too much overlooked, that it would have been a simple matter for a confusion to arise, by which the Synoptic evangelists have been affected, as to the day of the Last Supper, which it would be so natural to take to have been the regular Paschal meal.

The Last Supper

Of what passed at the Last Supper, and during the whole three or four hours, and perhaps somewhat more, which Jesus and His disciples spent together in the Upper Chamber on that last evening, Mark has only related, and this in the concisest manner, two incidents, namely the prediction by Jesus that one of the Twelve would betray Him, and the breaking and blessing of the loaf which He gave them as His body, and the blessing of and participation in the cup as the New Covenant in His blood. Matthew, too, has only given us the same two incidents in a slightly expanded form. Luke, perhaps because he felt the blank in the Marcan account, which told so little about an evening with which there were such touching associations, has introduced here a reference to contentions among the disciples about precedence, and has recorded the teaching of Jesus called forth thereby. This added section as a whole has probably been suggested by the Request of the Sons of Zebedee and reply of Jesus, placed in St Mark on the last journey to Jerusalem, though some of the sayings may be compared with those which in the Fourth Gospel are connected with the Feet-washing.

That the last-named act of Jesus was in accord with His character as depicted in the Synoptic Gospels will not, I think, be disputed; but that it should not appear in them, if it actually took place, may be thought strange. If so, I believe this may well be because it is not easy in our day to realise how the brevity of the Synoptic account and the immediate purpose out of which it arose have determined what has or has not been recorded.

On the other hand, in a circle such as that in the midst of which the Fourth Gospel primarily took shape and was put forth, a circle consisting of disciples of the New Truth, who fully understood that they were cut off from the surrounding world, lessons needed by disciples in their life among themselves would be specially likely to be recalled. Such is the lesson taught by the Feet-washing. It is an application to their relations to one another of the general duty of humility and readiness to serve, which holds such a prominent place in the teaching of Jesus.

As in the opening incident on the last evening, so in the

whole following account in the Fourth Gospel of discourses and conversations in the Upper Chamber, it is the life of discipleship which is in view, and moreover that life in a still more peculiar and intimate relation, that of dependence upon a Master and Lord Who would be spiritually but no longer visibly present.

That the thought of the position of His little band of devoted disciples, and their great moral and spiritual needs when He would no longer be in their midst in the flesh to instruct and guide them, should have occupied the mind of Jesus on the eve of His departure and have suggested His words to them at that time, is evidently probable in the highest degree, and to that extent it is certainly likely that the subject and tenor of the contents of Jn xiii–xvii corresponded with what was actually spoken. Whether the beliefs by which He there consoles and fortifies them, and the conception of His own personality which He displays, have a historical foundation can best be considered in connexion with the Johannine representation as a whole of His teaching and self-consciousness in relation to the Synoptic one; and our examination of this subject must still be deferred for a little longer.

That there should be no reference in the Johannine account to the Breaking and Blessing of the Loaf and Blessing of the Cup of the New Covenant necessarily excites surprise. Two motives may have combined to dictate its omission. The constant repetition in the Christian assemblies of the rite which recalled this act of the Lord at the Last Supper may have made it so familiar that it did not seem necessary to record it. While the teaching which the evangelist would have desired to connect with it had already been introduced as a sequel to the miracle of the Feeding of the multitude.

The fourth evangelist could not pass over the other incident at the Last Supper mentioned in the Synoptic Gospels, the prediction of the betrayal, for it fell in with his whole idea of the situation. It was necessary that the false disciple should be distinguished from the true ones, and the little company be purged of his presence. The announcement is made in the Fourth Gospel as in St Matthew and St Luke that "one of them should betray him." The important point of difference in the

The Garden

various accounts lies in what they do or do not imply as to the indication of Judas individually as the traitor. The words in St Mark, "he that dippeth with me in the dish," and in St Luke, "the hand of him that betrayeth me is with me on the table," seem to hold of all the disciples and vividly to express the same idea as "he that eateth with me." But in St Matthew "he that dipped" may be specific, and at all events at the end it is added that when Judas asked "Is it I?" Jesus gave an affirmative answer, which, if heard by the rest—and there is nothing to shew that it was not—must have marked him out to them. In the Fourth Gospel the beloved disciple at the instigation of Simon Peter inquires of Jesus whom He meant, and Jesus then employed a sign whereby the former at least, and probably also Simon Peter, was informed of this. But apparently the rest did not learn it; for when Judas left the room, it did not occur to them that he had any malign object in view.

It seems most probable that Jesus, though He might foreshadow betrayal, would not point out to the other disciples who the guilty man would be; or at most would communicate it only to one or two specially trusted disciples. The account in the Fourth Gospel is therefore more natural than that in St Matthew, but less so than that in St Mark or St Luke.

The fourth evangelist describes the place to which Jesus and His disciples went from the Upper Chamber in different terms from the Synoptics, but he indicates the same locality. He does not mention the Mount of Olives or "the piece of ground called Gethsemane," but he says that it was a garden on the further side of the torrent-bed, variously given in the authorities for the text as the Kedron (τοῦ Κέδρου or Κεδρών), or of the Cedars (τῶν Κέδρων). The latter would not correctly represent the Hebrew name. But it may have been adopted even by Jews as more euphonious in Greek, when they were writing for Greeks. If the evangelist actually used this form it would not go far towards proving him not to have been a Jew, as against all the evidence of an opposite kind that there is[1].

---

[1] On the text here and its bearing on the question of the author's knowledge, see especially Lightfoot, *Biblical Essays*, pp. 172 ff. Also see Additional Note at end of ch. XVIII in Westcott's *Commentary on St John*, or *Select Readings in Westcott and Hort's Greek Testament*.

From St Mark, if not otherwise, the fourth evangelist knew of the Agony in the Garden. He may have omitted it because he had nothing to add, or because it did not illustrate the special themes of his Gospel, and because he feared lest the narrative should be misunderstood from the prominence which it gave to a moment in the life of Jesus which seemed like one of weakness. There is instead an echo of it in the words of resolve which he gives as spoken just after it (Jn xviii. 11). He refers indeed to the mental distress and perturbation of Jesus on an earlier occasion (Jn xii. 27)[1]; then, however, it passed more quickly. The misgiving was not so profound, or the struggle to master it so severe.

In the Fourth Gospel a cohort of Roman soldiers, led by its commander, a tribune, and accompanied by servants (ὑπηρέται) from the chief priests and Pharisees, come to arrest Jesus. In the other Gospels we hear nothing of Roman soldiers on this occasion. It is possible, or even probable, that there might have been negotiations on the part of the Jewish authorities with Pilate about Jesus before He was handed over to him. But one would imagine that if Roman soldiers had joined in the arrest of Jesus they would have led Him off direct to the Roman governor. The Jewish authorities also would not have exceeded their powers in merely making the arrest, and they doubtless had, in connexion with the guardianship of the temple, a sufficient police-force for the purpose at their disposal; and they must have preferred the comparative privacy with which the arrest could be made, if they managed it themselves, to any support which the Romans could give them in case of resistance. In the number given for the Roman force there must certainly be exaggeration[2].

The part of Judas was confined, according to the Fourth Gospel, to leading the way to the place which Jesus frequented. Instead of waiting to be marked out by the sign which the traitor had agreed to give, Jesus comes forward at once and

[1] In referring to the approaching betrayal also it is said (Jn xiii. 21) that Jesus ἐταράχθη τῷ πνεύματι.

[2] σπεῖρα, according to Polybius, is the term used for a maniple (200 men), but in the New Testament apparently it denotes a cohort (600), of which a χιλίαρχος (=a military tribune) is the commander. See Acts xxi. 31 and cp. x. 1 and xxvii. 1; also Mk xv. 16 (Mt. xxvii. 27).

Jewish examination and trial

offers Himself to be seized, whereupon the company of people that came to arrest Him "went backward and fell to the ground." Jesus then asks why they do not take Him, and requests that His disciples may not be interfered with.

The narrative seems to have been shaped to shew that the ignorant and indifferent heathen and the hostile Jews were alike constrained to pay a tribute to the Divinity of Jesus, and that certain significant doctrinal sayings were fulfilled. One is expressly referred to, and another comes to mind, namely Jn x. 18, where Jesus says, "No one taketh my life from me, but I lay it down of myself. I have power to lay it down and I have power to take it again."

It cannot be claimed that these features in the Johannine account have the appearance of coming from one who was present. The description indeed of the persons sent by the Jewish authorities gives us a better idea of what they were than the "crowd" referred to in St Mark and St Luke (in St Matthew the "great crowd"), and the names "Simon Peter" and "Malchus" which it introduces may, perhaps, not be merely feigned. But in more important respects the simpler Synoptic narrative is to be preferred.

On the other hand, in some of the following sections of the narrative in the Fourth Gospel there are peculiarities which suggest the possession of sound information. Those who arrest Jesus take Him "to Annas first." This "first" reads like a correction. Anyway there could be no motive for adding this interview with Annas except the knowledge that it actually took place. Moreover the appearance of Annas here accords well with the position which, as we learn from Josephus, he for a long time occupied. The fourth evangelist also states that he was Caiaphas' father-in-law, a point mentioned by no one else, but which helps to explain that position known from general history.

Annas does not hold a trial. He merely seeks to satisfy his own curiosity about the teaching and disciples of Jesus and then sends Him to Caiaphas. There is no reference at this point in the Fourth Gospel to any assembling of the Sanhedrin, or trial before it with Caiaphas presiding. The reason may be that in the view of its author the Jewish authorities had already, on that occasion on which Caiaphas had spoken the words which are now recalled, resolved upon the death of Jesus. It may have seemed to him therefore unnecessary here to record a trial in which a verdict of condemnation to death was a foregone conclusion.

According to St Mark and St Matthew the whole Sanhedrin after having tried and condemned Jesus in the night assembled again early in the morning—not that they might hold another trial and register their sentence in a more formal manner (as some have supposed in order to harmonise these Gospels with St Luke), but to convey Jesus to Pilate in a body. That they should have done this is quite probable; in any case a deputation sufficient in number and importance to impress Pilate would go with the prisoner.

It is a defect of literary construction in the Fourth Gospel that we are not told who "they" are who bring Jesus to, and parley with, the Roman governor; but from earlier notices in this Gospel it is evident that the Jewish authorities are intended; and both their conduct and that of Pilate, and in one instance the course adopted by Jesus, can be better understood here than in the Synoptic Gospels.

Naturally Jesus is brought inside the governor's palace and interrogated by him there, while the latter converses with the accusers outside, in concession to their scruples, seeing that they feared defilement if they entered. More than once he passes from the one to the others. The successive scenes and the play of different motives can be clearly distinguished. The fear that Pilate would be likely to have of popular disturbance is first appealed to, and the claim of Jesus to be "king of the Jews" insisted on. But that Jesus would simply allow Pilate, which according to the Synoptic account He did, to understand the description "king of the Jews" as the Roman would, and not as in the Fourth Gospel indicate the spiritual character of His work and claims, is far from being in agreement with the idea of Him which we form from what we are told of His work and teaching in the Synoptic Gospels as well as in the Fourth.

The Roman governor evidently did not consider that Jesus and any movement connected with Him constituted a danger to Roman rule, and he may have held that in gratifying the chief priests he might provoke hostility in other quarters. According to all the Gospels he tried what the effect would be of proposing that Jesus should be the prisoner released to the people after the custom of the feast. But we gather from the Fourth that he made more than one other attempt to avoid putting Jesus to death[1]. He suggested to the Jews that they should judge Him according to their law. It is not likely that he meant to grant them a power which they did not under the Roman Government possess; nor is it probable that he is merely speaking in irony. We may suppose him to mean that the case was one suitable for them to deal with by the jurisdiction still left them, and they reply: "this man deserves to die, and we cannot condemn him to death." The evangelist sees in the mode of death, which was the consequence of the Romans being the executioners, the fulfilment of another saying of Jesus. But here the reality of the principal fact which gave point to the words, namely the contrivance by the Jews that the Romans should put Jesus to death, cannot be challenged. According to the Fourth Gospel, also, by the scourging, which in St Mark and St Matthew is only inflicted when crucifixion has been determined upon, Pilate hopes to satisfy the Jews; and when he observes how, during a pause in the proceedings, his soldiers have dressed up Jesus in mockery as a king, it occurs to him that he will try to dispose of the affair by ridicule, and therefore presents Him in that fantastic garb to the people assembled without, while declaring that he finds no fault in Him. When, however, the Jews prefer against Jesus the charge of blasphemy Pilate realises the seriousness that the case has in their eyes, and resumes his examination. Yet it is still only when the cry that if he releases Jesus he will not be acting as Cæsar's friend has brought home to him how fatally for himself a lenient course may be misrepresented, that he can make up his mind to condemn Jesus to death, and that he proceeds to pass sentence on Him in the place for formal judgment, "the pavement."

We have no other reference to this "pavement" as the Roman governor's tribunal at Jerusalem; but the form was customary. It is possible that for this very reason the evan-

[1] On Pilate's desire to release Jesus cp. Acts iii. 13.

gelist may have assumed its existence. He adds, indeed, an Aramaic name for it; yet this cannot be taken to prove accurate local knowledge, owing to the philological difficulties connected with the word. On the other hand, it would not be fair to infer want of knowledge from these difficulties, especially when we consider how easily in a case of this kind error might have been introduced through a very early copyist.

The sentence of death was passed, according to the fourth evangelist, "about the sixth hour." The discrepancy which there is between this statement and those in the other Gospels with regard to the time of the Crucifixion, if they are using the same mode of reckoning the hours of the day, has (as all students of the Gospels are aware) often been explained by assuming that while the Synoptics count the hours as was usual from sunrise, the fourth evangelist counted from midnight. Even so, and allowing for considerable latitude owing to the want of precision in the measurement of time which was customary in that age, "about the sixth hour," that is about sunrise at that season, would hardly allow time for all that is related to have occurred in that night and early morning, and would leave more time than necessary before the Crucifixion, which took place according to Mark at the third hour, that is, by the reckoning from sunrise, at 9 a.m. But apparently there is in point of fact no satisfactory evidence that the practice of counting hours from midnight was anywhere followed[1].

The apportionment of the day by Mark appears to be the most probable. But the fact chiefly deserving of notice in connexion with the difference in the present instance is perhaps that the fourth evangelist, who (as it seems) knew St Mark, has treated him with so much independence; while that he should have had a doctrinal motive for so doing is far from evident, as I have pointed out when discussing the *day* of the Crucifixion. He does, however, in describing the death of the Crucified single out for emphasis anything that seemed to him to be specially significant through its fulfilling prophecy, or otherwise illustrating the Divine purpose in the whole transaction. And one or more of the touches peculiar to this

---

[1] See arts. by Sir William Ramsay in the *Expositor*, IV. vii, pp. 216 ff. and v. iii, pp. 457 ff.

The Teaching of Jesus 263

Gospel may have suggested themselves to his mind in consequence of his desire to do this; but there is nothing in them that is unnatural, or savours of an exuberant fancy.

We may here end our comparison of the narrative portions of the Fourth Gospel with the Synoptic narrative. The words of Jesus as given in the different sources have yet to be considered; and I do not propose after this has been done to pass to the Appearances of the Risen Christ. In recounting these the Synoptic Gospels differ widely from one another in the lines they take, as well as from the Fourth, and we have not the original ending of St Mark. Moreover, I have already had occasion to discuss several points in regard to those Synoptic narratives in a preceding volume of this work[1], and in regard to the last chapter of the Fourth Gospel, in the present one[2].

In the comparison of representations of the Utterances of Jesus upon which we are about to enter, some of the opening reflections in the present chapter should be borne in mind. And there are some others partly in further development and application of those already made, partly independent ones, which I would here add as bearing specially on the judgments to be formed in this part of our subject.

Although I have kept the inquiry into the value of the discourses in the Fourth Gospel separate so far as possible from that into the historical value of its account of the movements of Jesus and His relations with different classes and persons, because the discourses require a different kind of testing, yet in the work itself discourses and other matter are closely interlaced; and the impression produced by the former is probably upon the minds of most readers predominant. In modern times the didactic aim of the discourses has often given rise to an unfairly biassed view, I believe, of the narrative portions, as though all that is peculiar must have been invented with a like intention. One object I have had in examining the narrative portions in themselves independently is that we are able thus to judge of them more fairly. That is at least one way in which they should be studied. And when we do so it seems to me that, especially in certain broad

[1] Vol. II, pp. 200 ff.   [2] See above, pp. 17–32.

features in the course of events as he depicts it—the visits of Jesus to Jerusalem before the last in order that He might deliver His message there, the number of disciples of a superficial kind from among Pharisees as well as other classes which He made in the earlier part of His Ministry, and the crises both in Galilee and Jerusalem in which they fell away —but also in some individual statements and scenes, we see signs of a source being open to the evangelist from which he obtained sound and important information. But if so, we have not only the gain of this material itself for forming our conception of the Life and Work of Jesus, but the possibility is suggested that through the same channel Utterances of Jesus may have been handed down, which have been preserved in this Gospel.

The contrast between the simple teaching of Jesus, on the one hand, recorded in the first three Gospels, concerning the relation of men to their heavenly Father and to one another, the true way of life, the aims to be pursued, the dangers to be feared and guarded against, the hopes to be cherished, and on the other the sayings and discourses attributed to Him in the Fourth Gospel, at once presents a difficulty. It may seem impossible that both should proceed from the same lips. Great caution is, however, required ere we rely on this contrast for such a conclusion. Wide differences of character between different portions of the utterances of the same person are possible, which might well lead us to declare, if they reached us separately, that all the reports could not be authentic. Suppose, for instance, one of the longer pieces of the ethical teaching of St Paul, say the contents of Rom. xii–xiv, had been recorded by one disciple, and his argument on Justification earlier in the Epistle by another, might it not have been held that both could not express the same man's thoughts?

But, indeed, if the matter be well considered it will, I believe, appear that the essential difficulty does not consist in the two forms of teaching being given by the same person so much as in one of these in itself. If Jesus knew and declared that He had come into the world as the Divine Saviour of mankind, it would not be strange that He should have made provision for the moral and spiritual needs of men in widely different stages of spiritual knowledge. The chief characteristic in which the Johannine teaching differs from that large portion of the Synoptic teaching to which I have referred is not one of style but of subject, namely, that in the Fourth Gospel we meet everywhere with the consciousness of His own Person and Mission to the world, His own relation to the Father and of the Father in and through Him to men, and it requires a wholly different attitude of mind to give assent to these claims, to embrace them as true, from that which it does to perceive the excellence and acknowledge the truth of instruction of that other kind.

It was probably the desire to concentrate thought in his Gospel upon the supreme question in regard to Jesus Himself, whether He was the Christ, the Son of God, which led the fourth evangelist to omit that simpler, more popular teaching. And it may be observed that for the most part the manifestation by Jesus of the consciousness of His own unique Person and Mission and assertion of His claim upon the faith of men take place either in the innermost circle of His disciples, or in controversy with opponents.

We have still to take account of the fact that in the Synoptic Gospels, too, Jesus makes tremendous claims for Himself, though they are presented there in some respects differently. And they raise questions as to the personal consciousness of Jesus, and the light in which He offered Himself to human faith, hardly, if in reality at all, less difficult than those in the Fourth Gospel. In this connexion there are some special grounds for making allowance for the modes of thought of our informants in the first three Gospels, when we are endeavouring to get as near as we can to the thought of Jesus. The minds of all men to some extent, but especially of the majority of ordinary men, must make what they can of new ideas that are put before them by the aid of those which they have already. If they do not reject new teaching they will not merely adapt themselves to it, but most often will in considerable measure adapt it to their own previous way of thinking. Imperfectly educated men, as the majority of the first generation of disciples of Jesus were for the most part, it is probable that they often understood literally words which He used figuratively to express profound spiritual truths. The point of view of those preachers of the Gospel whose testimony lies behind the earliest records was that of men of strictly Jewish upbringing. Their hearers, too, were to a large extent ordinary Jews, in addressing whom they would be tempted to emphasise Jewish features in the message they had to deliver. What we observed in a preceding volume as to the eschatological element in the Synoptic Gospels enforces this point[1]. Sayings indeed of Jesus of which there is no reason to question the genuineness serve to shew that to a certain degree He shared the eschatological ideas of contemporary Judaism, and also that He saw marked out for Himself a unique place in the things of the end. But in the Synoptic Gospels eschatological matter has also been introduced from sources or current traditions that were purely Jewish, or narrowly Jewish-Christian, so that eschatology of this type has been made to appear considerably more prominent in the teaching attributed to Jesus than it probably was in reality. And to speak more generally, there is reason to think, even from the study of these Gospels, that the conception of Messiahship in the mind of Jesus Himself was not altogether the same, not one determined to the same extent by inherited ideas, as that held by the evangelists. There are also sayings about Himself in these Gospels in which He does not make use of the current terms of Jewish expectation, and which, without interpretations such as the latter require, are capable of giving us glimpses into some of His deepest thoughts about His own unique relation to the spiritual order of the world and the working-out of the Divine purpose. In these especially we shall find correspondences with sayings in the Fourth Gospel, in some of which at all events, if I mistake not, we are brought into contact with the living consciousness of Jesus,—with revelations of His thoughts concerning His Mission from the Father to the World, and of the communion which His Spirit held with the Father. If our minds are not obsessed with the notion that in the Fourth Gospel throughout we have simply deductions from, or various restatements of, a philosophical theorem by a theologian of the second, or a later, Christian generation, these sayings will, I believe, give us a

[1] II. 116 ff.

strong impression of authenticity, and the comparison of sayings in the Synoptics will help to shew that it is a right one.

1. In the remarkable account in St Matthew and St Luke of the Temptation in the Wilderness the trial described is not merely such a one as any child of man may have to undergo. It is a challenge by Satan to Jesus as Son of God. A consciousness on the part of Jesus of a character and mission which are unique is plainly implied in each temptation. In particular in the last temptation according to Matthew's order (the second in Luke's) He is addressed as an aspirant to a world-wide authority; and unless He had in some sense regarded Himself in this light, this attempt of Satan to mislead Him could have had no appropriateness and no apparent chance of success. And on the other hand Satan presents himself as the actual ruler of this world. The significance both of this narrative and of the reply which Jesus gave a little later to those who charged Him with casting out devils by Beelzebub (Mk iii. 27 and parallels) is enhanced by their being considered in close connexion. A similar conception in the mind of Jesus of His position relatively to the Evil One is implied in the former and is expressed by Him in the latter. He declares Himself to be mightier than the Wicked One, able to despoil him of his goods, to liberate his slaves. He has come as the Protagonist against the evil that is in the world. He is pitted in combat against, and He is overthrowing, one who through his mysterious and malign power was the chief adversary of God in the world. Sayings of Jesus in the Fourth Gospel which are in the same vein come to mind: xii. 31, xiv. 30, xvi. 11.

2. In the Parable of the Vineyard (Mk xii. 1–12 and parallels) Jesus indicates His own place relatively to the past dispensations of God to Israel, who were in a special sense the people of God. This people had been committed to the charge of men whose duty it was to guide them in ways of truth and righteousness, and who in so doing would themselves have reaped a reward, as vine-dressers might tend a vineyard in order that it might produce abundance of fruit for its owner, of which they themselves would receive an equitable share. But they have neglected their duty and made a purely selfish use of their opportunities. Messenger after messenger has

been sent in successive generations to warn them, but to no purpose. Now the Son of the Owner of the Vineyard—the Heir—has come to take possession.

After nineteen Christian centuries we can enter in some measure into the greatness of the conception of Jesus as "the Heir." He has in part, though not yet wholly, entered into His inheritance. And we have an ideal in our minds of what it would be for Him to do so completely. We can also appreciate the force of the distinction drawn through the use of this title and all the servants (δοῦλοι) of God who went before, including even the greatest of the prophets and other exponents of God's Will. But let it be considered what it meant for Jesus in that day to have this conception of Himself, and to hold it so clearly and undoubtingly that He was willing to claim this, albeit through a parable, as a true description of Himself.

There is a passage in the Fourth Gospel in which in a lesson given to His own disciples He implies a similar view of His relation to the past:

Say not ye, There are yet four months and then cometh harvest? Behold I say unto you, Lift up your eyes and look on the fields, that they are white already unto harvest. He that reapeth receiveth wages and gathereth fruit unto life eternal; that he that soweth and he that reapeth may rejoice together. For herein is the saying true, One soweth, and another reapeth. I sent you to reap that whereon ye have not laboured; others have laboured and ye are entered into their labours (Jn iv. 35–38).

I have dwelt above on the difficulty of tracing a clear line of thought throughout this passage, and of supposing the latter words to the disciples, implying that they had already been sent forth, to have been spoken at that early time in His Ministry[1]. But imperfectly as the words of Jesus may here have been arranged, we discern in them the thought that He Himself is the great Harvester. He Himself is beginning the work of ingathering, and His disciples when they take part in it will go forth in His name as sent out by Him.

3. We pass now to the saying in our First and Third Gospels (Mt. xi. 27, Lk. x. 22) which is most remarkable for similarity to many in the Fourth. As our first and third

---

[1] See above, p. 64 f. on "Conglomerates."

evangelists worked independently of one another[1], so that one could not have taken it from the other, it is evident that each separately had met with it somehow or somewhere, and consequently that before their time teaching attributed to Jesus of a Johannine type had been known at least to this limited extent in circles outside that in which the Fourth Gospel arose. This would be interesting even if the saying in question had only come to the knowledge of the two evangelists through their having heard it repeated orally, or through its having been circulated in some little collection of Sayings of the Lord, like that which was found in 1897 on a papyrus at Oxyrhynchus[2]. But in point of fact the probability is that they derived it from the main source of the matter common to them which is not found in St Mark[3] and this increases the importance of the saying in question. It is in each Gospel preceded by another which is the same in each: "I thank thee, O Father, Lord of heaven and earth, that thou didst hide these things from the wise and understanding, and didst reveal them unto babes; yea, Father, for so it was well-pleasing in thy sight." So that these two at any rate were probably found together. And there is a connexion of thought between the two. The clear recognition of and entire and joyful accord with the Father's Will in choosing "babes" as those to whom Divine truth shall be revealed, expressed in the first saying, are an instance of the Son's knowledge of the Father declared in the second, where He also declared that it is through Himself, the Son, that the revelation is made.

[1] See vol. II, pp. 29 f., 140 f.
[2] Prof. P. Gardner makes this latter suggestion in *The Ephesian Gospel*, pp. 296 f.
[3] Prof. Gardner, *ib.*, combats this view on the grounds that the saying here is plainly an insertion from some other source than those in the context, and that Jesus would not so have spoken to simple Galilean disciples. He adds, "Nor do I believe that during His earthly Ministry our Lord gave utterance to metaphysical views." It will be seen in the sequel that there seems to be a connexion of thought quite sufficient to have brought the sayings together. We cannot venture to say in this or in many another case whether sayings were in the source rightly placed as to time. But I must add that I cannot regard it as a sound assumption that Jesus would never utter mysterious sayings which His disciples could not at the time understand, or that they may not sometimes have faithfully remembered and repeated such sayings. The saying appears to me to be chiefly noteworthy as expressing a living experience; it is metaphysical only as including the assumption of a permanent relationship of being, implied in that experience.

Further, the first saying is introduced in St Matthew with the words ἐν ἐκείνῳ τῷ καιρῷ and in St Luke with ἐν αὐτῇ τῇ ὥρᾳ—just such a difference as would arise from the habits of revision to be noticed in the latter; so that it is probable that there was the same phrase in the source of each. Moreover this phrase is itself a link with something going before. In point of fact the denunciation of the towns of Galilee which had rejected the teaching of Jesus precedes immediately in St Matthew and occurs only a little before in St Luke. Luke has, however, interrupted the series of sayings in order to relate the return of the seventy, and has made ἐν αὐτῇ τῇ ὥρᾳ refer to this moment. In another way also he has slightly altered the setting of the denunciation of the hard-hearted, worldly towns. The order in which we have this and the other sayings in St Matthew is probably in this instance that in which they stood in the common source. There is thus brought out for us by close juxtaposition the contrast between those who have rejected and those who have accepted the message of Jesus[1].

In the saying now specially under consideration[2] we have to notice:

(a) The name "the Son" implying a unique sonship. The

---

[1] For "Clues for the reconstruction of the lost common source, and a review of the non-Marcan matter common to St Matthew and St Luke," see vol. II of the present work, pp. 76–102, and for discussion there of the present passage, p. 88.

[2] Schmiedel (*Vierte Evang.* in *Religionsgeschichtliche Volksbücher*, p. 49) asserts, as if there could not be any doubt about it, that the original form of the saying was οὐδεὶς ἔγνω τὸν πατέρα εἰ μὴ ὁ υἱὸς καὶ τὸν υἱὸν εἰ μὴ ὁ πατήρ; although the evidence decidedly favours the text as we have it in our New Testament both as to the present tense of the verbs and the order of clauses. Irenæus says that the Gnostics changed the form to suit their views (*Adv. Hær.* I. xx. 3). He may be right or wrong in this account of the matter, but he is at all events an unhesitating witness himself to our present text before the end of the second century.

If the original form were that which Schmiedel declares it to have been, there would still be a question of the meaning. Justin M. who in one place quotes the saying in that form (*Apol.* I. 63; at *Dial.* 100 he has one with the present) no doubt gave it an orthodox meaning. The Gnostics interpreted it as meaning that before the Advent of Christ, men knew only the Demiurge, who was not the same as the Father. Schmiedel refers the knowledge exclusively to a time after the earthly life of Jesus began:—"only Jesus had won this knowledge that Jesus is a loving Father." In more ways than one this surely is an inadequate interpretation of the words, even with the reading which he adopts; and it would seem still more unsuitable if only Schmiedel had given the aorists their proper force instead of rendering by perfects.

title ὁ υἱὸς τοῦ θεοῦ is hardly[1] used at all by Jesus according to any of the Gospels. It is found for the most part on the lips of others, but He is plainly represented by all the Gospels as accepting it, and as having in effect claimed to be this. The title which in the Fourth Gospel Jesus constantly uses is ὁ υἱός simply. It occurs on His lips fourteen times in this Gospel, but in a limited number of passages, v. 19-26 (8 times), vi. 40, viii. 35, 36 (twice), xiv. 13, xvii. 1 (twice); and in comments by the evangelist four times in iii. 17, 35, 36. In all these passages, save viii. 35, 36, "the Father" also occurs, and the subject is the relations of the Father and the Son.

In the Synoptic Gospels, besides the saying in Mt. xi and Lk. x, we have "the Son" followed by a mention of "the Father" at Mk xiii. 32 and Mt. xxiv. 36. And though here there is mention of something which is not communicated to the Son, its being withheld from Him is referred to as a fact not less strange, or even stranger, than its being withheld from the angels.

There are also the sayings in which Jesus speaks of God as "my Father," where He is declaring the Mind and Will of God evidently as One specially entitled to declare it. There are not only many of these in the Fourth Gospel, but no less than sixteen in St Matthew, and three (all different from the former) in St Luke, besides the instance common to both in the first clause of the saying now under consideration.

Further I would suggest that the history of the remarkable name for God used several times in Epistles of St Paul (Rom. xv. 6; 2 Cor. i. 3, xi. 31; Eph. i. 3; Col. i. 3) and at 1 Pet. i. 3 —"the Father of our Lord Jesus Christ"—is that Jesus was remembered to have spoken often and with emphasis of God as "my Father."

(*b*) The reciprocal knowledge of the Son by the Father and the Father by the Son, implying deep spiritual intercommunion. The statement most similar in the Fourth Gospel is at x. 15. But the idea is included in sayings there on the indwelling of the Father in the Son and of the Son in the Father (x. 38, xvii. 21), and on the union of the Father and the Son (x. 30, xvii. 25), which also imply the communication to the

---
[1] Jn. v. 25 is an exception.

Son of more than knowledge, namely, life, power. As regards that communion which is the source of knowledge the present tense of the verbs is very expressive. It is a knowledge which is continuous. In two respects also the form of the saying in St Matthew conveys more fully the idea of communion than that in St Luke does. According to the former the Father knows the Son, not merely "Who the Son is," and the Son knows the Father, not merely "Who the Father is"; and in St Matthew also the intimacy of the knowledge is expressed by the strong word ἐπιγινώσκειν.

(c) The Father is revealed through the Son. With this we may compare sayings of Jesus in the Fourth Gospel at vi. 45, 46, viii. 19, 38, xiv. 6–11, xv. 15, as well as i. 18 in the evangelist's Prologue.

We may note under this head that, as in the two sayings which in St Matthew and St Luke are placed together we have the two ideas combined of the Father as revealer and the Son as revealer, so at Jn vi. 45, 46 Jesus says that "every one who hath heard from the Father and hath learned, cometh unto me," and then it is added almost like a correction, " not that any man hath seen the Father, save he which is from God, he hath seen the Father."

(d) Finally we turn to the comprehensive statement with which the saying opens: "all things have been delivered unto me of my Father." The words in the Fourth Gospel which correspond most closely with this occur in a comment by the evangelist (Jn iii. 35). But in sayings attributed to Jesus Himself, xvi. 15 ("all things that the Father hath are mine") is similar. The prerogatives, also, of judging (v. 22, 27), of answering petitions (xiv. 13), of exercising authority over all flesh that He may give eternal life (xvii. 2) may be taken to be specially intended.

With the first of these the claim of Jesus to forgive sins on earth (Mk ii. 10 and parallels) as the Son of man, and the judgment at the last day by the Son of man (Mt. xxv. 31), should be compared.

4. Jesus compares the relation that His disciples will bear to Himself, as sent by Him and His representatives, with His own relation to the Father, as sent by and representative of

Fourth Gospel on His Person and Mission

the Father (Mk ix. 37 = Lk. ix. 48; and Mt. x. 40 = Lk. x. 16). Cp. Jn xiii. 20, which is virtually the same saying; also cp. Jn xx. 21, spoken after His resurrection. The profound sense which Jesus had of His Mission stands out prominently in the Fourth Gospel. See the frequency there of the expressions ὁ πατὴρ ὁ πέμψας με, and ὁ πέμψας με, and cases of these; also the use of ἀποστέλλειν in connexion with His own commission from the Father[1]. He also declares it to be the purpose of His life in the world "to do the will of him that sent him" (Jn iv. 34, v. 30, vi. 38). No one will be disposed to doubt that these are genuine sayings, yet there is no close parallel to them in the Synoptic Gospels. There is, however, a striking indirect confirmation of the presence of this thought in His mind, where He says that those who do the Will of God are His brother and sister and mother (Mk iii. 34, 35 and parallels).

5. At the Last Supper according to the Synoptic Gospels Jesus bade His disciples eat of the bread which He blessed and brake and gave them as though it were His body, and drink of the cup which He blessed as though the wine in it were His blood. So far as one can see this must have meant that their life was to be mysteriously dependent upon and nourished from His own, and have involved ideas similar to those in Jn vi, or in passages where without metaphor He speaks of His dwelling in them and they in Him.

It has been held that the words attributed to Jesus in the Synoptic account of the Last Supper in respect to the bread and the cup, "Take ye; this is my body," "This is my blood," were derived from St Paul, whose conception of the mystery of the death and resurrection of Christ, perpetually renewed in the Eucharist, they expressed, and who imagined that the Lord Himself had in a vision taught it him, apparently in the form of a narrative of what took place at the Last Supper[2]. This theory of the origin of the words we will briefly consider. In the growth that is sketched for us of this supposed myth there are two main stages, each of which it is difficult to regard as

---

[1] On the shade of difference between the meaning of πέμπειν and ἀποστέλλειν, see Westcott, *Commentary* Additional Note on xx. 21.

[2] This view has been skilfully expounded recently in *Les Mystères Païens et le Mystère Chrétien* by A. Loisy; see pp. 284 ff.

possible. At 1 Cor. xi. 23, where (it is said) the reference is to a communication made directly to him by the heavenly Christ, the same expressions "I received" and "I delivered to you" are used as in a passage a little later in this same Epistle where unquestionably he has in view not something learned in a vision but the common tradition of the Church. It is suitable to take them in the same sense here. The addition in this earlier passage of the words "from the Lord" is natural, because that which was received and was to be handed on was an injunction to be traced back to Himself, though reported by those who heard it.

Further, that which is related is not after the manner of a vision. In a vision the Lord would not have spoken of Himself in the third person, nor is it likely that He would have described the origin of the Eucharistic rite as a narrator; He would, as speaking in the present, have interpreted its significance. A passage earlier in the Epistle where the Apostle is interpreting it will suggest what he might have said[1]: "The bread which ye break is a communion of my body"; "The cup of which ye partake is a communion of my blood."

Moreover, although the truths which the words at the Eucharist, "This is my body," "This is my blood," plainly seem intended to convey are fundamental ones for the Apostle, the actual words come before us in his writings as found by him, and having to be interpreted, not as belonging to his own phraseology, or as directly proceeding from his own mode of thought. He feels that they need paraphrasing as in the passage to which reference has been made just above. But on the hypothesis which we are discussing, the spread of a narrative based on a Pauline vision, so generally and so early that it could come to be embodied in the tradition of the Gospel-history preserved in the Synoptic Gospels, has also to be assumed. Now, however much influence we allow for the attractiveness of the belief which would thus be authoritatively taught, it is not easy to understand how those preachers and teachers and their disciples among whom and through whom the primitive tradition of the facts of the Gospel took shape, could have accepted a fresh account of incidents at the Last Supper from

[1] Ch. x. 16.

Fourth Gospel on His Person and Mission

St Paul, to whom they certainly were not accustomed to look for the facts of the Gospel-history. There is, therefore, good reason to regard the words, "Take ye; this is my body," "This is my blood of the covenant, which is shed for many," as authentic, and they afford a most remarkable parallel to teaching contained in the Fourth Gospel.

6. Devout Jews were able to infer from prophecy that the Messianic times would be signalised by an Advent of the Spirit, and that the Messiah Himself would be endowed with the power of the Spirit. According both to the Synoptic Gospels and the Fourth Gospel John the Baptist foretold that He Who was about to come would baptize with the Spirit, and a sign was granted of the endowment of Jesus with the Spirit at His own baptism. In the power of the Spirit He went forth from the wilderness to begin His Ministry, and by that power He preached and performed miracles (Lk. iv. 1, 18; Mt. xii. 18; Mk iii. 29).

In the Fourth Gospel His endowment with the Spirit for teaching is, in a very interesting comment by the evangelist, represented in a manner which is not essentially different (Jn iii. 34): "he giveth not the Spirit by measure." $\delta \ \theta\epsilon\delta s$ of text. rec. is not part of the original text, but seems to be a gloss which rightly brings out the meaning[1]. On the other hand, the gloss of the English A.V. "unto him" obscures the line of thought. Primarily the words state a general proposition; but when they are read with the context we gather that the Christ is the supreme example of the principle. The thought is that to each of His messengers God has given the Spirit abundantly for the work he had to do; and that this must be and is surpassingly true of Him of Whom it is said in a sense that is unique that God sent Him.

Jesus also promised the Holy Spirit to His disciples: Mk xiii. 11; Mt. x. 20 = Lk. xii. 12. This subject is of course treated far more fully in the Fourth Gospel, especially in the discourses of the last evening. After His resurrection, according to Lk. xxiv. 49, Jesus tells them that He is on the point of sending—such seems to be the force of the verb—the

[1] Cyril took "Christ" to be the subject, but this does not suit the context so well.

"promise of my Father upon you," and they are to wait in Jerusalem till they receive it. In Jn xx. 22, He is described as actually bestowing it on them.

The sayings in the Synoptic Gospels of the kind we have been considering are few, but their significance is not to be measured by their number. They express thoughts which, if they were entertained at all, cannot have been merely passing ones; they must have been constantly recurrent and dominant ones. They must have proceeded out of deep experiences of the inner life, and be revelations of a fully established self-consciousness, if they were anything better than the ravings of a fanatic. They must have determined the whole point of view of Jesus in regard to His Mission in the world, if His character was one of any consistency and solidity. Even, therefore, if such words were actually uttered only to the extent that might appear to have been the case from the Synoptic Gospels, the emphasis laid upon them in the Fourth Gospel, through being oft repeated and enlarged upon, might well serve as a challenge to us to make sure that we had rightly estimated their importance. But it is improbable that such sayings could have been spoken, and yet have stood alone in the intercourse of Jesus with His disciples. Even in order that they might be rendered intelligible and be duly impressed upon their minds, they would need to be repeated and explained.

EPILOGUE

I HERE bring this work to a close. It will not surprise anyone that in the prosecution of labours extending over many years I should not have found it expedient in all respects to conform to the plan originally sketched[1]. So far as Pts I—III now completed are concerned, the line of investigation indicated at the beginning has been adhered to in the main. But I spoke there of an intention to add a fourth Part in which an endeavour would be made to apply two tests to the Gospel narratives; viz. that " we would seek (*a*) to ascertain the degree of accuracy by which their representations of Jewish life and thought for the period to which they refer are marked; (*b*) to see how far the conception of the history of the rise of Christianity which can be formed from them agrees with that which is to be derived from other very early Christian writings, especially those contained in the New Testament."

It has already been found convenient to treat of some points belonging to (*a*); and in like manner some phenomena of contemporary Gentile thought have been touched upon. I do not think I could here usefully engage in a fuller discussion of those subjects. There are works generally accessible to all students from which information about the facts can be obtained, and much further weighing of the facts does not seem to be necessary for the purposes of the present work.

It is otherwise with the topics indicated in (*b*). Our view of the value of the Gospels as historical documents cannot but be dependent in divers ways on our view of the significance of the whole movement of life and thought which sprang from Him Who is their great subject. In part we have to judge of the truth of what is recorded about Him from the consequences of His presence among men. The effect which the place of the supernatural element in the Gospels should have upon our estimate of their historical trustworthiness is a case in point, and one the consideration of which I said that I would defer till

---

[1] See Preface to vol. I, p. vi.

the last stage of our inquiry[1]. I have now decided to forbear from the attempt to do so, because it would necessarily open out into discussions of wide range in regard to fundamental beliefs, which could not suitably be entered upon merely in subordination to and with a view to the completion of investigations of the kind in which we have been engaged and which have already been sufficiently diverse and complicated. This work will retain more unity and the relation of its several parts will be more apparent, if it is concluded at the point now reached, than it would be if I proceeded now to examine the grounds of belief in the Divinity of Jesus. It has been so far and must remain simply a study preliminary to such an examination.

It is to be freely admitted that even in such a preliminary inquiry some points, as has been already implied, may have to be left undetermined for want of our being able to bring to bear upon their decision some of those conclusions which depend upon wider considerations; and also that in the preliminary inquiry itself there is the possibility that the positions reached may be affected by an investigator's general outlook, anxious though he may have been to avoid making any assumptions illegitimate at that stage. One must be satisfied with the reflection that through controversy between men whose principles and tendencies of thought differ, facts which pass unnoticed, or the importance of which is unperceived, on the one part are better appreciated on another.

On reviewing the results, as they appear to the present writer, of this survey of the principal sources for the knowledge of the life of Jesus, these sources appear to be all more nearly on the same level in respect to their value as historical witnesses, than they have been represented as being on the one hand in old Church tradition, or than they have been and are held to be by many modern critics on the other. From the latter part of the second century onwards two of the four Gospels, our first and our fourth, were held to have been the actual composition of two members of the Twelve. As regards our first Gospel this has been seen to be impossible from the time that its relation to St Mark had been duly realised. But for the discovery that our first evangelist, as also our third, was in large

[1] Vol. II, pp. 2 f.

of the Fourth Gospel

measure dependent upon, and so in authority secondary to, a writer who was not one of the Twelve, we have a very considerable compensation in the identification, by means of the careful comparison of our first and third Gospels with St Mark and with each other, of another source, the form of which cannot be fully determined, but much of the matter of which we possess in substance. And there is good reason to believe that ultimately at least this source was the Aramaic document by the Apostle Matthew to which Papias refers.

For the Fourth Gospel, too, we have been led to claim a high degree of importance as a historical witness to the Person and Work of Jesus, though not that which would arise from its being actually composed by John the son of Zebedee. Less progress towards agreement has indeed been made hitherto in regard to the history of the composition of the Fourth Gospel than of the other three. But the cause of this, if I mistake not, has largely been that even more than in most hotly disputed questions opponents have exaggerated, or even essentially misapprehended, the force and significance of the pieces of evidence on which they have respectively placed their chief reliance, while ignoring such as did not support their own view. If the weight and bearing of each piece of evidence are correctly estimated, and an endeavour is made to do justice to each, the right conclusion in the present instance is not difficult to arrive at.

For the fact that John the son of Zebedee lived and taught in Asia in his latter years the reminiscences of Irenæus of what he had heard in his youth from his elders, and the general tradition of the Church in the latter part of the second century may (as I have maintained) be thoroughly trusted, because this would be matter of common knowledge, about which it would have been exceedingly difficult for an error to arise and to hold its ground, all the more so in this case because there were those whose interest it would have served to have cast doubt upon it in a bitter controversy at a time when it would not have been too late to call it in question[1]. But the authorship of the Fourth Gospel by the Apostle John, though included in the second century tradition about him, cannot be regarded

---

[1] See vol. I, ch. V, and present vol. ch. IV.

as therefore established. For the writing of the Gospel would be a work performed in private, of which few could have direct knowledge, while from the first there would be a general disposition to magnify the Apostle's connexion with the book if he had, or could be supposed to have had, any at all. For these reasons also the statement by a later hand at xxi. 24 in regard to the contents of the preceding work cannot be taken as decisive, at least to the full extent of what it declares. On the other hand a later date for the composition of the Gospel than there is any ground for has often been, and is still, in modern criticism inferred from internal features. In reality there are not any such which make it unsuitable to suppose that it was produced in the last decade of the first century[1]. Nor is the mental growth which must be assumed to have taken place in the evangelist, if he was one of the Twelve, through having been brought under new influences, and called to meet new intellectual and spiritual needs, perhaps an *inconceivable* one. But is it *probable*; more particularly is it probable if John, the son of Zebedee, was the disciple in question? I do not think it can be held to be so by anyone who will duly consider the course of his life so far as we know it. When St Paul wrote his Epistle to the Galatians he refers to the fact that on one of his visits to Jerusalem he found John, who must have been already middle-aged, holding the position of one of "the pillars" of the Church there, and closely associated with James the Lord's brother, and with Simon Peter, who were unquestionably representatives of Jewish Christianity[2]. And we cannot suppose him to have gone to Asia for a good many years after this. Tradition itself concerning his work in Asia connects it with his old age. It is reasonable to imagine that he migrated there from Palestine either during the troubles which immediately preceded, or subsequently to, the Destruction of Jerusalem. Now although the composition of the Fourth Gospel did not require the Alexandrian training on the part of

---

[1] See above, ch. v, esp. pp. 202 ff.

[2] Gal. ii. 9. It has been disputed whether the visit of St Paul to Jerusalem to which he here refers took place fourteen years after his conversion, or after that previous visit which was itself three years after his conversion. See *ib.* i. 18 and ii. 1. The date of his conversion has also been a subject of controversy. It is unnecessary to go into these questions here.

of the Fourth Gospel

its author which some have held that it did[1], and although there need not have been any fundamental difference between the conception of the Person and Work of Jesus in the mind of a primitive apostle and that which we meet with in this Gospel, yet it would be strange that one who had come among the Greek or Hellenised population of Western Asia Minor in the last two or three decades of a long life should have been able in his presentation of the truth to adapt himself to his hearers and readers, laying aside earlier habits of speech and points of view, and should shew also that in his own thought he has undergone development, to the extent that we find here.

The argument that the author of the Fourth Gospel had been a disciple of Jesus in the days of His Ministry on earth which most deserves attention is that in the Prologue to the Gospel the writer classes himself with those who had "seen the glory" of the incarnate Son of God, and that at the commencement of the First Epistle of St John expressions to be compared with this are used, which are equally pertinent as to the advantages which had been enjoyed by the evangelist, if (as there is good reason to think) Epistle and Gospel are from the same hand. These expressions cannot be interpreted of spiritual sight and touch and hearing because these would not have been referred to merely as experiences in the past; this meaning is also inconsistent with the general tenor of the contexts. One can, however, understand that the claim in question might be made by a youth or boy, younger by some years than the Apostle John even if the latter was the youngest of the Twelve, but who could remember having sometimes himself seen and heard Jesus, and who had derived a sense of a knowledge, which was at least almost immediate, of the Divine revelation made in the Lord, by intimate association with His personal disciples very soon after His departure[2].

It fits in with this view of the writer that the acquaintance with Palestinian localities shewn in the Fourth Gospel suggests that the writer had at some time lived there[3]. He may have gone to Asia before John did, and at all events probably he did so at an age when his mind was more supple; and it is

[1] See above, pp. 161 ff.   [2] Cp. above, pp. 141 ff.
[3] *Ib.* pp. 155 ff.

more natural to attribute to him the capacity for producing the Fourth Gospel in the last decade of the first century, earlier than which it is difficult to place its composition.

Hardly less important than the question of the authorship of the Gospels, for judging of their value and of the use to be made of them as historical witnesses, are the history of their composition in other respects, their approximate dates and the conditions generally under which they were produced. In the reaction from the theory that oral instruction could of itself account for the resemblances between the first three Gospels, the signs have been too often overlooked that the main outlines and contents of the Synoptic narrative, which has come down to us most nearly in its original form in St Mark, were first determined through oral teaching as required by people living far from Palestine, but who had been impressed by the preaching of the Gospel of the Risen Lord, and that this brief account was then written down much in the form in which it had usually been spoken[1], and again that the other early document, embodied in our first and third Gospels, and which we can recover in considerable measure through a comparison of them, plainly seems to have consisted of little collections of sayings of the Master on particular topics made for the benefit of followers of His in divers circumstances[2].

But even the Fourth Gospel is to be regarded as a work which arose from the writing down of teaching given in the first instance orally in the Christian assembly, though teaching of a different kind—repetitions of and meditations upon Utterances of the Lord relating especially to His own Person and Mission, and expositions of the significance of particular episodes in His life through connecting such Utterances with them[3]. Although there is a certain homogeneity in the thought throughout, the whole has not been, as has often been supposed, reasoned out from the conception of the Logos set forth in the Prologue as a premise[4]. That conception was reached by a process of thought which was going on in the teacher's mind while the instructions which make up the body of the Gospel were being given, and which was prefixed to them

---

[1] See vol. II, pp. 130 ff.   [2] *Ib.* ch. II.   [3] Present vol. pp. 50 ff.
[4] *Ib.* pp. 161 ff.

the Fourth Gospel upon its interpretation 283

when they were ultimately thrown together. Some features in the account which this Gospel gives of the discourses of Jesus, appearing in their manner, as distinguished from the substance of the declarations contained in them, can thus be explained. The setting of the sayings came often from the evangelist. It would have been so even if from the first his object had been to compose a record of the Master's life and teaching. Still more evidently, however, it must have been so, and to a greater extent, if the accumulation of the material had gone forward during that period of oral instruction, to which the circumstances point as probable, and of which there are indications in the actual form of the Gospel. The whole work as it stands is evidence of the impression which Jesus had made; and it may be claimed, as will presently be seen, that the great themes at least, dwelt upon in the discourses which are attributed to Him, proceeded from Himself. But there is less reason to put confidence in the historical correctness of the connexions in which the discourses are represented as having been spoken, or in the number of times that a particular thought recurs, or in all the forms in which it is expressed. This is to be borne in mind in connexion with that monotony of self-assertion which in some parts of the Gospel we meet with, in the conflicts of Jesus with His opponents, and which we do not expect to find in Him to Whom the words could be applied, " He shall not strive nor cry." So also, in regard to the representation of this Gospel that He placed before men who had never been sincerely attached to Him, and who had now broken away from Him, or were on the point of doing so, an aspect of His Person and Work, which was at once peculiarly lofty and deeply spiritual, and that He condemned them for rejecting claims hard for them to understand and admit with a severity which seems excessive, guilty though they might be of disloyalty to their own consciences in their general attitude to Him and His teaching.

Again, if, as I have contended, the conception of Jesus as the spiritual Life and Light of men was not a deduction from the doctrine of the Logos but a stepping-stone to it, then where He is spoken of as the Life and the Light in the body of the Gospel we are at least brought nearer to the original form of the teaching. We have to do with the evangelist at an earlier stage in the development of his thought. It might still be the case that his exposition of his subject has been affected by a Christology of his own; but it is not likely to have been so much affected as would be probable on the other view. But this is not all; these conceptions—regarded as suggested by the Old Testament, and not by a Hellenistic system of philosophy—can also far more probably have had a place in the teaching of Jesus Himself.

Further, the circumstance that those who first read the Gospels, or heard them read, had already been instructed in much that they contained bears upon the question of their historicity. In some degree the truth of the Gospels is guaranteed not merely by the writers but by the Church of the time when they were put forth. In the case of the Synoptic Gospels the generality of Christians could remember to have heard delivered for a good while past what could now be read in scrolls; some could even recall having heard it from those disciples of Jesus of the first generation who had been His constant companions. The men who now committed it to writing would not have ventured, if they had desired to do so, to depart in what they wrote from what had often been repeated in the Church assemblies.

It is no less true that strong protests would have been called forth if the teaching in the Fourth Gospel had differed essentially from the faith held by the Christian believers among whom the work was promulgated. That substantially the belief concerning Jesus Christ set forth in it was that which had been embraced in the Church at least of a particular region is clearly shewn by the First Epistle of St John[1]. And from studying the form of the Gospel we have seen that not improbably large portions of its contents had been imparted to the Church before they were here put together.

At the same time this teaching, which had been communicated to, and we must suppose accepted as true by, a portion of the Christian Church, is marked by special characteristics; and we must consider the significance of their appearance in

---

[1] We have seen (pp. 83 ff.) that the writer was in all probability the same, and that at all events he held substantially the same faith and was a man of the same spirit.

teaching given to the Church in the region in question, and at the time to which the Johannine writings ought to be assigned. The region was the Western provinces of Asia Minor; this is not disputed. The time was near the close of the first, or quite early in the second century. The allusions to errors that were rife are compatible with this time, and would not be with a later one, when more elaborate heretical doctrines had appeared of which clearer indications would have been given. The position of authority, also, alongside of the other three Gospels which the Fourth Gospel occupied in the Church in the last quarter of the second century points to its having been known and esteemed for a period not much shorter than they had been. And the history of the reception of the Fourth Gospel in the Church, upon the investigation and discussion of which so much labour has been expended, has not ceased to be an important matter, even though we cannot obtain from it proof of its Apostolic authorship, owing to its bearing upon the probable date of the Gospel.

The Christians of Ephesus and other cities of the Western part of Asia Minor would be more open to new ideas, more willing to accept new statements of Christian belief, than those of many other parts of the world. Theosophic speculations had found a congenial soil there even before the Gospel was brought to this district. The defenders of Christian truth, even while striving to protect it from corruption through contact with such speculations, were here led to see it in new lights. The Epistles of St Paul to the Colossians and Ephesians are evidence of this; and the author of the Johannine writings and those whom he addressed were no doubt affected not dissimilarly by their environment in the same part of the world. Contact with new and alien speculations, and the controversy thereby provoked, while they lead many men to adhere more rigorously to old formularies, undoubtedly in another order of minds, equally zealous for the preservation of a faith they have held dear, have the effect of calling forth the expression of their faith under new forms. But controversy does not usually of itself tend to create faith.

Further, if the conception of the Person and Work of Jesus Christ had in the mind of the author of the Johannine writings undergone development in the course of years, as undoubtedly it had, it was a development in which he had been able to carry the generality of his children in the faith with him, and in which he would certainly have been anxious that they should participate. He would have viewed with suspicion any ideas which could cause a breach in the unity of the Christian body. Largely for this very reason he felt it necessary to restrain the disposition to intellectual speculation of some Christians, and to remind them that love was requisite for attaining to true "gnosis[1]." The same consideration would act as a guiding principle of his own thought.

But it would also be a mistake to think of the communities of Christians in the cities of the Western districts of Asia Minor in the Apostolic and Subapostolic age as sharply separated from those in other parts of the world, so that transformations of belief could take place there without reference to what was held elsewhere. There might well be differences of *ethos* in the Christianity of different regions, and movements of thought could then arise and spread here or there more freely than in later generations when the Church throughout the world was coming to be more and more united into one body through a formal organisation. But from the first there was intercourse between different portions, which must have acted as a check upon radical changes anywhere. And in Asia Minor certainly such intercourse cannot have been lacking, lying as its cities did either upon or close to one of the greatest highways of the world between East and West.

Among others, Jewish Christians from Palestine came there, probably in considerable numbers, and in many instances came to settle, in the years immediately preceding and following the Destruction of Jerusalem; and the majority of them were merged in the Christian communities which they found there. The Jewish Christians who remained in Palestine, or settled on its Eastern borders, came to be cut off from the remainder of Christendom. But there is no sign that in the Jewish Dispersion in the West distinct bodies of them were formed. The fact that, as appears from the Acts of the Apostles, in the Churches founded in Gentile lands there was an element of

---

[1] 1 Jn iv. 7, 8 etc.

The only development conceivable 287

converts who were Jews by birth would make fusion all the easier; while such later accessions, bringing with them as they did traditions from the birth-place of the Christian faith, must have exercised an appreciable influence.

The consideration of what was possible under these conditions, and up to the time when the fourth evangelist wrote, must determine our view of the nature and extent of the development which can have taken place in his beliefs.

It was mainly under the influence of an exaggerated estimate of the gap which separated the doctrine of the Fourth Gospel from primitive Christian belief that critics of the Tübingen School felt compelled to place the time of the composition when they did, in defiance of the evidence of history as to the reception of the Gospel, and of the indications of its internal character, and of those in the First Epistle of St John; and to conceive of the evangelist also far too much as an independent thinker who could work out his own theories without concerning himself about what was commonly held among his Christian brethren. But it seems to me that as yet many critics who recognise that those positions are untenable have not faced the consideration of what is involved in the abandonment of them. The vital matter now in the problem of the Fourth Gospel for every student of it is that he should be able to form an intelligible and just conception of the development of the Christian faith which could have taken place in the writer's thought and teaching. When we bear in mind the relation in which he stood to those among whom he ministered, and their relation to Christians in other parts of the world, it should (as it seems to me) be evident that such a development can have amounted only to an unfolding of what had virtually been contained in the faith of Christians from the beginning.

We ought also to trace out as far as we can the probable course of the evangelist's own mental history. The degree to which he need have come under the influence of Alexandrian philosophy in order to make use of the idea of the Logos in the manner that he does in the Prologue should not be overestimated. A right view of the relation of the First Epistle of St John to the Fourth Gospel in doctrinal position and in date, and of the body of the Fourth Gospel to the Prologue, are also of assistance, as enabling us to mark a stage, or stages, through which the comprehensive idea of the Logos was approached. But for my own part I cannot understand the process as a whole unless for its foundation and starting-point it had great Utterances of Jesus concerning His unique communion and fellowship with the Father, and knowledge of the Father's Mind; and concerning His Mission to make known to men, through His Teaching and Life of Ministry and Death, with a fulness and clearness that were altogether new, the Father's Character and Will.

INDEX

Aall, A.; on the doctrine of the Logos, 161 n. 1, 163 n., 166 n.
Abrahams, I.; on Jewish characteristics in the Fourth Gospel, 154 nn. 1 and 2
Alexandrian Judaism; 161 ff.
Allegory; use of in the Fourth Gospel, 179 ff.
Alogi, The; 123 ff.
Anrich, G.; on the Mystery-religions and their influence on Christianity, 188 n. 1; on P. Gardner's theory of the origin of the Christian Eucharist, 200
Aphraates; 117
Apuleius; on new birth, 197 n.
Bacon, B. W.; on Jn xxi, 18 n. 8, 19, 22, 23, 27 nn. 2 and 3, 31; on the process by which the Fourth Gospel has reached its present form, 41 f.; on the arrangement of passages from the Fourth Gospel in Tatian's *Harmony*, 42, 75 f.; on the prediction at Mk x. 39, 117 n. 2, 119 f.; on Irenæus and the Alogi, 123 ff.
Baldensperger, W.; his theory of the aim of the author of the Fourth Gospel, 10 f.
Baumgarten, O.; he attributes 1 Ep. Jn to same author as Fourth Gospel, 83 n. 2
Baur, E. C.; his theory of the Fourth Gospel, 3 ff., 12 f.; on the type of Gnosticism referred to in the Johannine writings, 202
Bernard, J. H.; on the Syriac Martyrology, 113 n. 2
Beyschlag, W.; referred to by Schürer, 8; on Jn xxi, 22 n. 4
Blass, F.; on the text of the Fourth Gospel, 33
Bousset, W.; he attributed the authorship of the Fourth Gospel to a "John of Asia Minor" distinct from the son of Zebedee, 9 f., 82 n. 1, 106 n. 2, 108 n. 3, 109 n. 1; on the question of the unity of the Fourth Gospel, 33, 43, 54
Bretschneider, K. T.; his *Probabilia*, 1 n. 1
Brooke, A. E.; he attributes 1 Ep. Jn to the author of the Fourth Gospel, 83 n. 2; holds that it was written after the Gospel, 86 n. 1, 97 n., 102 n. 1; on the difference between the two writings in point of view, 90, 93 n. 3, 101; comparison of grammatical usages in the two writings, 91 f.
Burkitt, F.; on the Syriac Martyrology, 113 n. 2
Cerinthus; 202 f.
Chapman, J.; on John the Presbyter, 110 f.
Chwolson, D.; on Jewish characteristics in the Fourth Gospel, 154 n. 2; on the day of the Last Supper, 249 ff.
Clemen, C.; on Partition-theories, 44 n. 5; on the false doctrine combated in 1 Ep. Jn, 93 n. 4, 94 n. 1; on question of the fourth evangelist's knowledge of localities in Palestine, 156 n. 2; on the influence of the Mystery-religions, 188 n. 1
Clement of Alexandria; on the ethical teaching of certain schools of Gnostics, 205 n. 1.
Cone, O.; his view of the Gnostics referred to in 1 Ep. Jn, 204 n. 2
Corssen, P.; on Irenæus and the Alogi, 123 ff., 127
Cumont, F.; on the Mystery-religions, 188 n. 1; on the civilisations of Persia and ancient Egypt, 195
Cyril of Alexandria; on Jn iii. 34, 275 n.
Delff, H. K. H.; he attributed the authorship of the Fourth Gospel to John the Presbyter, 9
Development in the evangelist's Christology; 89 f., 96 f., 178 f., 287 f.

Index

Dieterich, A.; on the Mystery-religions, 188 n. 1
"Disciple whom Jesus loved"; 54 ff., 134 ff.
Dobschütz, E. von; on strata in the Fourth Gospel, 44
Dölger, F. J.; on the connotation of θεός in the second century, 199 n. 1
Drummond, J.; held that the Fourth Gospel embodied the testimony of, and was probably by, John the son of Zebedee, 15; an instance of acquaintance with Jewish ideas in the Fourth Gospel, 154 n. 1; on "Bethany beyond Jordan," 158 n. 3.; on Philo's doctrine of the Logos, 186 n.
Duchesne, L.; on the Syriac Martyrology, 113 ff.
Eberhardt, M.; on Jn xxi, 17 n., 18, 20 n. 1, 22 n. 4, 28 f.
Ebrard, J. H. A.; his idea that 1 Ep. Jn was written to accompany the Gospel, 101
Edersheim, A.; on the day of the Last Supper, 249 f.
Erbes, C.; on the Syriac Martyrology, 113 n. 1, 116 n. 3; on the prediction at Mk x. 39, 117 n. 2, 119 f.
Eusebius; on the two Johns, 110 f.
Franke, A. H.; on the knowledge of the Old Testament displayed in the Fourth Gospel, 153 n.; an instance of acquaintance with the ideas of later Judaism, 154 n. 1
Furrer, K.; on the fourth evangelist's acquaintance with localities in Palestine, 155 n. 2, 156 n. 1, 159 n. 1
Gardner, P.; on the influence of the Mystery-religions, 188 n. 1, 200 n.; on the saying at Mt. xi. 27 and Lk. x. 22, 269 nn. 2 and 3
Gnosticism; 93 ff.; 201 ff.; pre-Christian, 194 ff.
Goguel, M.; on the sources of the narrative of the Passion in the Fourth Gospel, 43
Grau, R. F.; referred to by Schürer, 8
Gregory of Nyssa; on the days of commemoration of John and other apostles, 116

Grill, J.; on the Prologue to the Fourth Gospel and the relation of the remainder of the work to it, 9 n. 2, 168 n., 173 ff.; on Philo's doctrine, 164 n.; on work still required for a truer understanding of the Fourth Gospel, 12 n. 3
Grotius, Hugo; on Jn xxi, 17
Güdemann, M.; on the fourth evangelist's acquaintance with the ideas of later Judaism, 154 n. 2
Harnack, A.; on the relation of the Prologue to the remainder of the Gospel, 9, 162, 167 ff.; he attributes 1 Ep. Jn to author of Fourth Gospel, 83 n. 2; makes a suggestion as to a connexion between 2 and 3 Jn, 105 n. 2
Harris, Rendel; his theory as to the derivation of the Logos-idea in the Prologue to the Fourth Gospel, 162 n. 2, 182 ff.
Heitmüller, J.; on the Logos-idea in the Prologue to the Fourth Gospel, 161 n. 3
Hermeticum, Corpus; 165 n. 2; it illustrates pre-Christian Gnosticism, 195 f.; 197 n.
Hilgenfeld, A.; on Jn xxi, 18; on the date of the Gospel, 160 n. 2
Holtzmann, H. J.; on the date of the Fourth Gospel, 15 n. 3; on Jn xxi, 18 n. 8, 19; a criticism on Partition-theories, 44 n. 6; held that Fourth Gospel and 1 Ep. Jn were from different hands, 84, 90; and that the Epistle was the later, 85 nn.; comparison of grammatical usages in the two writings, 91 n. 2, 92 n. 1; comparison of their theology, 96 n. 1, 97 n. 1, 102 n. 1; on "we beheld his glory," 141 n. 1; on citations from the Old Testament as an indication of a writer's Jewish origin, 152; he supposed that the fourth evangelist imagined the high priest's office to be an annual one, 155 n. 1; allowed that in the Fourth Gospel elements from different doctrinal systems are combined, 161, 179 n.; his reply to Har-

Index

nack in respect to the use of the term λόγος in the body of the Fourth Gospel, 168 n.; his paraphrase of ἐγώ εἰμι, 176 n.; on the position relatively to the Church of the Gnostics referred to in 1 Ep. Jn, 207 n. 2

Ignatius; on lack of care for the needy on the part of heretics, 206 n. 1

Irenæus; on Papias, 110 f.; his reference to Polycarp's statements, 121 f.; on the Alogi, 123 ff.; on the ethical teaching and practice of certain Gnostic sects, 205 n.

Jackson, L.; on the statement of Georgius Hamartolus, 112 n.; on the prediction at Mk x. 39, 117 n. 2

John the Presbyter; 82, 108 ff.

Josephus; on death of James "the brother of Jesus" and "certain others," 119 f.; his definition of Galilee, 156

Jülicher, A.; his change of view as to the character of the Fourth Gospel, 12; the date he assigns for it, 15; on authorship and purpose of Jn xxi, 18, 27; holds 1 Ep. Jn to be by the fourth evangelist, 83 n. 2; 2 and 3 Jn not by writer of 1 Jn, 108 n. 1

Keim, T.; 7 f.

Kennedy, H. A. A.; on the Mystery-religions and their influence, 188 n. 1

Klein, G.; on the fourth evangelist's acquaintance with the ideas of later Judaism, 154 n. 2

Klöpper, A.; on Jn xxi, 18 n. 8, 23 n. 1, 28

Lewis, F. W.; his theory of accidental displacements in the Fourth Gospel, 74 f.

Lightfoot, J. B.; on authorship of Jn xxi, 18; his idea that 1 Ep. Jn was written to accompany the Gospel, 101

Logos, The; the Logos-doctrine of the Prologue to the Fourth Gospel compared with that of Philo, 162 ff.; the conception absent from the body of the Gospel, 166 ff.; how the evangelist may have met with the conception, 178 f.; compared with that of "Sophia" and of "Memra," 182–6

Loisy, A.; on the relation of the Fourth Gospel to Gnosticism, 13, 208 n.; on Jn xxi, 19 n.; on the lack of evidence in respect to the origin of the Fourth Gospel, 123 ff.; on the reception of the four Gospels in the Church, 129 f.; on "the disciple whom Jesus loved," 136, 138 n.; on "we beheld his glory," 141 n.; on the Pharisees as they appear in the Fourth Gospel, 152 n.; on the reference in "one that cometh in his own name," 160; on the Logos-idea in the Prologue, 161 n. 3; on ἐγώ εἰμι, 176 n.; an allegory in the Fourth Gospel, 180 n.; on the Mystery-religions and their influence, 188 n. 1; on St Paul and the Institution of the Eucharist, 273 n. 2

Loofs, F.; on the historical value of the Fourth Gospel, 15

Lücke, F.; on Jn xxi, 18, 21 n. 1, 31 f.

Luthardt, C. E.; referred to by Schürer, 8

"Mediate" Johannine authorship; 5 ff.; 51

Memra, The; comparison of the idea with that of the Logos, 185

Metaphysics; their relation to experience, 169 ff.

Meyer, A.; his review of recent criticism of the Fourth Gospel, 8 n. 3, 12; he holds that the Fourth Gospel does not add anything trustworthy to the statements of the Synoptics, 14 n.; his criticism of Partition-theories, 44 n. 5; on the influence of the Mystery-religions, 188 n. 1

Moffatt, J.; on the *entweder-oder* view, 209

Muratorian Fragment on the Canon; 127 f.

Mysticism; a style natural to a mystical writer, 45; the significance for mystics of external acts and events, 14 f., 59

Norris, J. P.; his theory as to a supposed displacement in the Fourth Gospel, 73

Oakesmith, J.; on Plutarch, 192 n. 1

Index

Oral instruction; as a preparation for the composition of the Fourth Gospel, 50 ff., 282 ff.
Palestine Exploration; views on position of Ænon, 157; "Bethany beyond Jordan," 158
Papias; on John the Presbyter, 82, 108 f., 110 f.
Partition-theories; 33 ff.
Pfleiderer, O.; held 1 Ep. Jn to be addressed to the whole Church, 92 n. 2, and to have been written with a controversial purpose, 93 n. 2; 2 and 3 Jn not by writer of 1 Jn, 108 n. 1; his view of the Gnosticism combated in the Johannine writings, 202 n. 2; his misrepresentation of Lightfoot, 203 n. 1
Philo; his doctrine of the Logos compared with that in the Prologue to the Fourth Gospel, 162 ff.
Plan of the Fourth Gospel; 49
Platonism; its influence in the first century A.D., 193
Plutarch; on the Mystery-religions, 188 n. 2, 191 n., 192, 194
Poimandres; its references to Life and Light and the Logos, 165 n. 2; the *Shepherd* of Hermas has been held to have been suggested by it, 195 n.
Polybius; on the term σπεῖρα, 258 n. 2
Poseidonius; the character of his influence, 193
Pre-existence of Christ, The; 171 f.
Quartodecimanism; 122
Ramsay, W.; on modes of reckoning of the hours employed in the Gospels, 262 n.
Reitzenstein, R.; on the Mystery-religions, 188 nn. 1 and 2; on the date of the basal document in the *Corpus Hermeticum*, 195 n.; his unfounded suppositions as to the influence of the Mystery-religions on pre-Christian Gnosticism, and Christian teaching, 196, 200 f.
Réville, J.; on "the disciple whom Jesus loved," 138 n.; on the fourth evangelist's view of the Pharisees, 152 n. 1; on the Alexandrianism of the Fourth Gospel, 161 n. 1; on Philo's doctrine of the Logos, 163 f.; on the use of allegory in the Fourth Gospel, 180 n. 1
Sabatier, A.; on 1 Ep. Jn, 103 n.
Salmon, G.; on John the Presbyter, 110
Sanday, W.; his review of the history of the criticism of the Fourth Gospel, 8 n. 3; his view of the authorship of the Fourth Gospel, 15; on localities in Palestine, 155 n. 2
Schmiedel, P. W.; date to which he assigns the Fourth Gospel, 15; on Jn xxi, 18 n. 8, 29; holds that the Fourth Gospel and 1 Ep. Jn were from different hands, 84 n., 91; the reference he sees in "if another shall come in his own name," 160 n. 2; on the text at Mt. xi. 27, 270 n. 2
Scholten, J. H.; on Jn xxi, 18 n. 8
Schürer, E.; on a "mutual approach" from different sides among students of the Johannine problem, 2 n.; on publication of Baur's views by his pupils, 3 n.; on Weizsäcker, 5 ff.
Schütz, R.; on the earliest form of the Fourth Gospel, 42 f.
Schwartz, E.; his theory of the compositeness of the Gospel, 40 f., 47 n., 49, 52; on the prediction at Mk x. 39, 117 f.; 2 and 3 Jn not by writer of 1 Jn., 108 n. 1
Scott, E. F.; on the Logos-idea in the Prologue to the Fourth Gospel, 161
Sinaitic-Syriac; the arrangement in its text of the matter in Jn xviii. 12–27, 72, 75
Smith, G. A.; on localities in Palestine, 155 n. 2; on Sychar, 159 n. 1
Soden, H. von; on John the Presbyter, 82 n. 1; holds that Fourth Gospel and 1 Ep. Jn are from different hands, 84 n.; and that the Gospel was the later work, 89; on the type of erroneous teaching referred to in 1 Ep. Jn, 208 n.
Soltau, W.; his theory of the compositeness of the Fourth Gospel, 35 f.

Index 293

Soulier, H.; on Philo's doctrine of the Logos, 186 n.
Spitta, F.; his theory of the compositeness of the Fourth Gospel, 43, 57 f., 68; his theory of accidental displacements, 73 f.
Syriac Martyrology, The; 113 ff.
Tatian; his *Diatessaron* and the present form of the Fourth Gospel, 42, 75 f.
Thoma, A.; on the Alexandrianism of the Fourth Gospel, 161 n. 1; on use of allegory in the Fourth Gospel, 180 n. 1
Tiele, C. P.; on Jn xxi, 18 n. 8, 28 ff.
Tübingen School; Baur's views were modified by successors, 11; its view of the date of the Apocalypse, 81
Turner, C. W.; on the text at Jn xviii, 12 ff., 72
Unity of the Gospel; 49, 73
Weiss, B.; reference to him by Schürer, 8; examination by him of Partition-theories, 44 n. 5; he accounts for errors in the Fourth Gospel by failure of John's memory through age, 210 n.
Weisse, C. H.; on the compositeness of the Fourth Gospel, 34
Weizsäcker, C.; adopted the theory of "mediate" Johannine authorship, and substantially adhered to it, 5 ff.
Wellhausen, J.; on Jn xxi, 28 ff.; his theory of the compositeness of the Fourth Gospel, 36 ff., 52 ff., 66; on the prediction at Mk x. 39, 113 n. 1, 117 ff.; on the length of the interval between the Triumphal Entry and the Crucifixion, 232 n. 1
Wendland, P.; on Hellenistic culture in the Roman Empire in its relations to Judaism and Christianity, 187 n. ; quotes Seneca on a moral change, 197 n.
Wendt, H. H.; his theory of the compositeness of the Fourth Gospel, 33 ff., 57 ff.
Westcott, B. F.; his point of view, 8; on authorship of Jn xxi, 18; his recognition of comments by the evangelist added without clear break to recorded discourses, 62 n., 63 n., 171 n. 2; his view of the reckoning of the hours in the Fourth Gospel, 156; his view of the sources of the Logos-doctrine in the Fourth Gospel, 162 2, 182 ff.; on ἐγώ εἰμι, 176 n. 1; on Jn iii. 35, 178; on the day of the Last Supper, 248; on the difference between ἀποστέλλειν and πέμπειν, 273 n.
Wetstein, J. J.; an instance taken from him of acquaintance with Jewish ideas in the Fourth Gospel, 154 n. 1
Wette, W. M. L. de; pointed out a want of lucidity in the fishing-scene narrated in Jn xxi, 20 n. 1
Wetter, G. P.; his treatment of the idea of divinity, 199 n.
Wisdom; the idea of in the Sapiential books, 184 f.
Wrede, D. W.; his view of the Fourth Gospel, 12
Wright, W.; on the Syriac Martyrology, 113 n. 2; on the Homilies of Aphraates, 117 n. 1
Wurm, A.; on the false doctrine combated in 1 Ep. Jn, 93 n. 4, 204 n. 1
Zahn, Th.; on the authorship of Jn xxi, 18
Zeller, E.; on Philo's doctrine of the Logos, 186 n.

www.ingramcontent.com/pod-product-compliance
Lightning Source LLC
Chambersburg PA
CBHW070234230426
43664CB00014B/2299